D0319707

WAL

**This book is to be returned on or before
the last date stamped below.**

T

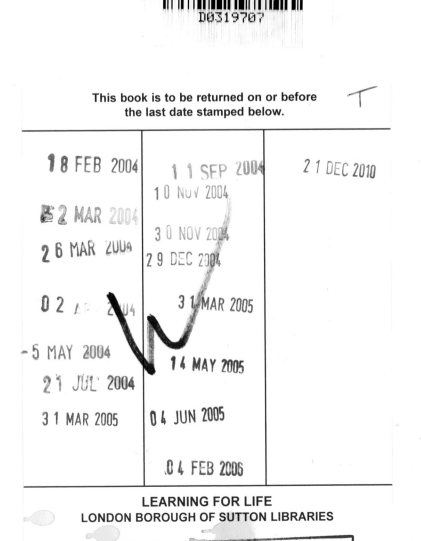

1 8 FEB 2004	1 1 SEP 2004	2 1 DEC 2010
	1 0 NOV 2004	
2 2 MAR 2004		
	3 0 NOV 2004	
2 6 MAR 2004	2 9 DEC 2004	
0 2	3 1 MAR 2005	
- 5 MAY 2004		
	1 4 MAY 2005	
2 1 JUL 2004		
	0 4 JUN 2005	
3 1 MAR 2005		
	0 4 FEB 2006	

**LEARNING FOR LIFE
LONDON BOROUGH OF SUTTON LIBRARIES**

WALLINGTON LIBRARY
SHOTFIELD
WALLINGTON, SM6 0HY
TEL: 020 8770 4900

RENEWALS   Please quote: date of return, your ticket number
and computer label number for each item.

THE
MAN WHO
INVENTED HITLER

THE
MAN WHO
INVENTED HITLER

DAVID LEWIS

headline

LONDON BOROUGH OF SUTTON LIBRARY SERVICE

022735320	
Askews	Jan-2004
943.086	

Copyright © 2003 David Lewis

The right of David Lewis to be identified as the Author
of the Work has been asserted by him in accordance with the
Copyright, Designs and Patents Act 1988.

First published in 2003
by HEADLINE BOOK PUBLISHING

David Lewis would be happy to hear from readers with their comments on the book at
the following e-mail address: david@dlcltd.com

10 9 8 7 6 5 4 3 2 1

All rights reserved. No part of this publication may be reproduced, stored in a retrieval
system, or transmitted, in any form or by any means without the prior written
permission of the publisher, nor be otherwise circulated in any form of binding or
cover other than that in which it is published and without a similar condition being
imposed on the subsequent purchaser.

Cataloguing in Publication Data is available from the British Library
ISBN 0 7553 1148 5

Every effort has been made to fulfil requirements with regard to
reproducing copyright material. The author and publisher will
be glad to rectify any omissions at the earliest opportunity.

Typeset in Caslon by Palimpsest Book Production Limited,
Polmont, Stirlingshire
Printed and bound in Great Britain by
Clays Ltd, St Ives plc

HEADLINE BOOK PUBLISHING
A division of Hodder Headline
338 Euston Road
London NW1 3BH

www.headline.co.uk
www.hodderheadline.com

To Rudolph Binion and Eléna Lagrange
(not forgetting Titi), with grateful thanks

CONTENTS

Introduction and Acknowledgements   ix

Chapter One   **'HITLER LACKED THE PERSONALITY EVER TO BECOME A LEADER!'**   1

Chapter Two   **THIRTY DAYS AT THE SHOOTING HOUSE**   13

Chapter Three   **THE HITLERS OF BRAUNAU-AM-INN**   23

Chapter Four   **THE FORSTERS OF AMSTERDAM**   39

Chapter Five   **DOWN AND OUT IN VIENNA**   53

Chapter Six   **JOURNEY INTO MIND**   75

Chapter Seven   **HITLER GOES TO WAR**   91

Chapter Eight   **FORSTER GOES TO WAR**   113

Chapter Nine   **BATTLEFIELDS OF THE MIND**   131

Chapter Ten   **GAS ATTACK**   147

Chapter Eleven   **THE WAYS OF THE WOLF**   165

Chapter Twelve   **BEFORE THE DELUGE**   197

Chapter Thirteen **VISION AT PASEWALK**   213

Chapter Fourteen **DECLINE AND FALL**   235

Chapter Fifteen   **THE STRANGE SUICIDE OF
                  EDMUND FORSTER**   261

Chapter Sixteen   **AFTER THE FUNERAL**   277

   Notes   285

   Archival References and Bibliography   309

   Index   329

INTRODUCTION AND ACKNOWLEDGEMENTS

'To know everything', claimed Madame de Staël, 'is to forgive everything.' Where Hitler is concerned, however, even the profoundest knowledge offers no mitigation. By describing the events that helped to shape the thoughts, words and actions of so monstrous a tyrant, I am seeking neither to excuse nor diminish an evil so immense as to defy understanding, let alone allow forgiveness.

Nevertheless, I feel it is important to gain a better understanding of the psychology behind the history by closely examining the experiences that changed a purposeless drifter into a merciless dictator.

The key to Hitler's transformation may be found in treatment he received, some time between 21 October and 19 November 1918, at a nerve hospital in Pasewalk, Pomerania, at the hands of an eminent German neuropsychiatrist named Edmund Robert Forster. This book recounts, for the first time, the life story of the man who, Frankenstein-like, unintentionally and from the best of motives, may fairly be said to have 'invented' Adolf Hitler.

My interest in Forster was first aroused some thirty years ago while researching an article on German psychiatry during the First World War for the *International History Magazine*. In the *History of Childhood Quarterly* I came across an article by Rudolph Binion, today Professor of History at Brandeis University, which described Forster's role in the career of Adolf Hitler. At that time both Pasewalk and the University at Greifswald, where Edmund Forster had been Professor of Neurology and Director of the Nerve Clinic, were behind the Iron Curtain, which made research there both difficult and politically problematic. Rudolph Binion, who is fluent in both German and French, had become intrigued by the story of Edmund Forster after reading a then-classified 1943 United States Naval Intelligence report on an Austrian doctor named Karl Kroner. While living in Iceland as a refugee from the Nazis, Kroner had described how, in 1918, Forster had diagnosed and treated Hitler as a hysteric. Earlier Binion had read *Der Augenzeuge* (*The Eyewitness*) by Czech novelist Ernst Weiss, which describes in great detail the treatment of a patient known only as A.H. for hysterical blindness. Determined to discover more about these events, Binion took a year's leave from the university and, at no small risk to himself, penetrated the tangled communist bureaucracy to carry out original research at both Pasewalk and Greifswald. There he discovered transcripts of an internal investigation into Professor Forster, initiated by the Prussian Minister of Education, Bernhard Rust, which ended only with the fifty-five-year-old neuropsychiatrist's violent death. For reasons of security, these transcripts had been recorded using an archaic and almost-forgotten form of short-hand, making them unintelligible to anyone not versed in this long-abandoned code. Fortunately, Binion was able to track down two archivists in the Greifswald University Library who had worked there in Forster's time and were among the few people able to decipher the text. At his request, they produced a full typescript in German, thereby saving for posterity an invaluable historical document.

Later, in his ground-breaking book *Hitler among the Germans*, Binion provided some details about Forster's treatment of Hitler. As a psychopathologist, with both a clinical and an academic background, I became fascinated by Forster's story and was eager to know more about this eminent German physician whose unor-thodox therapy, while successful in curing the hysterical blindness, had wrought such a catastrophic change in Hitler's personality. To many, it may seem incredible, perhaps even implausible, that the actions of one individual over such a short period of time could so profoundly change the outlook and actions of another, but, from my own experience, I knew that the outcome of therapy may depend on the most seemingly inconsequential words or actions on the part of the therapist. Was this, I wondered, what had happened in the case of Dr Edmund Robert Forster and Lance-Corporal Adolf Hitler?

The search for an answer to this question took me to the United States, Germany, Austria, France, Switzerland and the Netherlands, and required the co-operation of many individuals whose assistance I am pleased to acknowledge here.

My greatest debt of gratitude is to Professor Rudolph Binion for his extraordinary generosity and untiring assistance. He not only granted me access to his own unique and remarkable archive but, with his charming French wife Eléna, provided me with superb hospitality at their delightful home outside Boston.

My warm thanks are also due to my two senior researchers: Eva Magin-Pelich MA, in Berlin and Jacqueline Holzer MA, in Austria. Their skill and dedication made it possible to unearth many previously unpublished documents and to obtain interviews with individuals who had never before disclosed what they know about the life and times of Edmund Forster. Not only that, but their tireless and enthusiastic collaboration made the lengthy research an enjoyable and exhilarating experience.

My thanks go also to Charles de France and Michele Frouge-Noret of Librarie Thierry Corcelle (Paris) and Jill and Roger Bromiley (Amsterdam) for their contribution to the researches.

I owe special debts of gratitude to Edmund Forster's grand-children, Arne Forster and Mechthild Mudrack, to Marie Rose von Wesendonk MA (granddaughter of Edmund's brother Dirk), and to Pam Forster (widow of Dirk's son Vincent) for their tremendous assistance and for kindly allowing me access to their extensive family archives and personal photographs. Special thanks to Professor Dr

Dirk Ropohl, University of Freiburg, for his assistance in contacting Edmund's surviving relatives.

As always when researching books or articles concerning war history, I received co-operation and guidance from one of Britain's major authorities on Nazi Germany, Terry Charman, of the Research Department at the Imperial War Museum, London, as well as from the staff of the museum's library. I am grateful to Matthew Buck, researcher at Firepower, the Royal Artillery Museum, for advice on the use of gas in the First World War, and to Major Tonie and Valmai Holt, authors of the invaluable guides to the battlefields of that war. Dr Sean Kelly, one of Britain's foremost specialists in nerve gases, was kind enough to provide expert advice on the effects of mustard gas and nicotine poisoning.

I also wish to acknowledge the assistance of Frau M. Schumann, archivist at Ernst-Moritz-Arndt-Universität Greifswald, Herr W. Brose, curator of the Pasewalk Museum, Frau Neitzel, from the Greifswald town's archive, Pastor Hanke, the curator and staff of the Museum of Nonnenhorn, and Sheila Noble, senior librarian at the University of Edinburgh.

I am grateful to Icelandic historian Thor Whitehead for his assistance, and, especially, to Dr Klaus Kroner, son of the late Dr Karl Kroner, for reliving the still-painful memories of his family's flight from Nazi persecution.

I received invaluable assistance from German linguist Heike Rünger-Field with translation. My ever-patient and consistently reliable PA Elaine Franks put in painstaking work tracking down references, and Steven Mathews LLB took great care reading and commenting upon early drafts of the text.

Finally, my gratitude and thanks to Ian Marshall, my editor at Headline, for having faith in this project at the outset and for his consistently helpful and encouraging advice during the writing and to managing editor Celia Kent. I am additionally greatly indebted to my copy editor Philip Parr for his meticulous work on the text and invaluable suggestions for changes.

Chapter One

'HITLER LACKED THE PERSONALITY EVER TO BECOME A LEADER!'

My Führer! As we have performed our duties in the past, so shall we also in the future, wait solely for your order and your order alone. And we, comrades, know only one thing: to follow the orders of our Führer and to prove that we have remained exactly the same – to be loyal only to our Führer – Adolf Hitler. Sieg Heil! Sieg Heil!

Viktor Lutze, September 1934[1]

Tuesday, 7 September 1948 was a warm but overcast day that threatened rain and allowed only occasional glimmers of sunshine to penetrate the grime-smeared windows of Number Two Courtroom in Nürnberg's vast and rambling Palace of Justice.[2]

In the well of the darkly panelled chamber court, wearing the uniform of a US Army captain, stood Robert Wasili Kempner, a stocky, forty-nine-year-old lawyer and the only German-born Jewish member of the USA's prosecution team at the International Military War Crimes Tribunal. Kempner,[3] who started his legal career as an adviser to the Prussian police, had once tried to have the Nazi Party declared illegal, and, when that failed, had attempted to indict Adolf Hitler on treason charges and have him deported as an illegal Austrian immigrant. It was hardly surprising, therefore, that within days of Hermann Göring's appointment as Prussian Minister of the Interior and political head of the Prussian police in 1933, Kempner found himself sacked, arrested by the Gestapo and thrown into prison.

Released only thanks to the intervention of some influential friends, he wisely fled to the United States where, two years later, he became Professor of Law at the University of Pennsylvania. In 1945 he returned to Germany as a deputy counsel to assist in the prosecution of Nazi officials who, in the words of United States Chief Counsel Justice Robert H. Jackson, had: 'created in Germany, under the "Führerprinzip", a National Socialist despotism equalled only by the dynasties of the ancient East. They took from the German people all those dignities and freedoms that we hold natural as inalienable rights in every human being . . . Against their opponents, including Jews, Catholics, and free labour the Nazis directed such a campaign of arrogance, brutality, and annihilation as the world has not witnessed since the pre-Christian ages.'[4]

While Kempner came across in court as a meticulous if unin-spiring jurist, the same could not be said of the man who now faced him from the witness-box. Fritz Wiedemann was a tall and distinguished fifty-nine-year-old ex-professional soldier and former diplomat, whose charismatic personality was such that, despite a greyish pallor from four years' detention and a drab prison-issue suit, he still managed to bring a splash of flamboyance and colour to the sombre courtroom. A graduate of the Munich Military Academy and a professional soldier from the age of nineteen, Wiedemann had been Regimental Adjutant with the 16th Bavarian Reserve Infantry Regiment, known as the List Regiment after its first commander. In 1916 he had met twenty-seven-year-old Lance-Corporal Adolf Hitler for the first time and been left singularly unimpressed by his encounter: 'Hitler did not cut a particularly impressive figure,' he later observed. 'His posture was careless and his answers when one asked him a question were always sloppy. He held his head a little to the left and all these things made him look very unmilitary.'[5]

But if Hitler failed to impress Wiedemann, the Regimental Adjutant's organisational ability had left a lasting and favourable impression on the future Reich Chancellor. At the end of the First World War Wiedemann bought a farm in southern Germany and might well have remained a simple farmer for the rest of his life had he not, in 1933, stage-managed an apparently 'chance' meeting with Hitler at Munich station. This, as he had hoped, led to an offer of employment as the Führer's personal adjutant, a position he held until 1939, when he had the temerity to question Hitler's determination to go to war. Banished from Berlin for this impertinence, he went, at his own request, as Consul-General to San Francisco. American journalist Sidney Roger, who met him frequently during his time in California, remembers him as: 'One of those tall, handsome men, with a title like Baron So-and-so. [He] drove a super-expensive Mercedes-Benz sports car and played polo. The social upper crust of San Francisco went wild for him, paraded him at their posh parties and were not fazed by the fact that he flew the swastika banner over his residence.'[6]

When, at the end of June 1941, some time before Pearl Harbor, the German consulates were closed in the USA, Wiedemann was transferred to the Chinese coastal city of Tientsin and it was there, in 1945, that the Americans took him into custody as a potential witness in the forthcoming war crimes trials.

The proceedings involving Kempner and Wiedemann, listed on the court's schedule as Case Number 11, soon became known as the Wilhelmstrasse Trial, since all twenty-two defendants had worked for various Nazi ministries. Among them was Otto Meissner, once State Secretary in the Presidential Chancellery and, in the words of Otto Friedrich: 'A factotum of such chameleon talent that he served in the same capacity under both [Social Democrat leader] Friedrich Ebert and Adolf Hitler.'[7] Summonsed as a character witness by Otto Meissner's counsel, Wiedemann's testimony had made a favourable impression on the judges. Now, as he rose to start his cross-examination, Kempner knew he must try to discredit this impressive witness by branding him an unrepentant disciple of the Führer. With this in mind he started by asking:

'You knew Hitler from the First World War when he was your messenger?'

'Yes!'

'Can you tell us what this job entails?'

'A messenger has the assignment of collecting messages dictated by Regimental and Battalion staff and delivering them to companies. I believe that the right English expression is "Dispatch Rider".'

'Hitler was a lance-corporal, is that right?'

'Yes.'

Kempner smiled wanly and brushed back his thinning grey hair before slyly enquiring: 'Can you explain why you did not consider him suitable for promotion?'

Wiedemann paused for a moment and then, choosing his words with care, responded: 'Hitler was an excellent soldier. A brave man, he was reliable, quiet and modest. But we could find no reason to promote him since he lacked the necessary qualities required to be a leader.'

Robert Kempner smiled and savoured what he believed to be his moment of triumph. He now intended so to denigrate Hitler's leadership abilities that Wiedemann would be compelled to leap to his defence and, by doing so, reveal his Nazi sympathies.

'In a word,' he suggested mockingly, 'Hitler lacked the personality ever to become a leader!'[8]

But the plan failed miserably when Wiedemann immediately and firmly responded: '*Genau das!* [Exactly that!]'

So emphatic and unequivocal was this reply that all those in court, including the defendants, burst out laughing. 'Professor Kempner considered he had made a good joke,' Wiedemann remembered. 'Yet what he had said was perfectly true. When I first knew him, Hitler possessed no leadership qualities at all.'[9]

In this comment lies the significance of the Kempner – Wiedemann exchange. For it throws into sharp focus one of the most baffling questions about Hitler's rise to power. By what strange alchemy was this once aimless, front-line soldier, who lacked any leadership qualities, transmuted into the twentieth century's most powerful, most ruthless and most charismatic despot? 'The aftermath of the First World War found Adolf Hitler a charismatic political orator spewing rage and hate,' notes historian Rudolph Binion. 'The war itself had seen the same Adolf Hitler as an innocuous underling in a front-line Bavarian regiment . . . What then wrought that change in Hitler?'[10]

While Wiedemann's assertion that Hitler – a man Lloyd George once described as 'a born leader, a magnetic, dynamic personality with a single-minded purpose'[11] – 'lacked the personality ever to be a leader' struck those in court as risible, his statement appeared even more bizarrely humorous because he had uttered it in, of all places, Nürnberg. For nowhere else – including Munich, which was the birthplace of Nazism, and Berlin, from where Hitler exercised his despotic power – was so intimately linked to the cult and creed of National Socialism as was this medieval German city. Over a six-year period it had not only played enthusiastic host to the party's grandiose annual rallies, but it was there, on 15 September 1935, that the Nazis promulgated their infamous Law for the Protection of German Blood and German Honour, which, by expelling Jews from mainstream German society, opened the way for *Einsatzgruppen* (death squads), concentration camps, gas chambers and the whole evil industry of the Holocaust.

Nürnberg had first attracted the attention of the Nazis in 1923 when Julius Streicher, a one-time secondary-school teacher and an anti-Semitic rabble-rouser, was searching for a suitable venue for their rallies. The city's location at the junction of seven main railway lines made it easy for party members to travel there from all over Germany. Furthermore, because the old centre was relatively compact, even the fledgling Nazi Party's modest membership could make an impressive show of strength as Storm Troopers paraded down the narrow streets and massed in the ornate squares. Practicalities aside, the eleventh-century city, with its steeply pitched roofs, narrow, winding cobbled streets and ornate bridges, was also in perfect accord with Nazism's pseudo-mythological and romantic 'volkish' roots. It was in Nürnberg that the nineteenth-century poet Ludwig Tieck rediscovered German art and culture, and here too that the cobbler–poet Hans Sachs sings of the mysterious violence found in the heart of all men in one of Hitler's favourite operas, Wagner's *Die Meistersinger*.

Hitler was so captivated by Nürnberg that no sooner had he come to power than he set about transforming it into a citadel of National Socialist culture. On the south-east outskirts he ordered his architects to construct a vast complex of buildings and open-air arenas to provide dramatic backdrops for the rallies. These ultimately included three gigantic parade-grounds, each capable of holding around half a million people, the Märzfeld (one of a number of arenas in which military manoeuvres were held under public gaze) and the Grosse Strasse, a one-mile-long, hundred-yard-wide paved area along which massive formations of troops and armoured vehicles could parade. 'No cheap theatricality was omitted nor expense spared in the gigantic melodramas glorifying the implacable monster of Nazism,' says author Alan Wykes. 'In a blaze of searchlights, framed by towering banners, fireworks and mock battle, thunderous martial music and mesmeric chanting drown rationality – but not the Führer's screeching, hate-filled tirade.'[12]

There were Wagnerian overtures, tens of thousands of banners, streamers, flags and standards surmounted by eagles, heel-clicks and endless salutes, impassioned speeches and ecstatic responses from the hundreds of thousands of party loyalists assembled in tightly disciplined formations. There were goose-stepping marchers, massive bonfires, human swastika formations and awesome firework displays. Observing the 1934 Nürnberg Rally, American journalist William Shirer described how:

> Like a Roman emperor Hitler rode into this medieval town . . .
> past solid phalanxes of wildly cheering Nazis who packed the

narrow streets that once saw Hans Sachs and *Die Meistersinger*. Tens of thousands of swastika flags blot out the Gothic beauties of the place, the façades of the old houses, the gabled roofs. The streets, hardly wider than alleys, are a sea of brown and black uniforms . . . About ten o'clock tonight I got caught in a mob of ten thousand hysterics who jammed the moat in front of Hitler's hotel shouting: 'We want our Führer.' I was a little shocked at the faces, especially those of the women, when Hitler finally appeared on the balcony for a moment. They reminded me of the crazed expressions I saw once in . . . Louisiana on the faces of some Holy Rollers . . . They looked up at him as if he were a Messiah, their faces transformed into something positively inhuman.[13]

As Shirer noted, at the heart of the spectacle was Adolf Hitler, the divinely inspired leader and mesmerising orator with his intense blue eyes and brisk, aggressive gestures, working his magic on the masses and, through the use of repetitive rhythms of speech, generating in them an almost hypnotic state so that they came away with 'shining faces and dreamy eyes'.

'No one in history has understood the basic principles of mass persuasion better than Hitler, and no organisation expended more labour and material in perfecting and using its techniques than did the Nazi Party during its turbulent and productive life,' comments Barrie Pitt. 'Every art, every subterfuge and contrivance was employed to hammer into the spectators and participants the message that Nazism was the only religion and Hitler its God.'[14]

Nowhere is this portrayal of Hitler as Germany's Messiah more vividly apparent than in Leni Riefenstahl's *Triumph of the Will*. This chilling documentary of the 1934 Nazi Rally opens with a slow and lyrical depiction of mountains of cumulus clouds. As the clouds slowly disperse an aircraft can be seen flying over thousands of brown-shirted Storm Troopers marching in a seemingly endless procession. To a symphonic rendition of the Nazi anthem, the

'Horst Wessel March', the shadow of the aircraft appears as a black crucifix moving over the swarming masses.

By means of such apocalyptic symbolism Leni Riefenstahl sought to liken Adolf Hitler to the resurrected Christ descending from the heavens and bringing not merely military and political glory but redemption from past sins to those who were followers less of a political creed than of a new religious order. 'Nazi devotion took many forms,' observes Ernst von Weizsäcker. 'Some tried to touch Hitler, as though he were endowed with thaumaturgic powers. Others built little domestic shrines to him. Widows sent him small gifts. A tubercular party member gazed at the Führer's portrait for hours "to gain strength".'[15]

Schoolgirls painted swastikas on their fingernails, and one group of blonde maidens vowed to 'Heil Hitler' at the point of orgasm. 'There was only one thing for me,' explained one devout male believer, 'either to win with Adolf Hitler or to die for him. The personality of the Führer had me in its spell.'[16]

It was largely because Nürnberg so potently symbolised all that was most bestial and malign about Nazism that the Allies earmarked the city for destruction. As a Bomber Command intelligence report in 1943 makes clear, the medieval city was condemned to obliteration mainly because it represented 'a political target of the first importance and one of the Holy Cities of the Nazi creed'.[17] Nürnberg had supped with the devil and now the ancient city and its quarter of a million inhabitants had to pay the price. The dropping zone for the first major raid against the city, on 30 March 1944, was carefully selected in order that 'the bombs would fall in the very centre of the city, that is in the Altstadt and the surrounding residential areas, rather than in the southern suburbs, where the main factories, main railway yards and the Nazi Party buildings were situated'.[18] Later, in one of the final raids of the war, on the night of 2 January 1945, in only twenty-five minutes, five hundred RAF Lancaster bombers dropped two thousand tons of high-explosive and incendiary bombs on to a city centre once considered the most beautiful in Germany. By the time the aircraft had turned for the long flight home, two-thirds of the Altstadt had been virtually obliterated by what one expert described as a 'near perfect example of carpet bombing'. Among the six thousand-plus buildings either razed to the ground or opened to the sky were the homes of Albrecht Dürer[19] and Hans Sachs.[20]

While all this tawdry pageantry, all this moral collapse and physical destruction, did not result from a single mind (National Socialism was a many-headed monster), it may be argued that it would never have occurred but for the supremacy of one man's will. 'Will-power, latent and then deliberately cultivated, is what Hitler was about,' comments journalist Neal Ascherson. 'Hitler is the supreme product of the "Age of Will" . . . He cultivated his will-power as other boys cultivate their physical muscles – to the same end of acquiring forms of influence over others.'[21]

In the chaos of the early Weimar Republic there was, to be sure, no shortage of would-be despots only too eager to seize power, and each, whether from the political far left or far right, certain that only they possessed the answers to Germany's immense social and economic problems. Nor is it conceivable that Hitler, no matter how spell-binding his oratory or passionate his self-belief, could have achieved power without the muscle of Ernst Röhm's Brownshirts, the ruthless organisational brilliance of Hermann Göring or the Machiavellian propaganda skills of Joseph Goebbels. But what may reasonably be asserted is that without the triumph of Adolf Hitler's will, National Socialism could neither have gained nor sustained its hold on power.

Although *Triumph of the Will* was not Leni Riefenstahl's choice of title for her documentary,[22] it perfectly encapsulates the essence of Hitler's conviction that only through an unwavering faith in the ultimate and predestined triumph of his own will could Germany regain its former power and glory. 'The Führer was able to transmit this faith not only to his immediate followers, most of whom, like

Goebbels, allowed themselves to be mesmerised by him,' notes Piers Brendon. '[H]e could also project his charismatic presence onto a wider screen. At such an apocalyptic moment the power of his personality cult was overwhelming.'[23]

Indeed, Hitler's hold over his supporters was such that even with Berlin in flames around him, Propaganda Minister Goebbels could still proclaim:

> The times through which we are passing demand of a Leader more than vision and energy. They need a kind of toughness and endurance, of courage of heart and soul such as seldom appear in history, but when they do lead to wonderful achievements of the human spirit. To whom but our Führer could these words apply . . . Who but the Führer can show the way? If history tells of this country that its people never abandoned their leader and that their leader never abandoned his people that will be victory.[24]

That Hitler genuinely believed himself guided and protected by a divine power is apparent from his frequent references to providence and predestination. Emerging unscathed from a serious car accident during the twenties, for example, he reassured his aides by saying they had no need to be concerned about his physical safety because it was impossible for anything to happen to him until his mission had been completed.[25]

Similarly, as early as February 1930, at a time when the party's future remained uncertain he confidently and presciently predicted that 'the victory of our movement will take place . . . at the most in two and a half to three years.'[26] On another occasion he confided to an associate: 'The impossible will become possible, miracles will happen.'[27]

Once in power, his conviction that his every action was predetermined and therefore infallible grew only stronger. Nazi Foreign Minister Joachim von Ribbentrop once remarked on 'the absolute certainty' with which Hitler took major decisions on the basis that, because his judgement was infallible, a favourable outcome must be inevitable.[28]

Exactly when and where Hitler came to be possessed of this unshakeable belief in his divinely ordained mission is not in doubt. He often recounted how in 1918, while being treated for gas-induced blindness in a military hospital at Pasewalk, his historic mission as the 'people's deliverer' had been revealed to him supernaturally by means of 'ecstatic visions of victorious Germany'.[29] 'It came over me that I *would* liberate the German people and make Germany great,' Hitler told Karl II von Wiegand, a pro-Nazi German-American journalist during the early twenties. 'That word "*would*"', Wiegand later commented, 'contained in it the promise, the assurance that he would succeed in the mission.'[30]

But if the *where* and *when* of Hitler's extraordinary epiphany have long been known, until now *why* and *how* it came about have never been fully explained. Although the notion of Hitler's 'ecstatic vision' was certainly little more than Nazi myth-making, it is equally apparent that an event of great significance in his life occurred at Pasewalk between 21 October 1918, when he was admitted to hospital, and 19 November 1918, when he was discharged to rejoin his regiment in Munich.

In this book I shall explain how his life-changing experience was the direct consequence of an idiosyncratic form of psychiatric therapy conducted by Dr Edmund Robert Forster, an eminent neuropsychiatrist. For, while restoring Lance-Corporal Adolf Hitler's sight, Edmund Forster unwittingly and unintentionally opened his eyes in a way that neither he nor his patient could possibly have foreseen.

Chapter Two
THIRTY DAYS AT THE SHOOTING HOUSE

The suspicion will always be there that the patient is in fact malingering. The final distinction between hysterical blindness and malingering is almost impossible to make.

Hanus J. Grosz and J. Zimmerman,
Experimental Analysis of Hysterical Blindness[1]

Although Hitler was never a stylish dresser,[2] the shabby lance-corporal emerging from the gloom of Pasewalk station into bright autumnal sunlight[3] on Monday, 21 October 1918 appeared more like some desperate vagrant than a soldier of the German Kaiser. An ill-fitting hospital uniform, rendered even more shapeless by five nights on the train from Flanders, hung in folds around his emaciated frame. The gauntness of his pale, exhausted features was accentuated by a thick, black moustache drooping beneath the long nose. His piercing blue eyes, which would one day capture the admiration of ardent female followers, were covered by a stained gauze dressing. Totally blind, he shuffled uncertainly along behind the orderly, grasping the man's belt with one hand while the other timorously brushed the air around him as if fending off invisible obstacles.

According to his medical notes, Lance-Corporal Adolf Hitler had been blinded by poison gas early on the morning of Tuesday, 15 October,[4] during a British assault on German lines at Wervicq-Sud in the Pas-de-Calais region of northern France. The attack had occurred just as he and a number of other message-carriers attached to the 16th Bavarian Reserve Infantry Regiment were about to eat breakfast. Before the men could pull on their masks, the gas was upon them and they immediately started coughing and choking from the dense and pungent fumes. Soon after, Hitler later recalled, 'My eyes had turned into glowing coals; it had grown dark around me.'[5] One of the other soldiers, Hermann Heer, who had been gassed less seriously than his comrades, led them all to the nearest casualty clearing centre at Linselle. He recalled how 'Everybody took hold of the jacket of the man in front and all went marching in Indian file.'[6]

Doctors at the aid station had immediately diagnosed gas poisoning (*Gasvergiftung*). After washing out the soldiers' eyes and disposing of their contaminated uniforms the doctors had dispatched all but one of the men by ambulance to the army's large military hospital in the suburbs of Brussels. The one exception was Adolf Hitler. He alone was driven to a hospital thirty miles away in the Belgian town of Oudenaarde for further assessment. After one night's stay there the doctors took the apparently odd decision to transfer him again: not to rejoin his comrades in the well-equipped military hospital outside Brussels, but to a small sick-bay, or *Lazarett*, in the little Pomeranian town of Pasewalk, not far from the Polish border. It was a journey of some six hundred miles! With their army in retreat and thousands of seriously injured soldiers urgently needing transport back to Germany for treatment, such a decision would seem to be a perverse waste of scarce resources. But the Oudenaarde medical staff had no choice in the matter.

Despite Hitler's red-raw swollen eyelids and his plaintive insistence that he was totally blind, the experienced military physicians had little difficulty in diagnosing the lance-corporal's blindness as being caused not by any injuries related to the gas attack but by *hysteria*. The doctors used this term to describe not a hyperemotional state accompanied by histrionic and attention-seeking behaviour, but a functional disorder lacking any discernible organic basis.

Hysterical soldiers, as we shall see later, could display an astonishing range of disabilities, from stutters, stammers and tics to paralysis, blindness and deafness.

Having diagnosed Hitler's blindness as hysterical in origin, his doctors were forbidden, under a Prussian War Ministry decree, from treating him alongside physically injured soldiers on the ward of a general hospital. Rather, he must be sent to one of the specialist 'nerve' hospitals that, since 1917, had been created throughout Germany. In that year the Berlin War Ministry had decreed that 'All eligible patients be directed from unsuitable hospitals into these sections . . . no neurotic may be released as unfit for duty until the vigorous attempt has been made to cure him, or at least rid him of the symptoms of his illness, under the full guidance of a specialist.'[7]

To satisfy the rapidly growing demand for psychiatric beds this decree created, the government was obliged to take over existing mental hospitals and requisition a wide variety of other properties, including convalescent homes, inns, hotels, schools and even large houses, the majority of which were located in remote rural areas. This was both time consuming and costly, but the military and medical authorities believed they had no other option. Psychiatrists on all sides in the conflict believed that, like an infectious disease, hysteria could rapidly spread throughout a ward, or even an entire hospital, undermining morale and destroying the fighting spirit of all the other patients.

To be diagnosed as suffering from a 'hysterical disorder', as we shall see later, was to be branded as best weak willed or feeble minded and at worst a cowardly malingerer. Indeed, the diagnosis was considered so pejorative that, in the early months of war, many psychiatrists refused to make it.[8]

In the evening of the day following the gas attack Hitler had been transferred from the hospital at Oudenaarde to Ghent railway station, the point of departure for German ambulance trains. There, along with hundreds of other injured soldiers, some still able to walk but a majority prostrate on stretchers, he was helped on to the train at the start of his journey to Pasewalk. Loading the wounded, with stretchers being manhandled through open windows into the congested and already stuffy carriages, was a slow process, and it was late into the night before the steam train pulled out of Ghent.

Hitler, unable to move through the crowded train without a nurse or orderly to guide him, spent the time slumped on the hard, narrow seat, struggling in vain to sleep and aware only of the burning pain in his eyes and the cacophony of cries, groans and screams from the wounded men surrounding him.[9] When the train finally arrived at Pasewalk he was exhausted, dehydrated and desperate. Once disembarked, he was guided through the small station's arched and ivy-covered doorway and on to one of several horse-drawn ambulances waiting in the chestnut-tree-shaded yard[10] for the last stage of his journey to hospital.

Although historians have always referred to Hitler's stay at *the* Pasewalk hospital, there were *seven* different clinics and sick-bays in the town, some treating physically injured patients and others the mentally wounded victims of fighting. Soon after the war started the military authorities had selected Pasewalk, a twelfth-century walled town on the River Ücker,[11] as a suitable location for these sick-bays, largely on the basis of its excellent rail links with the rest of Germany. They had requisitioned a variety of buildings, including a school, a hotel and some large private houses, for conversion into temporary clinics, the most unusual being the Schützenhaus, or Shooting House. This was a mainly single-storeyed greystone building with a three-storey block on one wing and a timber-framed annexe on the other, situated on the south-east fringes of the town. Surrounded by extensive grounds, the Schützenhaus had views across open fields to the Pasewalker Forest in one direction and, perhaps less encouragingly for its patients, overlooked the Neuer Friedhof Cemetery in the other. Originally a brick factory, the Schützenhaus had been purchased in September 1859 by Christian Darling, a local entrepreneur, who had converted it into a restaurant and bar set in what his advertising leaflets described as 'attractively laid-out gardens'.[12] A few years later the timbered extension had been added to provide space for the indoor rifle range, from which the building derived its name, as well as the stage for variety entertainment. A poster advertising one of its shows in 1907 lists among the popular songs being performed such sentimental ballads as 'Dear Granddad' and 'War and Peace', alongside two eerily prophetic numbers: 'The Devil Laughs Aloud' and 'You Can't Do Anything about It'.[13]

This unusual combination of a restaurant, bar, meeting-rooms, rifle range and music-hall theatre proved so popular that the Schützenhaus was among the first premises in the town to have a telephone, Pasewalk 363, on which to take bookings. In a 1913 advertisement the landlord, Johannes Thom, proclaimed: 'I recommend my friendly hostelry with its garden, large room with a stage, shooting range etc. for clubs and private hire. Good food and beverages with courteous service.'[14] A few months after this notice appeared the hostelry was requisitioned by the authorities, who wasted no time in converting it into a *Lazarett* specialising in the treatment of hysterical disorders. The restaurant offices, shooting range and music hall were turned into wards, with beds for around thirty patients, who would be cared for by a staff of fifteen doctors, nurses and orderlies. By the time Hitler arrived these were under the command of Dr Wilhelm Schroeder.

On admittance he was bathed, issued with a clean hospital uniform and allocated a narrow, iron-framed bed in one of the five small wards. The following day his eyes were examined by Dr Karl Kroner, a forty-year-old Jewish neurologist whose knowledge of the effects of gas poisoning was both professional and personal. The son of a well-known Jewish physician, Kroner had served as a doctor with the 3rd Husaren Cavalry Regiment, seen action on both the Western and the Eastern Fronts, working mostly near the front lines, and been awarded the Iron Cross, First Class. Temporarily blinded in a gas attack in 1917, he was invalided out of the army and returned to Berlin, where he worked as a neurologist while remaining a consultant to a number of *Lazarette*, including those at Pasewalk.[15]

Kroner's examination showed that, while Hitler was still suffering from a measure of conjunctivitis, with the delicate tissue surrounding the eyes appearing red and swollen, this was most likely due to his constantly rubbing them in an understandable but self-defeating attempt to dispel the intense irritation. Kroner found no trace of mucopurulence, the presence of which would have indicated a secondary infection of the conjunctiva. Nor, more significantly, did Hitler's corneas have the grey, lustreless, 'orange-skin' appearance characteristic of acute mustard-gas blistering. Had his eyes been burned sufficiently severely to cause blindness, Kroner would also have expected to observe a whitish band of dead tissue across those parts of his eyes unprotected by the lids. This would have indicated a much more serious risk of permanent blindness since, by compressing the tiny blood vessels that feed the cornea, these areas of congealed fluid could have starved them to death. With none of these indicators present, and given Hitler's agitated mental state, Kroner confirmed the diagnosis of the Oudenaarde doctors: Hitler's loss of sight was due to hysteria.

Although Kroner's examination had taken him only a few minutes, even this brief involvement would prove sufficient to place his life in grave danger once the Nazis were in power. In November 1938 he was arrested and sent to Sachsenhausen concentration camp, where his life was saved only by the determined intervention of Iceland's Consul-General in Berlin.

After writing up Hitler's medical notes Kroner handed them to the clinic's director, Dr Schroeder, with his recommendation that the patient receive psychiatric treatment from their consultant neuropsychiatrist, Dr Edmund Forster. Schroeder, in turn, sent the notes on to the Neurology Clinic attached to the Charité Hospital in Berlin, marked for Forster's attention.

On the morning he read Hitler's case notes, Edmund Forster

had been back in his old job in the clinic for less than a month, having spent the previous four years working as a military doctor in Flanders. A neurologist and psychiatrist with extensive clinical and research experience, the forty-year-old Forster had spent his time in Flanders treating hysterical and brain-injured soldiers, lecturing at Bruges University and giving expert evidence at courts martial. A highly intelligent and well-educated man who spoke fluent Dutch, French and English as well as German, Forster had been born in Munich, spent his childhood in Amsterdam and obtained his medical degree in Germany and Switzerland. In the laboratory he had pioneered new techniques for the study of general paralysis of the insane (the result of a syphilitic infection), while during his leisure time he relaxed by painting delicate watercolours, for which he showed a fair talent. This was in keeping with the bohemian nature of Forster's character: his friends tended to be artists, writers and actors, rather than fellow doctors. Nevertheless, he also prided himself on his scientific rationalism.

Forster had long been interested in treating hysterical soldiers and had developed a controversial therapy based on his conviction that irrespective of how the hysterical condition was manifested, the underlying cause was *always* a lack of will-power on the part of the sufferer. Forster therefore favoured a therapeutic approach in which he used his domineering personality essentially to bully the soldier better. He would strenuously insist that however disabling and distressing the soldier's condition might appear, he was not really ill at all but merely showing a lack of fighting spirit, or what the British military authorities termed a 'lack of moral fibre'. As a German officer as well as their doctor, he forcefully commanded the injured men as a matter of patriotic duty and personal pride to abandon the imagined disability and immediately return to their duties. Surprisingly, his hectoring approach frequently produced remarkable cures, with those he verbally abused most vehemently often recovering fastest and expressing the greatest gratitude towards him.

So it was with a fairly jaundiced eye that he glanced through Hitler's medical notes. Here, it seemed immediately apparent to him, was yet another soldier seeking to avoid the dangers of the front line by consciously or unconsciously feigning a physical injury. Later that week he drove the eighty miles from Berlin on one of his regular visits to Pasewalk, where he met his new patient, Adolf Hitler, for the first time.

Even before their meeting it is likely that Forster's unfavourable opinion of the patient had been reinforced by comments from the resident medical staff. The lance-corporal was, they told him, a restless and agitated troublemaker, constantly grumbling over his fate and raging furiously against the Marxist–Jewish conspiracy responsible for betraying his comrades at the front. An insomniac, he spent much of the night stumbling around the wards raging about his blindness, demanding to know how he, an artist, would ever again earn a living, and expressing terror that he would end up begging on the streets. Each evening a small group of patients would cluster around his bed as he voiced disgust for Austria, which he condemned as soft and rotten, while extolling the virtues of strong and virile Germany. He would ask rhetorically why Austria was so corrupt and effete. Then he would snarl out his answer: because *der Jude* had infected and poisoned the nation. Repeatedly he returned to his theme that for the strong individual and the strong nation everything is possible and permissible, while one should never show even the slightest respect for a weak opponent. By what right, he once demanded, were crashed French pilots afforded the honour of a military funeral as if they had been German flyers? Far better to leave their corpses to rot on the battlefield where they had fallen.

While speaking to his superiors, however, Hitler's tone was completely different and his manner utterly subservient in a clear desire to remain on excellent terms with them.[16]

Edmund Forster, a man of democratic views with many Jewish friends, was in equal measure repelled by Hitler's opinions and intrigued by the psychiatric challenge his case represented.

When faced by hysterical paralysis of the arm or leg it was often possible to show the patient that his muscles still functioned by stimulating them with electric shocks. If treating hysterical deafness, a sudden loud sound might be used to trick the sufferer into displaying a 'startle' response, revealing that they could, after all, hear perfectly well. Far more brutal and painful electric shocks and other forms of punishment were also used to terrify the hysteric to such an extent that he preferred returning to the battle rather than being subjected to the horrors of the hospital ward. More benignly, some of Forster's colleagues were using hypnosis to produce rapid and apparently permanent cures. While Forster was certain Hitler's hysterical blindness was the result of a failure of will-power, he also formed the view that neither trying to restore his patient's sight through a terror of electric shocks nor attempting to bully him out of his condition was likely to prove effective.

Hitler, Forster concluded, refused to see because he could not bear to witness the defeat of Germany. Whichever treatment was finally devised would have to take this fact into account. But how should this be approached? With Germany now poised on the verge of defeat, its armies being routed in the west and its civilian population rioting at home, there was no way in which Forster could persuade Hitler victory was still possible. Since it was impossible to alter the external situation, all the doctor could do was attempt to change his patient's *perception* of the events now rapidly unfolding around them. For more than a fortnight he pondered this interesting psychological challenge. He interviewed Hitler on several occasions and gathered additional background information on this curious individual through conversations with the medical staff and fellow patients. Finally, in the first week of November, a possible therapeutic approach crystallised in his mind:

> I could attempt to find a way to free him of his symptoms through an ingenious coupling of his two ailments with his drive for status, his drive to be like God, his excessive energy . . .

21

I had to approach this man not with logical premises but with a tremendous lie in order to conquer him . . . for he was really one gigantic lie for whom there was no absolute truth but only the truth of his imagination, his striving, his urges.[17]

The success or failure of this approach would, Edmund Forster appreciated, depend on whose will was the stronger, his own or that of Adolf Hitler. If he failed, then the lance-corporal would probably never recover his sight. If he succeeded, then the return of vision should be almost instantaneous.

Edmund Forster's will triumphed, but it was a triumph that would ultimately cost the doctor his life.

Chapter Three
THE HITLERS OF BRAUNAU-AM-INN

What were God's intentions when he created this man?
August Kubizek, Young Hitler[1]

Adolf Hitler was born at 6.30 p.m. on Easter Saturday, 20 April 1889 in bedroom number 3 at the Gasthof-zum-Pommer in the little Austrian border town of Braunau-am-Inn. His father Alois was a fifty-one-year-old customs officer and his slightly built mother Klara a twenty-nine-year-old farmer's daughter. It was a gloomy evening with low clouds and the proximity of the River Inn making the bedroom dank. The birth had been so long and hard that by the time midwife Franziska Pointecker finally delivered Klara a baby son the mother was exhausted and soaked with perspiration.[2]

But it was fear as much as the humid atmosphere and exertion of childbirth that caused Klara to perspire so freely during the long hours of delivery. In four years of marriage she had already lost three children, two sons and a daughter, under the age of two. Now Klara and Alois, who desperately wanted a family, had pinned all their hopes on this, their fourth child, so that, holding the squealing infant in her arms, she vowed that no matter what sacrifices were entailed, this baby boy would grow to manhood. At 3.15 p.m. on the following Easter Monday, Alois and Klara had their son baptised by the parish priest, Father Ignaz Probst. They christened him Adolphus, a Germanic name meaning 'noble wolf'.

For much of his early adulthood Hitler was very much a lone

23

wolf, prowling the streets of Vienna and Munich in self-imposed isolation from his fellow man. Early in his political career he adopted the pseudonym 'Herr Wolf'. Later, he named his war headquarters in eastern France Wolfsschluchut (Wolf's Lair), that in East Prussia Wolfschanze (Fort Wolf) and his temporary base inside Russia Werewolf. The last of these was also the name chosen for the group of resistance fighters trained to operate behind the Allied lines after the invasion of Germany in 1944–5. His favourite breed of dog was the lupine German shepherd. One of these pets, Blondi, shared his last hours in the Führerbunker deep beneath the Chancellery. Of Hitler's relationship with the dog, Albert Speer observed, 'The German shepherd probably played the most important role in Hitler's life: it was more important than even his closest associates.'[3] By a bizarre coincidence, the name of his senior secretary during his final days in power was Frau Johanna Wolf.

While the personal opinions of Father Ignaz as he splashed Holy Water on to the infant and admitted him to the Catholic family were never recorded, it is unlikely that he regarded the youthful Klara and her burly, middle-aged husband as two of his Church's most devout followers. Alois, who described himself as a 'free-thinker', was frequently involved in heated attacks on clerics and religion. Apart from his marriage, or attending burials and baptisms (of which he admittedly had more than his fair share), he attended church only on the birthday of Emperor Franz Joseph of Austria-Hungary, the one man he revered. Even less commendable, from the priest's point of view, must have been Alois's private life, which, characterised by promiscuity and adultery, had long been a local scandal. In the late nineteenth century Braunau-am-Inn, with a population of around three thousand, retained the character more of a village than a town, and, as in every small community, the private affairs of its citizens were very much a matter of public discussion.[4] And, where Alois was concerned, the gossip was built on firm foundations. By the time Adolphus was born, his already twice-married father had not only taken a wife twenty-three years his junior but a woman closely related to him, and it was also rumoured, probably with justification, that he kept a mistress in Vienna. Although the townsfolk were always polite and respectful, a respect Alois pompously demanded in view of his official government position, relationships with his neighbours were formal rather than friendly. So when, several years after Adolf's birth, he was promoted to the rank of customs officer grade 1 and transferred to Passau, a paper-manufacturing town with a population of around sixteen thousand, we may presume that neither he nor Klara regretted the change. Alois regarded his promotion as a well-deserved reward for more than thirty years of loyal service to the Austro-Hungarian state and a fitting conclusion to the working life of a poor village boy who, through his own efforts, had managed to make something of himself.

Alois had entered this world burdened by the twin stigmas of poverty and illegitimacy. When his mother, Maria Anna Schicklgruber, a forty-two-year-old unmarried farmer's daughter, became pregnant, her outraged parents immediately ordered her to pack her bags and leave home (in spite of the fact that in this period four out of ten babies in the region were born out of wedlock). It was only through the kindness of a villager in the nearby hamlet of Strones that when Alois was born, on 7 June 1837, he was delivered in a cottage bedroom rather than an open field. A weak child who was not expected to live more than a few hours, Alois was baptised on the same day by the Döllersheim parish priest. Somehow he survived, and even contrived to flourish. In 1842 Maria Anna married Johann Georg Hiedler (or Hütler, the spelling of his name varies), a spendthrift journeyman miller who was so idle that he scarcely did a day's work in the five years between their marriage and Maria Anna's death in 1847. Although during those five years she struggled to provide for both her indolent husband and her child, the family gradually sank into destitution. Finally, with their furnishings sold around them, Johann Georg was forced to sleep in a cattle trough.

Following the death of his wife, the erstwhile husband disappeared from the scene, not to reappear in Alois's life for another
thirty years. The abandoned ten-year-old would have been in
desperate straits but for his uncle Johann von Nepomuk (he had been
named for the Czech national saint). Unlike his indolent younger
brother, Johann von Nepomuk (who spelled his surname Hütler)
was a hard-working and prosperous farmer in the nearby village of
Spital. Although he provided his nephew with board and lodging,
Alois's childhood does not seem to have been particularly happy. He
was known by his mother's maiden name of Schicklgruber, and was
thus branded with the stigma of bastardy; Johann von Nepomuk
also made it clear that Alois had no prospect of inheritance.

It would be nearly thirty years before Johann Georg Hiedler, by
then aged eighty-four, came back into Alois's life. In November 1876
he went with a group of neighbours to see Josef Zahnschirm, the
elderly Döllersheim parish priest, to have Alois's birth legitimised by
producing a legal document showing him as the father. Zahnschirm
obligingly changed the parish records by scratching out the remark
'Male, illegitimate' and filling in the name 'Georg Hiedler' in the
previously blank space under 'Father'. In the space for 'Remarks' the
priest noted: 'It is confirmed by the undersigned that Johann Georg
Hiedler, whose name is here entered as Father, being well known to
the undersigned did accept paternity of the child, Alois, according to
the statement of the child's mother Anna Schicklgruber.'[5]

Alois celebrated his legitimacy by subtly distancing himself from
both Johann von Nepomuk Hütler and Georg Hielder by combining
their surnames and thus producing a third spelling of the name:
henceforth, he and his family would be known as Hitler.

Early in Adolf Hitler's political life, researchers and journalists
– friends and foes alike – set about trying to establish the truth
of his father's paternity, for there was a rumour circulating that
Hitler's grandfather was not Johann Georg Hiedler but a wealthy
Jew. Some hinted he might even be a member of the Rothschild
family, who lived in Vienna. A more likely candidate, however, was

a Jew from the town of Graz named Frankenberger, for whom Maria Anna worked as a cook. In the early 1920s this rumour was used by Hitler's opponents at home and abroad, outside the Nazi Party and within its ranks, in an effort to damage his career. In 1921, for example, Ernst Ehrensperger, an early party member, wrote a leaflet attacking Hitler in which he stated: 'He believes the time has come to introduce disunity and dissension into our ranks at the behest of his shady backers ... And how is he conducting this struggle? Like a real Jew.'[6] In October 1933 the *Daily Mirror* published a photograph purporting to show the tombstone of Hitler's paternal grandfather in the Jewish cemetery in Bucharest.[7] A copy of this was forwarded to SS chief Heinrich Himmler and found its way into the rapidly growing file that he was keeping on his Führer. This article survives in the Federal Archives and carries the handwritten instruction: 'Please send here, Reichsführer wishes to retain.'[8]

Even Hitler himself appears to have had doubts about his grandfather and, in late 1930, sent for Hans Frank, his lawyer, whom he would later make Governor-General of Poland, and asked him to investigate matters. Shortly before he was hanged at Nürnberg in October 1946 for war crimes including the destruction of the Warsaw ghetto, Frank wrote: '[Hitler] showed me a letter which he described as a "disgusting piece of blackmail" on the part of one of his most loathsome relatives [this was his nephew William Patrick Hitler] and said that it concerned his, Hitler's, antecedents.[9] In this letter William Patrick Hitler threatened to tell the newspapers that his uncle was part Jewish. In the event, he did write an article on the subject for *Paris Soir* and went on a pre-war lecture tour of the United States. However, the French newspaper article is a somewhat self-pitying but innocuous account of their relationship.[10]

After his investigations, Frank claimed to have discovered that the Frankenbergers paid Maria Anna an allowance to raise her son and that there were letters showing a relationship between the family's nineteen-year-old son and their cook. 'Hence the possibility cannot be dismissed that Hitler's father was half Jewish as a result of the extra-marital relationship between the Schicklgruber woman and the Jew from Graz. This would mean that Hitler was one-quarter Jewish.'[11]

This was speculation on Frank's part: he found no hard evidence that Adolf Hitler's grandfather was 'the Jew from Graz'. Another candidate is the workshy Johann Georg, who in 1876 was made the 'official' father of Alois. While it is certainly possible that he was also the biological father, it seems more likely that his brother Johann von Nepomuk, who brought Alois up from the age of ten, was not only his guardian but his father. Perhaps he was willing to raise the boy as his own but was not prepared to admit to his adultery with Maria Anna. He was, after all, respected in the community as a happily married man.

The historical significance of Alois's legitimisation lies in the change of surname this allowed. From 6 January 1877, when the new name was registered at the government office in Mistelbach, Alois Schicklgruber was officially able to call himself Hitler. As Adolf Hitler's personal photographer, Heinrich Hoffmann, dubbed 'the court jester of the Third Reich' by the Führer's inner circle, once commented, without this change of name Hitler might never have achieved power. For while the masses would enthusiastically bellow 'Heil Hitler', Hoffmann suggested they would be less inclined to chant 'Heil Schicklgruber!'

At the age of thirteen Alois Schicklgruber, as he still was, left home to 'better himself' and – like his son almost half a century later – travelled to Vienna to seek employment. There he became apprenticed to a bootmaker and worked in this trade for five years while studying at night classes to make up for his lack of secondary education. In this he was successful and, at the age of eighteen, entered government service as a clerk with the Inland Revenue.

Within nine years the hard-working and ambitious young man had achieved the position of probationary assistant in the Customs

Service. In 1873, having already had one affair that led to the birth of an illegitimate son, Alois wed Anna Glassl-Hörer, the widowed daughter of an inspector in the imperial tobacco monopoly, and fourteen years his senior. The marriage brought him considerable financial benefits, for his bride came with a generous dowry from her father, and for the first time in his life Alois was able to enjoy a life of some comfort, and employ a housemaid. Two years later he was promoted to assistant inspector and transferred to Braunau-am-Inn. The following year, obviously feeling he had bettered himself sufficiently to return home, Alois travelled to Spital and stayed with his 'foster-father', Johann von Nepomuk. In the neighbouring cottage lived Johann Nepomuk's daughter, her husband and their three daughters. The eldest, Klara Pölzl, was a slim, dark-haired girl of sixteen who immediately caught Alois's roving eye. He somehow persuaded her parents to let her return with him to Braunau as his new maid and share his and his wife's rooms at the Gasthaus Streif. These lodgings were located conveniently close to his customs post at the Austrian end of the great iron bridge spanning the River Inn.

Working in the Gasthaus Streif's kitchens was a twenty-one-year-old cook named Franziska, 'Fanny', Matzelsberger, and within a few weeks of their return from Spital she had become Alois's latest mistress. When she learned of this affair his wife Anna immediately walked out and sued for a judicial separation, which was granted in 1880. No sooner had Anna left him than Alois invited Fanny to take her place. She agreed, but only on condition that his attractive young maid, Klara, was sent back home.

On 13 January 1882 Fanny gave birth to a son, named Alois after his father. On 6 April the following year Anna Glassl-Hörer, aged sixty, died of tuberculosis, and Alois wasted no time in marrying Fanny. Two months after the wedding Fanny gave birth to her second child, Angela. By now Alois was already sleeping with several other local women and having bitter rows with Fanny over her refusal to allow Klara to take up residence with them again.

Soon Fanny too was diagnosed with tuberculosis and sent to a sanatorium, giving Alois the opportunity to invite Klara back to Braunau. The young woman, who called Alois 'Uncle' – a habit she continued even after their marriage – seems to have had an almost daughterly affection for him. She gave up a job in Vienna to look after him and the two children he'd had with Fanny, two-year-old Alois Jr and ten-month-old Angela.

In August 1884, only a few months after her twenty-third birthday, Fanny died and was buried in the small country church at Ranshofen, the same parish in which she'd been married the previous year. Alois wanted to marry Klara, who was by now pregnant, immediately, but a delicate problem now arose. According to the birth certificate issued to him in 1877, Alois's father was Johann Georg Hiedler, the brother of Johann Nepomuk, and therefore Klara's great-uncle. The closeness of this blood tie meant that the relationship between Alois and Klara was prohibited under the consanguinity laws of the Catholic Church. If, as seems likely, Johann Nepomuk, Klara's grandfather, was Alois's father, then, of course, the blood tie was even closer: Alois was Klara's uncle. Had they even suspected this, one would presume that the church authorities would have forbidden them from marrying. In practical terms this would have made little difference, since the couple were living together and Klara was four months pregnant when Alois petitioned for a papal dispensation to permit their union. Father Kostler, the priest who was asked to deal with Alois's request, was initially reluctant to agree and lectured the unrepentant father on the dangers posed to their children by so incestuous a relationship. However, when Alois bluntly informed him not only that Klara was pregnant but that they intended to have several more children, irrespective of whether the Church granted them the dispensation, Kostler sent their request to the Bishop of Linz, who in turn forwarded it to the Vatican. Within three weeks the dispensation was granted, and on 7 January 1885 the customs official married his heavily pregnant bride. Alois, who was on duty at the customs post, insisted that the ceremony be held at the unusual hour of six o'clock in the morning and returned to work immediately afterwards.

Five months after the wedding Klara gave birth to her first son, whom they christened Gustav. In September 1886 she had a daughter, Ida, and, during 1887 (the date is unclear), another son, Otto. All three of these children quickly succumbed to diphtheria.[12] From this time onwards Alois's work frequently took him to Vienna or Linz, and even when not there he sometimes chose to stay in lodgings in a valley outside Braunau rather than in the town with his wife and children. One may presume that these absences, on top of the tragedy of losing three children in infancy, cemented the relationship between Klara and Adolf from his birth in 1889 onwards. While the Hitlers' family life was certainly unconventional – with the father frequently absent and the mother bringing up two children from Alois's previous marriage in addition to her own – with Alois's pension to look forward to on his retirement, their financial and material comfort was secure. But tensions between Adolf and his dominant and easily angered father meant that their relationship was turbulent and often violent. Those same qualities of self-reliance and ambition that had enabled a poor, illegitimate boy to rise above his humble origins also made Alois an obstinate and cantankerous parent, as is noted by B.F. Smith:

> At home he was more than a formidable character. He was master, and he impressed this fact upon every member of the household. He alone had raised the whole lot of them and he demanded the obedience and respect that he felt they owed him ... The old man's dominance made him a permanent object of respect, if not awe, to his wife and children. Even after his death his pipes still stood in a rack on the kitchen shelf, and when his widow wished to make a particularly important point she would gesture toward the pipes as if to invoke the authority of the master.[13]

Whenever Alois was away from home on a posting to Vienna or Linz, meek and submissive Klara strove to maintain discipline by warning Adolf and his older stepbrother Alois Jr of the severe punishment that awaited them on their father's return if they misbehaved. It was no idle threat. That Alois used corporal punishment on his sons is apparent from a comment Hitler made in 1942. Recalling the fate of a prisoner, he remarked: 'I told [Minister of Justice] Gürtner that had I, myself, received in one fell swoop all the thrashings I deserved (and had had) in my life I should be dead!'[14] As a child, he had expressed these fears in a poem, written in a guest book on 30 April 1905, when he was sixteen years old. The final two lines read: 'Then comes, poor man, his wife/And heals his bottom with thrashings.'[15]

Alois was away from home again when Adolf's brother Edmund was born in March 1894. A year later he returned and the family was reunited in a new home at Lambach-am-Traun. On 25 June 1895, with forty years' service behind him, Alois retired from government service and vowed to spend the remainder of his life running a smallholding and keeping bees. Adolf had just started attending a primary school attached to Lambach's ancient monastery, run by the local Benedictine monks. A bright and energetic child, he proved himself an adept pupil. Overawed by the splendour of the Catholic mass and captivated by the beauty of church music, he took singing lessons and joined the choir. For some years he was attracted to the Church as a career, convinced that the priestly vocation was the 'highest and most desirable ideal'.

Although Hitler remained on friendly terms with his sister Paula, who was born in January 1896, his relationship with his half-brother Alois Jr was always fraught. If Adolf did anything naughty, he would invariably blame his older brother, who received a beating. A year after his father retired, fourteen-year-old Alois Jr was unable to stand life at home any longer and ran away to Vienna. There he later married an Irish woman and they had a son, the aforementioned William Patrick. By the 1930s Alois Jr had opened a beer hall in

Berlin, where he traded on his relationship to Adolf, much to the latter's annoyance. William Patrick emigrated to America and served with the United States Navy during the Second World War.

With his stepbrother no longer at home, Adolf was left to bear the brunt of his father's increasingly vicious temper, a rage exacerbated by overwork. Like many men before him, Alois found his smallholding a burden rather than the pleasant retirement he had envisaged, and in 1897 he sold up. The family moved twice within the space of a year: first to a house situated next door to a blacksmith's shop, where the noise and stench from the smithy gave Adolf a lifelong loathing of horses; and then to a cottage with half an acre of land in the village of Leonding, outside Linz. Adolf, therefore, moved to his third primary school in as many years.

Under the German system, children started in a people's school (*Volksschule*), then moved to an elementary school (*Grundschule*) at the age of six. At ten those from the upper social classes, together with a handful of scholarship students from the lower classes, were sent either to a *Gymnasium* – where lessons were dominated by Greek, Latin and the humanities – or a *Realschule* – where the syllabus offered the chance to study science and modern languages. As a result of this practical approach to education, attendance at a *Realschule* carried far less status than going to *Gymnasium*. *Realschule* was intended for the plebeians (there were 110 such schools in Berlin alone), while *Gymnasia* (just 30 in the same city) were intended for the social elite. After studies lasting between eight and nine years, students were awarded a diploma, known as an *Abitur*, and left school. A minority went either to university or technical college while the majority set about finding a job. At all levels the regime within German schools was highly disciplined and based on rote learning, with accurate recall being encouraged and independence of thought or expression severely discouraged.

When, at the age of ten, Adolf transferred to the *Realschule* in Linz, he took an immediate dislike to the school, housed in a gloomy city-centre building, his teachers and the curriculum. From being a lively and high-achieving primary school pupil, Adolf became an apathetic and lazy student. His first end-of-term report describes his moral conduct as no more than 'adequate' and application to his studies as 'erratic'.

In February of 1900 his brother Edmund died of measles and the shock of his unexpected death may have contributed to a dramatic personality change that occurred in Adolf. He became increasingly rebellious, a change in his behaviour that brought him into even more frequent and violent confrontation with his father. The old man, perhaps recalling the early difficulties his own lack of education had caused him, furiously demanded Adolf work more diligently in class. But the rows and the beatings made Adolf only more determined to go his own way. 'It was', says Konrad Heiden, 'Adolf Hitler's first great struggle, and by his own admission he conducted it with great fears, with lies and with secretiveness.'[16]

In December 1902 Alois developed a bad chest cold and spent several days in bed, but at the start of the new year he appeared to have recovered, and on Saturday 3 January went to see a neighbouring farmer about buying some apples. It was a bitterly cold morning and on the way home he started feeling unwell and called at the Gasthaus Steifler for a glass of wine. Before the landlord could pour it, Alois collapsed and was carried into a back room where they placed him on a table while the pot boy was sent to fetch a doctor, but moments later the sixty-five-year-old man haemorrhaged and choked to death on his own blood. He was buried two days later in the cemetery opposite his house.

The local newspaper, *Linz Tagespost*, published a lengthy obituary that began: 'We have buried a good man – that we can rightly say about Alois Hitler, Higher Official of the Imperial Customs, retired, who was carried to his final resting place today.' The notice went on to remark that 'The harsh words that sometimes fell from his lips could not belie the warm heart that beat under the rough exterior.'

Hitler wept as the coffin was lowered into the grave, but he can hardly have been devastated by the old man's death, since not only did it free him from the endless arguments and frequent beatings but meant he only need share the affections and attentions of Klara with his young and slightly backward sister Paula.

Without his father's constant nagging, Hitler's schoolwork declined still further. He did the minimum possible and spent most of his time reading the stories of the German author Karl May, who wrote about the Wild West even though he had never visited the United States. His tales, therefore, were exciting but highly inaccurate.

On Whit Sunday, 22 May 1904, accompanied by an old friend of his father, Hitler was confirmed into the Catholic Church. The man tried hard to make a special occasion of the day, even going to the expense of hiring a horse-drawn carriage and taking the teenager to see his first movie, but fifteen-year-old Adolf remained sulky and ungrateful.

A few weeks later he suddenly left the Linz *Realschule* for reasons that have never become entirely clear. When his name was becoming more widely known around Munich during the early 1920s, this abrupt departure became a matter for wild rumours. On 27 May 1923, for example, the *Munich Post* alleged that he had been expelled because, during a school mass, he had spat out the Host and slipped it into his pocket. Other stories, circulated by his political opponents, claimed that he had been caught smoking, or that he had tried to seduce a girl. This last accusation would have been totally out of character, for, whatever personality traits his teachers may have attributed to the young Hitler (and one later described him as 'obstinate, high-handed, intransigent and fiery-tempered'), sexual precocity was never one of them.[17]

The most likely explanation is that Klara and his teachers felt that a change of schools might help improve his scholastic achievements, for he was considered an intelligent young man who lacked motivation and self-discipline. In September 1904 he entered the fourth form in the senior secondary school at Steyr, an industrial town some twenty-five miles from Linz. He shared lodgings with a boy of the same age and, according to his recollections, spent much of his spare time shooting at rats as they scampered across the gloomy courtyard below their window. At Steyr, while he remained rebellious and surly, his schoolwork showed some signs of improvement. A pencil sketch made by one of his classmates depicts Adolf as a slim fifteen-year-old with a high, receding forehead, prominent nose and jutting chin who appears to be prematurely old and far from well.[18] This was indeed the case, and a few weeks after leaving Steyr, which he celebrated by getting drunk for the first and probably the last time in his life, Hitler became seriously ill with a lung infection that might have been tuberculosis.

Concerned about his health, Klara took him and Paula to stay with her sister in the country. The weeks of rest, fresh air and good food soon helped bring about a recovery, possibly assisted by Klara bringing him a jugful of milk still warm from the cow to build his strength.[19]

In June 1905 Klara sold the cottage in Leonding and moved her family into a small apartment at 31 Humboldtstrasse in Linz, which had only two rooms and a kitchen with windows overlooking an inner courtyard. Klara and Paula slept in the living room, while Adolf was given the bedroom. Before long the sixteen-year-old's daily routine had become established. He read and sketched during most of the night and slept late. Sometimes, despairing of ever getting him out of bed, Klara would send Paula in to kiss him good morning. Adolf, who hated being kissed, would immediately leap out of bed.

With money from the sale of the cottage and Alois's pension, the family was comfortably off and Klara was able to give her son money to indulge his latest passion, attending the opera. He also had all the elegant clothes he craved. Hitler took a pride in his appearance and liked to stroll through the town swinging a small black cane. Not that he dressed smartly to attract others. He had no girlfriends and made no effort to strike up friendships with other boys. He saw himself as being above such mundane desires. As he wandered the darkened streets of Linz, he imagined himself not as a forlorn outsider but a noble wolf. Whenever anyone enquired what he intended to do with his life, he always announced proudly: 'I shall become a great artist.'

Chapter Four
THE FORSTERS OF AMSTERDAM

*Do not bow your heads. Do not know your place. Defy the gods.
You will be astonished how many of them turn out to have feet
of clay.*

Salman Rushdie, Step Across this Line[1]

Eleven years before the birth of Adolf Hitler and seventy-six miles
away from the petty intrigues of provincial Braunau-am-Inn, in the
heart of cosmopolitan Munich, the second player in the Pasewalk
drama, Edmund Robert Forster, was born into considerably more
emotionally secure and prosperous circumstances. His father Franz
Joseph was a rising young doctor and university lecturer, while
his mother Wilhelmina 'Mina' Emilie Louise von Hösslin came
from a wealthy Dutch-German family with extensive land holdings
around Augsburg in southern Germany. In the year of Edmund's
birth Russia was fighting with Turkey, the British government had
dispatched its Mediterranean squadron to Gallipoli, and England
was in the grip of war fever. At the London Pavilion, music-hall
artist the Great Macdermott[2] was performing a song whose chorus,
'We don't want to fight, but by jingo if we do/We've got the ships,
we've got the men, we've got the money too!',[3] added 'jingoism'
to the English language. Over the next half-century this word
was used to describe any expression of belligerent nationalism.
It would also provide the leitmotif for Edmund Forster's turbulent life.

Edmund's father was the seventh of eleven children born to Conrad and Elise Forster, who owned and ran a lucrative wine-trading business in the picturesque little town of Nonnenhorn on Lake Constance. The company had been started almost a century before Edmund's birth by Johann Georg Forster, a shrewd and energetic entrepreneur who travelled throughout the country securing contracts with major wine traders in most of the larger cities. By 1795 the business was prospering to such an extent that Johann purchased a vinegar factory and added it to his trade in wine and spirits. Edmund's grandfather began to manage the business in 1834, when he was only twenty. He proved so successful that two years later he felt sufficiently financially secure to marry. His chosen bride was the daughter of a wealthy Lindau merchant, and the couple set about starting what was to become a large family. By the time Edmund's father was born, on 6 April 1844, Conrad and Elise had become wealthy and respected members of Nonnenhorn's community, and were building an elegant, three-storey house that still stands today. Despite Conrad's affluence and bourgeois respectability this tall, imposing man with his bushy black beard and penetrating gaze did not, as might be assumed, epitomise all those inward-looking and narrow-minded social attitudes that Germans derogatively label as *Biedermeier*.[4] Not only did the heart of a revolutionary beat beneath his sober attire, but when the occasion arose he unhesitatingly risked his freedom for a just cause and, in doing so, played a significant role in the early history of the United States.

In 1848, when Conrad was thirty-four, the March Revolution plunged Germany into turmoil.[5] Triggered initially by discontent among intellectuals and students at their lack of personal freedom, the revolutionary spirit swiftly spread to the working classes. But while educated Germans were protesting at the authoritarian nature of the regime, workers had a more basic reason for dissent: many were starving to death. The combined effects of rapid industrialisation, urbanisation and population increase had caused hundreds of thousands to live in abject poverty, with even the hardest-working families unable to lift themselves above subsistence level. The widespread ownership of land by the Junker aristocracy and Church meant that in rural areas, where 80 per cent of the population still lived, pitifully low wages kept agricultural labourers in a state of permanent servitude and squalor. Four years earlier a minor uprising by destitute Silesian weavers had been savagely crushed by the army; protests about 'starvation wages' were met with the retort, 'Then eat grass.' Crop failures in 1847 resulted in famines, soaring unemployment and hunger riots. After these had been ruthlessly suppressed by the military, an uneasy peace lasted until March 1848. In Prussia, King Friedrich Wilhelm IV decided, against the advice of his ministers and generals, that the best way to control a revolution was to lead it. Accordingly, he agreed to almost all of the protesters' demands, including a written constitution, free parliamentary elections and the abolition of press censorship. These early achievements, however, proved very much a false dawn. Dogged by a lack of organisation and the conflicting aims of different leaders, including Karl Marx,[6] the revolutionaries were ultimately no match for a ruthlessly determined state. Within twelve months the idealists had been routed, leaders of the uprising were on the run and the general population too disorganised to continue the struggle. As a familiar militaristic authority was re-established, thousands of Germans, many of them the most highly educated, chose emigration over subjugation. Most of them settled in the United States.

A strong supporter of the March Revolution, Conrad had formed the Märzverein (March Association) in Nonnenhorn, and, with the backing of seven other prominent local businessmen, sent two resolutions to the Bavarian King Max II pleading with him to accept a new constitution. The King's response was to dispatch six hundred soldiers to occupy Nonnenhorn and stamp out any smouldering discontent. Within a year the garrison was firmly established, with regular street patrols and random house-to-house searches for fleeing revolutionary leaders. All of which placed Conrad in a precarious position.

One of the best-known and most rigorously hunted of these leaders was twenty-year-old Carl Schurz, a former student at Bonn University. After living underground in Berlin for almost a year, he had managed to reach Nonnenhorn, where Conrad concealed him in the firm's cavernous wine cellars while devising a plan to smuggle him across the lake to Switzerland. His already hazardous situation was made even more potentially dangerous when an informant tipped off the authorities that Schurz was being hidden in the town. The garrison's commander gave orders that every house was to be thoroughly searched and both the fugitive and those harbouring him arrested. Fortunately for Conrad, because the commander did not receive this tip-off until late in the afternoon, he decided to wait until first light the following day before starting the search. This delay gave Conrad an opportunity to pass a message to his fellow townsfolk, instructing them to invite the soldiers into their homes that evening and provide them with generous hospitality, including ample supplies of Nonnenhorn's excellent wines. He extended a similar invitation to the garrison's officers, and a long night of riotous drinking ensued. Cask after cask of his choicest vintages were broached, and bottle after bottle of his finest schnapps poured down eager throats. By dawn every one of the six hundred soldiers and their officers was too busy sleeping off the biggest hangover of his life to conduct the intended search. With the entire garrison sprawled in a drunken stupor, Conrad was able to row Schurz the nine miles across Lake Constance to freedom.

From Switzerland the young revolutionary made his way to the United States, where he became an early supporter of Abraham Lincoln. Later he fought as a Union general in the American Civil War, before ending a spectacular career as Secretary of the Interior. By the time of his death in 1906 Schurz had also gained an international reputation for journalism and authorship.[7] His most famous (and certainly his most misquoted) statement was 'Our country right or wrong', to which he added the frequently omitted, 'When right to be kept right; when wrong to be put right.'[8]

This escapade is still gleefully remembered in Nonnenhorn to this day, and in 1984 the townspeople commemorated their leading citizen's guile and courage with a four-act play, *Die Flucht* (*The Flight*).

In the 1850s and 1860s, with the March Revolution no more than a distant memory, Conrad continued the profitable if mundane business of trading wine and raising his growing family. He had become Nonnenhorn's most prominent citizen, and ultimately served as *Bürgermeister* from 1869 up to his death on 23 January 1878, as well as representing his community on the regional council. He was instrumental in setting up the town's fire service and helped run the Lake Constance Railway. There is a street named in his honour in the town.

On Conrad's death, since none of his many children expressed any interest in the wine business, it passed to Agatha Amalie, Conrad's niece, and her husband Friedrich Hugo May. They ran it successfully for another twelve years, until in 1890 Hugo May was convicted of embezzling 23,000 marks from the local chapel, where he kept the books. He was sentenced to three years' imprisonment. His disgrace led to the firm's bankruptcy and takeover, so ending a business that had been in the same family for more than a century. It also brought an end to the family's connection with Nonnenhorn, since neither Franz Joseph nor any of his relatives set foot in the town again.

By the time this happened, however, the wine trader's brilliant son had achieved a higher social status as a doctor and university professor. Conrad was a strong believer in the importance of an academic education and was eager for his children to receive the schooling he had been denied by beginning in the family business as a teenager. Of all his sons and daughters, however, it quickly became apparent that Franz Joseph was more than merely clever; he was brilliant. Realising that he would be unable to obtain the education he deserved in Nonnenhorn, Conrad and Elise sent him more than a hundred miles away to live with relatives while he studied at the *Gymnasia* of Augsburg, Munich and Leipzig. Their confidence in his precocity proved to be fully justified when, in his final exams, eighteen-year-old Franz Joseph achieved the highest marks of any student in Germany. His reputation as a scholar thus assured, he had no difficulty in gaining acceptance as a medical student at Munich University and, thanks to a generous allowance from his parents, was able to move into comfortable rented accommodation. Within four years he had qualified as a doctor of medicine, surgery and obstetrics, the viva for his thesis being examined and accepted on 29 July 1868.

After qualifying, Joseph worked for a time as an assistant to one of Germany's most eminent physiologists, Professor Karl von Voits, whose studies of metabolism were to lay the foundations for modern nutritional science. Voits had accurately measured the number of calories humans use when active and resting, and had demonstrated that metabolism occurs within the cells, rather than, as had been previously supposed, in the blood. Finally, he established the scientific basis of present-day diet regimes. Working with Voits on studies of nutrition had so fascinated Franz Joseph that he abandoned earlier ideas of becoming a physician and decided instead to make his career in the fields of hygiene and nutritional research.

Before he could take that step, however, the Franco-Prussian War of 1870 broke out and the twenty-six-year-old immediately volunteered as a battalion doctor with the 12th Royal Bavarian Infantry Regiment. He saw action in the Battles of Sedan, Coulmiers, Orléans, Loignay-Pomry and Beauganey, and was awarded the Military Order of Merit for his courage under fire. He gained a reputation among officers and troops for this bravery and for his humanity in the treatment of patients. One example that illustrates his generosity of spirit occurred after his assistant was killed during the Battle of Sedan. Franz Joseph requested another aide, preferably somebody with knowledge of French, and the regiment sent him a certain Johann Faist. To their mutual astonishment, the two men immediately recognised each other. Not only were they both from Nonnenhorn, but they had been friends at primary school. Later, when Faist was taken seriously ill and had to be invalided home, Franz Joseph wrote asking his father to care for him and to provide a bottle of good wine and a hearty meal each day until he had made a complete recovery.

On leaving the army Franz Joseph returned to Munich, where in 1874 he applied for and received a post-doctoral qualification essential for anyone wanting to lecture at a university. Since returning from the war, he had maintained a close friendship with his older sister Anna Juliana, who was married to August Voit, an eminent Munich architect. One evening, having accepted an invitation to dinner at the couple's Munich apartment, Anna Juliana introduced him to her husband's twenty-three-year-old cousin, Mina. It was love at first sight for both of them, and they were soon seeing each other regularly, despite their courtship initially facing strong opposition from Mina's wealthy and patrician parents. A brilliant doctor, decorated officer and academic Franz Joseph might be, but he was also the son of a tradesman. In the strictly hierarchical society of nineteenth-century Germany this was as great a barrier to marriage as it would have been in class-conscious Victorian England. Furthermore, Mina's family, the von Hösslins, were staunch members of the Dutch Reform Church, while their daughter's would-be suitor was a Catholic. Faced with such a daunting challenge, some young men might have bowed to the inevitable; but, like his father, Franz Joseph was not one to resign himself meekly to disappointment. Instead, he embarked on a relentless campaign to charm and reassure Mina's parents which, after two years of tactful persistence, finally succeeded in winning their consent. The only condition to the von Hösslins' consent was that Franz Joseph and Mina's children should be brought up in the Dutch Reform Church. Franz Joseph seems to have raised no objection to this, either because his religion was not especially important to him or because, like most German males of the time, he regarded the upbringing of children entirely as the responsibility of his wife. On 3 October 1876 they married in Munich and the following year his academic career was assured when, aged only thirty-three, he was appointed Professor of Physiology at Munich's Central Veterinary School.

On 28 July that year their first child, Margarethe 'Gretchen' Francisca Augusta, was born, and on 3 September 1878 the couple had their first son, Edmund Robert. Both infants were delivered by Franz Joseph himself in the family's spacious fourth-floor apartment on Lindwurm Strasse, a broad, tree-lined avenue whose tranquillity was disturbed only by the occasional rattle of passing trams and the steady click of hoofs as horse-drawn carriages trundled over the cobbles.

In 1879, through the influence of his wife's family, who were in contact with senior members of the Dutch government, Franz Joseph was offered and eagerly accepted the directorship of the new and not yet completed Hygiene Institute in Amsterdam. By the summer of that year the Forsters were comfortably settled into a gracious five-storey house overlooking a canal on the tree-lined Nicholaas Witsenkade. Already a Dutch speaker herself, Mina helped her husband master the language and ensured that all her children were raised to be fluent not only in German and Dutch but in French and English. Over the next four years three more children were added to the family, although one died in infancy.

Franz Joseph's time was fully occupied in supervising the completion of the Hygiene Institute, which was situated amid trees and gardens on the banks of a canal within a short cab ride from the centre of Amsterdam. Once it was operational he worked even harder to build an international research reputation for both the institute and himself. In addition to achieving practical advances in the fields of human and animal health, he co-edited a learned journal, the *Archiv für Hygiene*, which published papers on the hygienic aspects of nutrition, especially in relation to milk and meat. In 1883 he was elected a member of the German Academy of

Science, in 1884 to the Dresden Academy of Sciences, and in 1886 to the Scientific Department of the Royal Academy of Sciences in Amsterdam. In 1893 the Dutch government awarded him the Ritter des Ordens vom Niederländischen Löwen for outstanding services to his adopted country. Founded in 1815, this order is not only the Netherlands' oldest civil decoration but its most prestigious, being given only to those who have served society to an extent that goes well beyond what might have been expected of them in the normal course of their work. Three years after receiving this award Franz Joseph left Holland for Strasbourg to become Director of the city's Hygiene and Bacteriological Institute, and in 1903 he was appointed its Rector, a position he held until his death seven years later.

At the end of July 1898, he and his wife had travelled to Scotland, where he was awarded an honorary Doctor of Laws by the University of Edinburgh. On that occasion he was one of nineteen eminent medical men from many parts of Europe to be honoured. Had he been invited to the next awards ceremony, four months later, Franz Joseph would have found himself sharing the platform with Lord Kitchener of Khartoum, the general who would play such a prominent part in recruiting soldiers during the First World War.

By his mid-sixties, Franz Joseph Forster, admired and respected by his colleagues and adored by his wife and children, had reached the pinnacle of his academic career. A contemporary photograph shows him to have been portly, with receding grey hair and a thick, curling white moustache. While his steel-framed pince-nez glasses and very formal black morning-coat and high-collared shirt convey the serious demeanour expected of a Herr Doktor Professor, his dark eyes are kindly and the edges of his mouth appear on the point of twitching into a smile. It is clear from all the accounts of his life that the unknown portrait photographer had perfectly captured the rare blend of warm humanity and rigorous scientific objectivity that characterised his wise and generous nature. All his children remained close both to him and, to an even greater extent, Mina, with Edmund and his brother Dirk constantly writing letters and sending postcards home to keep their parents informed of everything that was happening to them, and to ask for advice and assistance. During the final months of his life, in 1910, Franz Joseph could look back not only on his considerable scientific achievements but on the academic success of his sons, especially Edmund, who had consistently gained the highest marks in all subjects during his school career.

In part, Franz Joseph's readiness to leave his homeland and work in the Netherlands may have been due to distaste for Germany's education system and a desire to have his children taught in a more enlightened and less authoritarian style. It was an aversion to Germany's rigid, militaristic schooling shared by many intellectuals, including Albert Einstein. 'To me,' Einstein recalled some years later, 'the worst thing seems to be for a school principally to work with methods of fear, force, and artificial authority. Such treatment produces ... the submissive subject. It is no wonder that such schools are the rule in Germany and Russia.'[9] In *Before the Deluge* Otto Friedrich quotes the views of an elderly German who believed that children's education at that time mirrored the cultural and social mores of the period:

> You must remember that the basic questions were not intellec-
> tual questions. The basic questions involved the development
> of character. I remember, for example, one day when we got
> a barrel of apples, and our governess always made us eat the
> bad ones first, the wormy ones, so that no apples would be
> wasted. And since we were only allowed to eat one apple a
> day, the good apples went bad while we ate the bad ones, and
> so most of the apples we ate had worms in them. But that was
> supposed to develop the character. And I remember that when
> I went to have my tonsils out, there was no talk of anaesthetic
> or anything like that. The doctor just stared at me for a long
> time, and then he said, 'Are you a brave German boy or are
> you a coward who cries because of a little pain?' Of course, I

had to say I was a brave German boy, and not a coward, and so he took his long shears and reached into my mouth and cut out my tonsils. And I didn't cry.[10]

With memories of his own school days fresh in his mind, the gentle and enlightened Franz Joseph may have felt a sense of relief that his sons would be able to experience the more liberal approach to education of Holland, where independent thinking rather than unquestioning obedience was more widely encouraged. From the age of six to twelve Edmund, along with his brothers, attended the Dutch-German School in Amsterdam, and from July 1890 to June 1896 he went to the prestigious *Gymnasium*, located in a building of imposing if austere architectural grandeur. Franz Joseph and his wife were clearly delighted with the education their sons had received at the Dutch-German School since they allowed their names to be used as endorsements in its prospectus.

Both Edmund and his brother Dirk proved to be exceptional students. Edmund's reports consistently gave him the highest marks in virtually every subject. While both boys excelled in English, French and mathematics, Edmund did especially well in science. However, he was a headstrong, stubborn and argumentative extrovert with a quick temper that he made little attempt to control and a readiness to take risks by rebelling against authority whenever he considered the rules arbitrary or unreasonable. He spoke his mind without considering the consequences and showed little patience with those who either remained silent in the face of injustice or expressed opinions he regarded as stupid or dull. In his view all such conflicts involved a battle of wills, and since he considered his own will-power superior to that of anyone else, the idea of defeat or surrender never entered his mind. Unsurprisingly, this brought him into regular conflict with the school authorities. On one occasion he became so angry with the philosophical opinions of one of his teachers that he struck him over the head with a salami and was suspended for the remainder of the term.

While disapproving of his rebellious nature, Edmund's teachers also recognised his original and painstaking approach to problem-solving and the eagerness with which he confronted unfamiliar intellectual challenges. He was, in the eyes of both his parents and his teachers, 'brilliant and outstanding'.

Dirk, although no less intellectually able, lacked his older brother's creative daring and innovative thinking. Where Edmund soared, Dirk plodded, and where the older son was inspired, the younger was merely industrious. Edmund was sociable and confident, while Dirk was quiet and more introspective. Cautious and dutiful, he preferred to guard his tongue and obey the rules, to avoid incurring anyone's disfavour, a habit he retained to the end of his life. His cautious nature is revealed in the account of why he never bothered to learn to drive. His daughter-in-law Pam Forster recalls how, when a young man, he went motoring with a friend who owned one of the first cars in Bavaria: 'It broke down and while the friend was lying under it attempting a repair, angry peasants came running from a field and chased Dirk down the road, thinking he had killed the man. It was only the quick action of his companion that saved him from their pitchforks! From then on, he stuck to taxis.'[11]

The Forsters' third son, Arne, who lacked his brothers' quick intelligence, found his studies more of a struggle, and had to work especially hard to keep up with their reputation for scholastic brilliance. While Edmund was a practical young man and Dirk a diligent conformist, Arne was a dreamer fascinated by romantic literature and often seeming to live in a fantasy world. On one occasion, after being given some money to pay for driving lessons, he spent it all on buying a Goethe first edition as a birthday present for Dirk.

All the children, including the rebellious Edmund, respected and admired their father without, as so often happened at the time, feeling intimidated or oppressed by him. Far from being the remote and unapproachable patriarch whose presence filled the house with silent dread, he was warm, loving and encouraging to all his children. However, it seems likely that Franz Joseph kept a special place in his affections for Edmund. Of course, Edmund was his first-born son and clearly had the same precocious intelligence as Franz Joseph himself possessed, but additionally, from an early age, Edmund was eager to follow his father into medicine. His two brothers, in contrast, plumped for the law and architecture.

On leaving the *Gymnasium* in 1896 at the age of eighteen, Edmund took his first steps to becoming a physician when he was accepted by the Medical School at Strasbourg's Kaiser Wilhelms University, the university to which his father had just transferred. It was an intellectual journey that would take him into one of medicine's most recent and least understood specialisations, neurology. He would spend the rest of his life attempting to make sense of that most impenetrable of all medical mysteries, disorders of the human mind.

Chapter Five
DOWN AND OUT IN VIENNA

And through this whole dismal, vicious life runs the desperate struggle against the city, the fatherland, the world which has not recognised the artist-prince in him, and whose judgement has made him shy of humanity.

Konrad Heiden, Der Führer[1]

Between the ages of fifteen and nineteen Hitler experienced two intense relationships, one with a boy of his own age and the other with a girl to whom he never spoke. The first served the practical purpose of giving him a sounding-board for his ideas and dreams, while the second was a romantic fantasy on which many of those dreams were centred. In November 1904 he met August 'Gustl' Kubizek, a gentle and rather naive youth, nine months his senior, who was working as an apprentice upholsterer in his father's workshop in Linz. Although his days were spent surrounded by dusty sofas and tattered armchairs, doing a job he loathed, Kubizek was no ordinary tradesman. He played the violin and piano, lived only for music, and had ambitions to study at the Vienna Conservatory and become a conductor. All his spare cash and every free moment was spent playing music or at the Linz Opera House, for which he could afford only the cheapest tickets, which permitted the holder to stand in one of the gangways. The most sought-after cheap position was beside one of the two ornate pillars holding up the royal box, as these provided a convenient support for one's back and a clear view of the stage. By missing his supper and racing to the opera house from work, Kubizek usually managed to gain one of these prime standing locations. But one night he arrived to find another young man occupying his favourite spot in the auditorium. In his book *Young Hitler* (on which all of Hitler's later biographers have relied for details of the dictator's early years), Kubizek recalled that moment:

> Half annoyed, half surprised I glanced at my rival. He was a remarkably pale, skinny youth about my own age, who was following the performance with glistening eyes . . . we took note of each other without exchanging a word. But in the interval of a performance some time later we started talking as, apparently, neither of us approved of the casting of one of the parts. We discussed it together and rejoiced in our common adverse criticism.[2]

According to Kubizek, it was through this shared love of music that they became friends, although just how close that friendship was remains open to question. Although Kubizek gives the impression of being genuinely fond of his strange and often difficult companion, Hitler's feelings seem a good deal less certain. For him, the main attraction of their friendship appears to have been that Kubizek provided an audience. 'Our characters were utterly different,' Kubizek recalls. 'I was a quiet, somewhat dreamy youth, very sensitive and adaptable and therefore always willing to yield. Adolf was exceedingly violent and highly strung.'[3] Hitler was apparently also extremely possessive, and jealously guarded the intimacy of their relationship. On one occasion, when Kubizek attended the funeral of his violin teacher Heinrich Dessauer, Hitler insisted on accompanying him, even though he had never met Dessauer and knew nobody at the service. 'I can't bear it that you should mix with other young people and talk to them,' he explained.[4]

When not going to the opera or concerts together, they spent hours walking in the countryside while Hitler declaimed his ambitions, philosophy and schemes. Sometimes he would stop and lecture Gustl – Hitler refused to call him August, a name he disliked, for some reason – as though addressing a large audience. His friend would listen patiently and attentively to the diatribe without making any attempt to contradict or disagree. The unconditional acceptance of his views and unquestioning obedience to his commands were precisely what Hitler expected, and it appears that Kubizek had no objection to playing such a passive role in their relationship, as 'it made me realise just how much my friend needed me'.[5]

On occasions, he reports, the vehemence of his friend's oratory surprised and startled him:

> These speeches, usually delivered somewhere out in the open, seemed to be like a volcano erupting. It was as though something quite apart from him was bursting out from him . . . again and again I was filled with astonishment at how fluently he expressed himself, how vividly he managed to convey his feelings, how easily the words flowed from his mouth when he was completely carried away by his own emotions . . . This to me was something new, magnificent . . . I had never imagined that a man could produce such an effect with mere words.[6]

This paean for the adolescent orator offers a clue to Kubizek's motive in writing his memories. As Rudolph Binion points out: 'This unctuous book was originally intended for the Nazi archive, and it shows. It mostly can't be confirmed, and his [Kubizek's] Linz townsman [Franz] Jetzinger [in his book *Hitler's Youth*] demolished lots of his yarns.'[7]

So it is with the caveat that Kubizek cannot be relied upon as an unimpeachable witness that the following incident should be judged. According to his account, Hitler's only other intense emotional relationship of his adolescence was with a girl about whom he fantasised but to whom he never plucked up the courage to speak. Kubizek remembers how, one evening in the spring of 1905, as they were walking down the Landstrasse in Linz, Hitler suddenly gripped his arm, pointed dramatically towards a slim, blonde girl strolling beside her mother, and whispered he had fallen in love with her. The Landstrasse at dusk was a favourite parading ground for chaperoned girls and hopeful youths who would promenade up and down, casting furtive glances at one another. Now and then the ladies would stop and stare with apparent fascination into a shop window, so as to watch the reflections of potential partners. Flower-sellers flanked the wide street, and a romance might begin with a would-be suitor presenting a bouquet to the girl of his choice, but Hitler lacked the boldness to make such a gesture. Instead, he persuaded the faithful Kubizek to turn detective and discover all he could about the girl. Thanks to a friend of his who knew her brother, August was able to report back that her name was Stefanie and she lived with her mother in the Linz suburb of Urfahr. Her father had recently died, Kubizek added, and the man who often accompanied her on walks was a brother who was studying law in Vienna.

Kubizek claims Hitler wrote mawkish love poems to Stefanie in which he depicted her as riding on a pure-white horse while the wind blew through her fair hair and disturbed the folds of her velvet robes. But these verses were never sent and he made no attempt to approach her directly. So Kubizek was compelled to stroll with his lovesick friend up and down the Landstrasse, always keeping a few yards behind her, with Hitler so lost in adoration that he ran a grave risk of being knocked down by the passing traffic. He had somehow persuaded himself that Stefanie knew about his love for her and shared all the dreams he had confided to Kubizek. When his friend had the temerity to question this curious assumption, Hitler flew into a rage, insisting that no words were needed, since his thoughts were instantly communicated to her through the power of their unspoken love. 'You simply don't understand,' he stormed at the bemused Kubizek, 'because you can't understand the true meaning of extraordinary love.'[8]

This delusion persisted for some time, even amid Stefanie's constant association with other young men. Hitler viewed this as simply a cunning diversion to prevent their own intense relationship being discovered. But, eventually, he started to doubt his theory, and, in the privacy of his apartment, he would burst into hysterical rages of jealousy and threaten suicide. Finally, though, his passion faded and Stefanie's name was never mentioned again.

His mother Klara had agreed to Adolf sitting the entrance examination at the Academy of Fine Arts, and in May 1906 he paid his first brief visit to Vienna, sending Kubizek a scenic postcard depicting the Karls Platz and writing that he had arrived safely, was going to the opera, but already felt homesick: 'Although I find everything very beautiful I am longing for Linz,' he wrote dejectedly. Throughout that year Klara's health had been poor, but it was not until 14 January 1907 that she finally visited the family physician, Eduard Bloch, a Jewish doctor who had trained in Prague and served in the Austro-Hungarian Army Medical Corps before starting his practice in Linz. Bloch was probably neither more nor less competent than any other doctor in general practice in the small town. However, his reputation as a humanitarian was higher than that of many other doctors in Linz, and he had earned himself a name as the 'friend of the poor' because he kept their bills as low as possible, and even on occasion waived his fee altogether. During his examination Bloch found a cancerous tumour in Klara's left breast. An immediate operation was essential and, four days later, she was admitted to the hospital of the Sisters of Mercy on the Herrenstrasse. There a surgeon named Karl Urban removed her breast during an hour-long operation.

On leaving hospital, early in February, Klara was very weak and found the stairs to the third-floor apartment more than she could manage, so that summer the family moved into three small rooms on the ground floor at 9 Blütengasse in the suburb of Urfahr, where Hitler's fantasy girlfriend lived. When next Kubizek called to visit them he was shocked by Klara's appearance: 'How wilted and worn was her kind, gentle face,' he recalled. 'She was lying in bed and stretched out her pale, thin hand to me.' Despite her pain, Klara's only concern was for Adolf's future. 'I never realised as clearly as on that visit how devoted she was to her son,' says Kubizek. 'She thought and planned for his welfare with all the strength that was left to her.'[9] She also expressed her fears for her son to Dr Bloch: 'She was softly spoken, patient; more concerned about what would happen to her family than she was about her approaching death,' he wrote many years later. 'She made no secret of these worries or about the fact that most of her thoughts were for her son.'[10]

In September Hitler was due to leave for Vienna to take the academy entrance examination, and Klara insisted that he go. On 1 and 2 October Hitler sat the test on which all his dreams depended. Although the examination had the reputation of being a formidable trial for any young artist, he sat it completely confident of his success. On the first day candidates had to make two paintings from a list of forty-eight subjects, including a number of biblical themes: *The Expulsion from Paradise, Adam and Eve Discovering Abel's Body*, and *The Return of the Prodigal Son*, among others. Hitler passed successfully, while 33 of the other 112 candidates failed at this first stage. The next hurdle was a presentation of original work to the selection board. Hitler, along with fifty-five other hopefuls, was now unsuccessful. The Malschule archive in the academy carries the notation 'too few heads', suggesting that his portfolio may have included too many street and architectural pictures and not enough portraits or life drawings to demonstrate sufficient overall ability. Bitterly disappointed, Hitler asked for, and was granted, an interview with Sigmund L'Allemand, Rector of the academy. He advised the young man to abandon any idea of becoming an academic painter and suggested he should concentrate on architecture instead. Hitler was convinced and applied to the Architectural School. He later explained that his rejection by that faculty was due to his lack of a *Gymnasium* diploma.

Hitler's rejection by the academy, bitter disappointment though it must have been, was far from the most devastating experience he was to endure that year. Although his mother's operation initially appeared successful and she seemed to make a good recovery, by 17 October Klara felt so unwell that she again called on Dr Bloch. He found that not only had her mastectomy scar become seriously infected, but that the cancer had metastasised to her lungs. It was a death warrant. Bloch told Paula her brother should come back home as soon as possible, and she immediately sent him a telegram. Adolf returned to Linz on the next train, paying a supplement to take an express that completed the 115-mile journey in three hours. On arrival he kept quiet about his failure, allowing his mother to believe he had gained a place at the academy. The following Monday Adolf and Paula called on Dr Bloch to discuss their mother's deteriorating condition. During that consultation one presumes that Hitler pleaded with the doctor to do something, anything, that might give his mother even the slightest chance of survival. Bloch, who would have known the case was hopeless, may have been persuaded by this meeting with Hitler to embark on the risky course of action he subsequently followed. Tragically, one consequence of the treatment was to make Klara's inevitable death even more agonising and devastating. Patient detective work by Rudolph Binion made sense of Bloch's almost unintelligible handwritten case notes, a task one reviewer described as being 'akin to deciphering Linear B',[11] and established that Klara was killed not by her cancer but by the drug Bloch had prescribed. This is not to say that Klara would have survived for much longer without Bloch's intervention or that he was anything other than well intentioned. But his prescription of great quantities of the antiseptic iodoform provides clear evidence of medical incompetence. Doubts about the drug had been voiced in the medical press for a quarter of a century before Bloch embarked on his 'treatment' of Klara. In 1882, for example, the *Wiener Medizinische Presse* published a lengthy article about the risks of using the antiseptic in large quantities. The article also pointed out that it could be absorbed into the blood through the raw wounds it was being used to treat. *Black's Medical Dictionary* from this period confirms this danger by stating that, while iodoform 'Relieves pain when applied to a raw or mucus surface and has the property of preventing putrefaction when brought in contact with discharges, when applied in large quantities to a raw surface it is absorbed.'[12]

In fairness to Bloch, it must be added that the decisive factor in iodoform poisoning, repeated application, was not firmly established until 1920 (and it was still being administered as late as 1945). Even so, by 1907 sufficient warning flags had been raised in medical circles to inhibit any well-informed doctor from prescribing the drug in large quantities. Given the extensive use Bloch made of the antiseptic in Klara's case, the only conclusion can be that he had failed to keep himself properly up to date by reading the relevant medical literature. While serving as an army doctor he may have used the drug, which, when administered sparingly, was a valuable antiseptic at a time when options were limited. In the light of that experience he presumably saw little risk in administering the drug to the sores on Klara's chest. As a humane man, he must have felt an overwhelming desire to try to assist the wretched woman. Certainly he seems to have entertained no real hope that his patient would recover, with or without iodoform treatment, a fact he made clear to Hitler and Paula on 21 October.

In Bloch's surgery, Hitler seems to have accepted the doctor's diagnosis that his mother's condition was incurable, but he would later yell at Kubizek: 'Incurable the doctor says. Incurable . . . what do they mean by that? Not that the malady is incurable but that the doctors aren't capable of curing it.'[13]

Klara's medical notes reveal that Bloch started the treatment on 22 October, binding saffron-yellow-impregnated gauze tightly around Klara's raw and wasted body. From then onwards, further applications were made almost daily, the stained gauze being gently removed and another strip of the expensive, pungent bandage applied. Later, as Klara's agony increased, Bloch administered morphine by injection, but within days whatever pain she was in from her ulcerating wounds must have been overwhelmed by the agony of iodoform poisoning. The antiseptic's distinctive odour would have filled the small apartment as it stained yellow her body and, as it was absorbed, her saliva. She developed a raging thirst, but could not drink without retching because the iodoform in her mouth made everything she ate or drank taste poisoned. On reaching her brain the drug would have produced increasing giddiness, hallucinations and insomnia. Research carried out in the 1920s indicated that death from repeated treatment usually occurred within twenty days. Perhaps because of her desperate will to live and protect her son, Klara managed to endure the pain for forty-six days.

Later, while living as a refugee in the United States, Bloch clearly had second thoughts about the vast quantities of iodoform he had administered. In his accounts of the episode (for *Collier's Magazine* and the Office of Strategic Services) Bloch made no mention of antiseptic, referring only to the injections of morphine, which, as he told and retold his story, gradually changed from being administered only occasionally to becoming a daily occurrence.

A copy of the billing record Bloch sent to Hitler survived intact in the *Cassette des Führers* in the Nazi Archive, where it was located by Rudolph Binion. 'Conceivably he did tamper with the original afterwards [in America],' says Professor Binion. 'As it did not survive him, I'd guess he ultimately destroyed it for the same reason that he spoke [to *Collier's* and the OSS] of morphine only, gradually upping the dosage, while omitting the iodoform from his later accounts.'[14]

During the final days of his mother's life Hitler was her tireless and devoted nurse. The boy who had been too idle to get up in the morning now worked around the clock to try to bring Klara what comfort he could. He moved her bed into the kitchen, which was warmer, and slept on a couch so as to be at her side during the night. He did all the cleaning and cooking. Each morning he would discuss the day's meals with Klara, finding out what she would like best and trying to encourage her appetite. Then he would hurry off to the market to buy it. Kubizek, who was all too familiar with his friend's obstinate nature and quick temper, was astonished by the change that had come over him: 'I had never before seen in him such loving tenderness. I didn't trust my own eyes and ears. Not a cross word, not an impatient remark, no violent insistence on having his own way. He forgot himself entirely in those weeks and lived only for his mother.'[15] Bloch too was impressed by the boy's devotion: 'His attachment to his mother was deep and loving,' he acknowledged in 1938. 'He would watch her every movement so that he might anticipate her slightest need. His eyes, which usually gazed mournfully into the distance, would light up whenever she was relieved of pain.'[16]

For Adolf, almost as much as for Klara, her final weeks must have involved great suffering. He had to watch the only person in the world for whom he probably ever felt any real love dying in agony. The sounds of her pain, the stench of the antiseptic and her unquenchable thirst must all have burned terrible images into his memory. On every visit he implored Bloch to administer morphine to relieve her pain, which the doctor did with increasing regularity. At two o'clock on the morning of 21 December, at the age of forty-seven, Klara died. Her last thoughts seem to have been for her son. Her last words to Kubizek, who visited her on 19 December, concerned Adolf's future: 'Gustl,' she said, 'go on being a good friend to my son when I'm no longer here. He has no-one else.'[17]

When Klara was buried beside her husband in the little cemetery at Leonding, Hitler broke down, remaining beside the grave long after the other mourners had left, as if unable to part from his mother even in death. Bloch, to whom bereavement was hardly a stranger, was deeply moved by the young man's desolation: 'In my entire career, I have never seen anyone so prostrate with grief,'[18] he later wrote. The following day Hitler called on the physician to thank him for his help: 'I shall be grateful to you for ever,' he said. At the time his gratitude was doubtless sincere, but as Rudolph Binion comments: 'Consciously or unconsciously the bereaved always blame the doctor for the patient's death.'[19]

Adolf spent a dismal Christmas with his sister before returning to Vienna in 1908 to seek his fortune in the big city. Klara's medical bills and funeral arrangements had eaten into his inheritance: Rudolph Binion has calculated that the lengthy treatment cost 359 Crowns, only slightly less than the 'hard polished wooden coffin with metal corners' Hitler ordered for the funeral and the interment charges.

Despite these expenses, Hitler was still a relatively wealthy young man who could afford to live in modest comfort while making no attempt to find work or earn money. He rented a room at 29 Stumpergasse and in February 1908 wrote to Gustl suggesting they share it. Kubizek, who had finally persuaded his parents to let him give up the upholsterer's trade and study music at the Vienna Conservatory, agreed. At six o'clock on 23 February he arrived at Vienna station to be met by his elegantly dressed friend. The young man's shoes were highly polished, his suit carefully pressed and he carried an ivory-handled stick beneath one arm. He greeted Gustl warmly and helped carry his baggage to their apartment, which, although located only a few blocks from the architectural glories of the Imperial Palace and the Ringstrasse, might just as well have been on a different planet. Stumpergasse was a narrow alley flanked by grey tenement blocks and small shops selling shoddy goods to the district's predominantly working-class population. With increasing concern, Kubizek followed his friend through an arched entrance into a dank courtyard, up some twisting stairs lit by a flickering gas mantle and down a gloomy second-floor corridor flanked by a dozen brown-painted doors. Hitler stopped in front of number 17, unlocked it and ushered his friend into a dingy kitchen. Kubizek, who was already taken aback by the small size of the dirty, dimly lit apartment, received a further shock when Hitler cheerily informed his friend that they had even less living space than he imagined, since they shared the three rooms with their elderly Polish landlady,

Frau Maria Zakreys. As her sub-tenants, he and Gustl would have to share a single room. In it, Kubizek found two narrow iron beds and a few items of cheap, shabby furniture. A guttering kerosene oil lamp filled the room with smoky light and the entire apartment with its stench. Gustl immediately protested that it was far too tiny for his needs because, as a music student, he must have sufficient space for the grand piano he proposed to rent. Hitler agreed they would move if they could find somewhere more suitable, but with limited resources their search turned into a depressing round of similarly dilapidated tenements in unprepossessing streets. The problem was finally somewhat solved when they managed to persuade Frau Zakreys, for an increase in rent, to exchange rooms with them. Kubizek hired his piano and it was duly installed, leaving just sufficient space for Hitler to pace up and down in the manner he claimed was essential for thinking. Within a few weeks their lives settled into a familiar pattern.

Kubizek would rise early to attend the Conservatory, while his friend stayed in bed until late in the day and then spent fine afternoons wandering the streets of Vienna and marvelling at the buildings (his ambition was still to become an architect). In order to pass the academy examination at his second attempt he began studying under the private tuition of a Viennese sculptor and art teacher by the name of Panholzer.

Despite the widely held belief that Hitler's time in Vienna was one of extreme poverty, a myth he himself assiduously promulgated, the death of Klara did not immediately plunge him into destitution. Indeed, research suggests that his monthly income from legacies in 1908 was around 83 Crowns – 58 Crowns from his father's estate since the age of eighteen and a 25-Crown orphan's pension – plus small and irregular amounts gained through sales of his pictures and drawings, ironically mainly to Jewish dealers. For comparison, a Viennese schoolteacher could expect to earn sixty-six Crowns each month, and a barrister would take home no more than Hitler. For around twenty-five Crowns one could purchase a monthly subscription ticket to an agreeable hotel and eat a hearty three-course meal every day. Hitler did not even stump up for that, though. His meals often consisted of no more than a bottle of milk and some bread; until Kubizek discovered this and insisted Hitler join him in the university's subsidised canteen. Depressing they may have been, but Hitler's lodgings cost only ten crowns a month, of which, of course, Kubizek paid half. Hitler's financial position was, therefore, reasonably secure, and he was able to spend much of his income on private art tuition and materials, as well as tickets for the opera and concerts, which he and Kubizek attended assiduously.

Vienna served this interest splendidly. At the Imperial Opera the finest singers in Europe could be seen and heard performing every major operatic work under the direction of Gustav Mahler. Night after night Hitler and Kubizek went to see such productions as Mozart's *The Marriage of Figaro* and Tchaikovsky's *Queen of Spades*. More important for Hitler than these, though, was Wagner, the Bayreuth master whose work received such devoted attention from Mahler's orchestra. When listening to Wagner, Hitler was a man transformed. 'His violence left him, he became quiet, yielding and tractable,' recalled Kubizek. 'His gaze lost its restlessness . . . He no longer felt lonely and outlawed and misjudged by society. He was intoxicated and bewitched.'[20]

For many months the two young men got along well, with Hitler even sketching out the design for a house they would one day share, and planning their lives together in meticulous detail. Each would have a separate room and work area: Kubizek for his music practice, Hitler for his drawing and painting. They would be looked after by a housekeeper and dress exactly alike. Hitler informed his friend that every summer they would travel around Germany studying architecture and listening to opera. This plan depended on his winning the lottery, which he was certain would happen imminently. When he failed to do so he became furiously angry, screaming that it was a fraud against honest men. But, despite Gustl's easygoing nature, their life together became increasingly fraught. Hitler would fly into sudden tempers and for days on end Kubizek could do nothing right. The situation finally grew so bad that Gustl began to believe Hitler's mother's death might have mentally unbalanced his friend, who now occupied his free time with extravagant and usually never-completed paintings and epic poems. His most ambitious project was *Wieland the Smith*,[21] an opera based on an ancient Norse legend, a subject on which Hitler considered himself an expert. He had made up his mind to control every stage of the production by writing the score and the libretto, arranging the choreography, designing the sets and handling the production. He would occupy hours scribbling down ideas and composing on Gustl's piano (he'd learned to play as a child). Unfortunately, he was unable to write the score correctly, and had to persuade Gustl to take over the task. For four weeks their every free moment was consumed with this project, Hitler frequently shaking his friend awake at night with fresh ideas. But, characteristically, his enthusiasm for *Wieland the Smith* soon waned, and he turned his mind to fresh subjects.

In the summer of 1908 Kubizek was called up for six months' military service, and on his return to Vienna, in November, he found that Adolf had disappeared from the lodgings without leaving a forwarding address. Frau Zakreys, who was as puzzled as Kubizek by this abrupt departure, could tell him only that Hitler had packed his bags, paid the rent due and walked out.

The two men were not to meet again for thirty years, when, in 1938, Hitler rode through Vienna like a triumphant Caesar.[22] Their failure to run into each other was somewhat surprising given that Hitler had moved only a few blocks away to a slightly larger room in the Felberstrasse, near the Western Station.

The most likely explanation for this sudden move was his second failure in October to gain a place in the academy. This time he had chosen his portfolio of pictures with greater care, and included much of the work painted under Panholzer's tuition. It was almost certainly good enough to have won him a place, but on this occasion Hitler did not even make it through to the selection board, having failed the first day's painting examination. Although he had been able to face his landlady after this setback, he probably felt too embarrassed and humiliated to admit his failure to Kubizek. Typically, he dealt with the problem by avoiding it, preferring to dispense with his only real friend rather than suffer a loss of prestige.

Police records show that by 18 November 1908 he was living in slightly larger and more upmarket lodgings at 16 Felberstrasse 22. For the next nine months little is known of either his lifestyle or his livelihood, but the more expensive accommodation, for which he had to pay without Kubizek's help, combined with his lack of application and commercial success as an artist, clearly placed a severe strain on his finances. In the spring of 1909 a relative of Frau Zakreys saw him queuing outside a convent soup kitchen and thought how pathetic it was that a young man who had always been so particular about his appearance should now look so dirty and ragged.

By the middle of August that year he was compelled to move to far dingier lodgings at Sechshauserstrasser 58, but remained there for only four weeks before abruptly leaving without completing the obligatory police registration form, providing any forwarding address or, most likely, paying the rent.

With his inheritance spent, he was now forced to live on his orphan's allowance of twenty-five Crowns, which enabled him, for a while, to become a *Bettgeber*, a slightly superior vagrant who had the price of a bed or couch in some cramped and dirty lodging. On other occasions he slept wherever he could, sometimes in a café but more often on a park bench. Because of this, he would have been familiar to the police, who repeatedly had to move him on. Once he even attempted begging, but fled when the well-dressed drunk whom he importuned raised his walking stick and threatened him with a thrashing.

The Viennese working class had always been inadequately housed and the situation was made worse by the steady drift from country to town that took place throughout Europe in the late nineteenth and early twentieth centuries. In 1880 some 60 per cent of Austria's population lived in the countryside, but by the time Hitler arrived in Vienna that had declined to 40 per cent. Even before this wretched tidal wave of humanity engulfed the capital, housing conditions for the lowest paid had been appalling, with more than a third of the city's population living in one- or two-room flats. Kubizek may justifiably have been dismayed at the drab apartment Hitler was subletting from Frau Zakreys, but the pair were better off than more than half of the city's population. Rooms the size the two of them shared would often accommodate five. One investigator reported he had found a tenement block in which 276 men, women and children shared 31 rooms. Facilities were minimal, with a dozen or more families sharing a single cold-water tap on a landing, and a hundred people using the same lavatory.[23]

For down and outs like Hitler, there were privately run flop-houses where for around forty Hellers (about five pence) a night's accommodation could be obtained. In such places men and women were packed together, with the consumptives spitting casually, drunks roaring their heads off and regular fights breaking out as ragged and filthy people disputed a square yard of floor space, a piece of bread, or the ownership of some tattered article of clothing: 'Dozens of illegal holes operated in the Leopoldstadt, whose winding alleys went back to the days when the ghetto existed,' wrote E. Kläger, an investigative journalist who posed as a down and out to obtain his information. 'Grasping tenants of old, half decayed houses sublet three or four rooms every night, often to eighteen or more persons of both sexes. At times their hapless guests were left only the windowsill on which to curl up.'

In one house the journalist came across an old man and a young girl sharing the same bed:

The politeness of their verbal intercourse indicated that acci-dent alone made them bed mates. In the same room, of course, were other 'boarders', including two children sleeping on wooden planks . . .

Another establishment sandwiched fifty persons into one diminutive hallway and a small room adjoining. Here shreds of blankets and sheets served as cover, and one needs little imagination to evoke the stench of such a hell . . . Filth, disease, agony of spirit, and degradation of body were the most obvious by-products of these supremely ugly habitations.[24]

'I owe it to that period that I grew hard and am still capable of being hard,' Hitler would later write in *Mein Kampf*, noting how by hurling him 'into a world of misery and poverty' the experience had made him 'acquainted with those for whom I was later to fight'.[25]

It was the lowest point of his life. Poverty had transformed him into an unshaven derelict, a thin and bedraggled twenty-year-old habitually dressed in a long, filthy and louse-ridden coat.

A few days before Christmas 1909 he turned up on the doorstep of a newly opened doss-house in Meidling, only a short walk from the Schönbrunn Palace, which provided a bed for the night but no other facilities. No matter how cold or wet the day, all the men would be turned out first thing in the morning and not allowed back in before seven. One night in the dormitory Hitler had a chance encounter with Reinhold Hanisch, a man of tremendous energy and ideas who provided the first step up the ladder back to respectability. At Hanisch's insistence, Hitler sought paid work for the first time in his life, initially by shovelling snow in the streets – the freezing cold and lack of warm clothing rapidly put paid to that job – and then by carrying passengers' luggage at the Western Station.

In January 1910, Hanisch wangled their transfer to a far superior hostel, the Home for Men at 27 Meldemannstrasse. This well-designed building, completed in 1905 under the patronage of the Emperor Franz Joseph I Jubilee Foundation for Citizens' Housing and Welfare Institutions, was no doss-house but a city-run hostel for single working men who earned less than 1,500 Crowns a year. The Home provided accommodation for 544 men in well-ordered if Spartan surroundings. Each lodger had his own sleeping cubicle that allocated him precisely four square metres of floor space and twelve cubic metres of breathing space. Each was furnished with an iron bed, covered with a horsehair mattress and a pillow bolster, two sheets, a double blanket and bolster cover, with a chamber pot beneath it. Clothes were hung on a rail beside the bed. There was no other furniture. Cleanliness was insisted upon and the Home was well equipped with a washroom and showers. Outside the washroom was a disinfectant chamber in which lice-ridden clothes could be treated. In order to shower, a guest had to pay ten Hellers for the towel and a bathing apron (nakedness in the shower rooms was forbidden). The rooms were closed during the day, but those residents who did not have a job to go to, or who were on holiday, could sit in the lounge, a reading room or a writing room. Only chess, dominoes and checkers were permitted, and these could be stopped if they led to noisy arguments. Spirits were forbidden on the premises and, if a man became drunk, he might be refused wine and beer as well. It was an austere, monastic-like institution much in demand during the cold winter months because it was warm, relatively comfortable and provided cheap but nourishing food.

Hitler's physical and mental state when he first arrived at the Home for Men is a matter of some dispute. A key source of information about his life during this period is Josef Greiner, who claimed to have known him well between the months of September 1907 and July 1908. In *Das Ende des Hitler-Mythos*, published in Vienna in 1947, Greiner asserts that when Hitler arrived at the Home he was in such a desperate condition, so dirty and ragged, that the Director, Johann Kanya, was inclined to throw him out. The Home was intended for men of some means, however minimal, not for those who had sunk beyond social redemption. According to Greiner,

Hitler . . . had neither shirt nor under drawers – they had

simply worn out. The coat Adolf wore was an old-fashioned salon model . . . its sleeves were ravelling and the lining was but a fragment of its original self. Grease and dirt were ground into the fabric, harmonising with the grey trousers and the disintegrating shoes. Only the young man's cultivated voice offset the dubious impression he made with his sunken and pale cheeks, his hurried manner, and his dirty rags.[26]

Greiner claims he saved Hitler from being expelled from the Home by persuading Kanya to loan him fifty Crowns against the security of a watch. This he then lent to Hitler to enable him to purchase some better clothes. His version of events has been severely attacked by historians, many of whom dismiss his stories as largely fiction. He certainly could not have met Hitler at the Home for Men during the period he claims, since Hitler was still living at 29 Stumpergasse. However, his confusion over the dates does not necessarily mean everything else was an invention. What can be said with confidence is that by January 1910 Hitler's plight was desperate and his transfer to the Home for Men marked a crucial step back up the ladder to respectability.

Another important move in that direction came when Reinhold Hanisch, according to his own account, persuaded Hitler to write to his half-sister Angela and ask her for some money. This he did only with the greatest of reluctance, but Angela wasted no time in responding. Virtually by return of post came a sympathetic letter and fifty Crowns, some of which Hitler used to purchase better clothes and buy painting materials. He began to work again, this time with the smooth-talking Hanisch selling his work and arranging some commissions. Most of Hitler's paintings were done from photographs rather than life, not through lack of ability (the paintings and drawings he made during the First World War show he was a competent draughtsman), but because it was so much more comfortable to paint in the Home's heated writing room than brave the cold Vienna streets. Hanisch found little difficulty either finding work for Hitler or selling any pictures he painted speculatively. His only complaint was that the artist was lazy and preferred to spend his time reading rather than painting.

Their collaboration ended acrimoniously in August 1910 when Hitler went to the police and accused his partner of embezzlement. There was a court case that resulted in Hanisch receiving a week in jail.

When Hitler later became an important political figure, Hanisch earned some money selling scurrilous stories to the press about their life together. One of the foreign journalists who tracked him down was the French writer Jean Constantinesco, who interviewed him in his Vienna apartment in 1933. Hanisch at first refused to talk to the Frenchman, saying that he was under contract to an Austrian publisher, but he was finally persuaded to recount some of his experiences with the new ruler of Germany. He said that many of the commissions had been from a Jew named Tansky, for whom Hitler had painted silhouettes of famous people on postcards, adding that Hitler was by no means anti-Semitic at this time and owed much of his livelihood to Jewish clients.[27] Although Hanisch had nothing sensational to reveal, his later attempts to peddle 'inside information' about Hitler to members of the Nazi Party made him a marked man. When Himmler's SS flew into Vienna in 1938 to prepare the security arrangements for the Führer's triumphal entry into the city, Hanisch was high on their list of those to be arrested and taken to Berlin for questioning. One account says he died of pneumonia, but it is more likely that he was murdered. This notion receives some support from the fact that in 1944 Martin Bormann, Hitler's secretary from April 1943, claimed that Hanisch hanged himself, suggesting an official cover-up.

After Hanisch left the scene, Hitler's life recedes into obscurity for almost three years. Presumably, with a market for his pictures developing, Hitler continued with his life of relative idleness at the Home for Men, and hawked paintings to art dealers, furniture manufacturers – who liked to include small pictures on some of their products – and picture framers – who were prepared to take almost anything in order to fill their empty frames.

On 24 May 1913 Hitler left the Home for Men for the last time and carried his few belongings down to the station, where he caught a train to Munich. As it pulled out of the Western Station that spring morning, Hitler could have had few regrets about leaving Vienna. He later wrote that in the Austrian capital he had experienced 'the saddest time of my life'.

Yet, while perfectly genuine, his sufferings were to a significant extent self-inflicted. Had he worked more diligently at his painting, he might have lived in reasonable comfort. Had he been more extrovert and sociable, he would have been less isolated. The conclusion must be that he was striving to create a lifestyle as different as possible to that of his orderly and industrious father. He felt little or no shame in his poverty, because he believed that it arose from a deliberate act of will. While, to an outsider, he might have seemed neither better nor worse than any jobless individual, Hitler was fully persuaded of the fact that he was *different*, and it was the certainty of this belief that enabled him to survive those months of dreary penury. Vienna, he says in *Mein Kampf*, taught him many lessons: to understand the poverty in which the majority of the working class lived and to see how this might be exploited politically; to realise the 'menace' of the Jew; to deplore the weakness of democratic political systems; and to despise the 'outworn' attitudes of trade unions. He also developed a profound contempt for the grey, anonymous masses among whom he lived but of whose lives he never felt a part. Perhaps the most crucial lesson Hitler took to heart was the belief that his will had triumphed. Later, he would come to regard his failure to enter the academy or make a living not as revealing any inadequacy on his part but as the diktat of destiny. 'What then seemed to be the harshness of Fate, I praise today as wisdom and Providence,' he proclaimed in *Mein Kampf*. 'While the Goddess of Suffering took me in her arms, often threatening to crush me, my will to resistance grew, and in the end this will was victorious.'[28]

But when Hitler abruptly departed from Vienna in 1913, he was neither obeying the will of Providence nor fleeing an existence that had become intolerable. His reason for flight was far more pragmatic: he was seeking to escape from what he considered the worst possible fate that could befall him – conscription into the Austro-Hungarian Army.

Chapter Six
JOURNEY INTO MIND

The selection procedure for those embarking on a career in medicine discriminates in favour of a certain personality type whose past history and present attitude denote them as being the sort of people who will be good at passing medical exams and can be relied upon to behave in a way deemed appropriate for members of the medical profession.

Garth Wood, The Myth of Neurosis[1]

In 1896 Edmund Forster began his medical studies at Strasbourg University. So keen was he to make a start that his father persuaded the authorities to let him attend lectures from November of that year, despite his course not officially commencing until the following February. Although unable to submit any written work, he was permitted to sit in on lectures and observe work in the dissection room, enthusiastically soaking up knowledge and counting the days until he could finally commence his medical training properly. This he did on 5 February 1897, joining 318 other would-be doctors out of a total university student body of 1,067.

After completing his first year at Strasbourg, he spent the next six months at the University of Munich, living in comfortable if modest lodgings on the third floor of 44 Sendlingerstrasse, funded by his parents. There was nothing unusual in his changing universities midway through the course. Many students lived a peripatetic existence at this time, moving from one place of learning to another in search of the most eminent lecturers or suitable topics. At the completion of each semester they would present a work book which, when signed by their lecturer, formed a sort of educational passport, enabling them to move between universities without prejudicing their final degree.

After the restrictions of living at home, twenty-year-old Edmund relished his new-found independence and quickly set about exploring the city of his birth and paying visits to family friends. An early call was on Karl von Voits, his father's former professor and mentor, who was also one of Edmund's lecturers. 'He teaches very well,' he wrote in rather patronising tones to his parents, 'but is worried that we do not pay enough attention!'[2]

In what were virtually daily postcards to his mother, which he wrote mainly in Dutch, Edmund reveals an enthusiasm for student life combined with the naive uncertainty and parental dependence of a young man let loose in a big city for the first time: 'I like it very much,' he assured them in one card. 'There is always so much to do and see. I went hiking and love the beautiful landscape. Can you please send me a bicycle and also a list of the people I should visit? I went to see Professor Bollinger and his wife, but she was unwell and could not receive me. Do you think I should call on them again?'[3]

Once his studies in Munich were completed he returned to Strasbourg, where he completed his degree on 21 July 1901, passing his final exams with the equivalent of a present-day upper-second-class degree. Among the Strasbourg lecturers who significantly influenced Edmund's later attitudes towards the treatment of mental illness, two names stand out: Karl Fürstner, his professor of psychiatry, who had conducted pioneering research into the relationship between brain tumours, hysteria and anxiety neuroses; and the physiologist Richard Ewald, who by means of delicate operations on pigeons had made significant advances in a scientific understanding of the role played by the semicircular canals in controlling head movements.

Edmund's interest in and talent for delicate experimental work in the laboratory are demonstrated by his choice of final-year research project. In this study, supervised by Professor Ewald, he examined the effects of electricity on the actions of nerves and muscles. The fact that muscles can be stimulated by passing an electric current through them had been known since 1791, when Luigi Galvani published an essay describing how, by means of an electrostatic machine, which produces electricity, and a Leyden jar, which stores it, he was able to make the muscles of a dead frog twitch vigorously. Edmund's breakthrough was to devise a method by which it was possible to apply these currents to individual nerves and muscles rather than, as had been done previously, to groups of them. This was a significant achievement demanding not only intellectual rigour but considerable manual dexterity in precisely positioning the hair-fine micro-electrodes into individual muscle spindles and nerve fibres.[4]

Under the influence of such mentors as Fürstner and Ewald, Edmund was being encouraged to take a strictly mechanistic view of brain function and psychiatric illness. In *The Myth of Neurosis*, Garth Wood writes of a tendency in medical education 'to emphasise the scientific method, which results in many doctors being ill at ease with, and therefore inclined to disregard, that which cannot easily be measured or inferred from measurement'. He goes on to point out that such doctors are usually 'conservative, conformist people who tend to believe in scientific solutions to the problems of the people who approach them. The medico-biological attitude is second nature to them, and because they may have little first-hand experience, in their own well-ordered lives, of the type of life problem that is frequently brought to them, they may have much sympathy for it, but little understanding of it.'[5]

While still a medical student, Edmund had joined the Field Artillery Regiment No. 15 as a part-time volunteer and, in August 1901, with his medical studies completed, he followed in his father's footsteps by volunteering to become a military doctor with the First Naval Division at the Kiel Naval Hospital in north-east Germany, as well as at the Royal Shipyard. It was there that he had his first taste of medicine on the wards, writing to his parents: 'Yesterday, I did my first surgery. I cut off a tumour of a man and vaccinated seven children and therefore have to be definitely called a benefactor of humanity!'[6]

After leaving military service in early 1902, Edmund took a crash course in tropical medicine before signing on as a ship's doctor aboard the *Suevia*, a small, six-thousand-ton cargo and passenger liner owned by the Hapag–Lloyd Line operating on the company's Far East Service. On 24 February he wrote to his parents from Hamburg: 'Right now, I am looking for malaria parasites in mosquitoes at the Institute of Tropical Medicine. I will start my journey to Japan on 10th.'[7] On Monday 10 March the *Suevia*, with twenty-two first-class passengers and a crew of forty, steamed out of Hamburg bound for Rotterdam, Port Said, Penang, Singapore, Hong Kong, Yokohama and Kobe. The first few days at sea were rough, and Edmund, between trying to help seasick passengers, was violently ill himself. By the time they reached Port Said, however, he had found his sea legs and began to enjoy himself thoroughly. At each port he spent his shore leave visiting hospitals, talking to doctors about tropical diseases and examining patients. He was also punctilious about sending cards home, most commercial but some featuring his own delicately executed watercolours of places of interest.

Late October found him back in Europe and ready to take up his new appointment as a clinical assistant in the Pathological Institute at the University of Geneva under Professor Frederick Zahn. It was during this period that Edmund took his first step up the academic ladder by publishing, with Zahn, a learned paper for the *Swiss Medical Review*, one of sixty-nine academic papers and articles he would write in French or German during his career. In it he gave a detailed account of two patients who had developed cancerous and abnormally growing polyps in their large intestines.[8] Although he found pathology interesting, however, he was eager to move into the field that had fascinated him from his days as a student under Professor Fürstner at Strasbourg: the study and treatment of nervous diseases and mental disorders. Furthermore, he loathed Geneva, and his postcards home became an almost unending grumble about the weather – 'still terrible, cold and rainy' – his lodgings – 'My accommodation is terrible and I am really fed-up with the food they serve at the pension. I am already looking forward to reasonable fodder!' – and the general tastelessness of his surroundings. Shortly before Christmas 1902 he wrote home apologetically: 'I could not find any presents for you. It is impossible to find anything worthwhile here as everything is unbelievably crude and bourgeois.'⁹ To add to these miseries, not only did he go down with tonsillitis and had to have one of his tonsils surgically removed, but found himself rostered for Christmas duty and unable to return home to share in the traditional family festivities, the first one he had ever missed.

It was with a sense of deep relief, therefore, that after working in Switzerland for a year he was able to transfer to more congenial surroundings at the University of Heidelberg, one of the most prestigious in the Wilhelmine Empire, where he was to learn experimental psychology with one of Germany's most notable specialists in this field, Emil Kraepelin. As a student, Kraepelin had worked under Max Wilhelm Wundt, the 'father of experimental psychology', who, while Professor of Psychology at Leipzig, had established the world's first psychological laboratory, the Institute for Experimental Psychology. Before long his Institute had not only become a Mecca for any doctor in Europe with an interest in experimental psychology, but the model for all other such laboratories. Edmund, therefore, could not have had a more knowledgeable or experienced teacher of experimental psychology than Kraepelin, who encouraged his students to carry out psychological experiments on their patients. While he found such studies of some interest, Edmund's strictly materialistic viewpoint left him unsympathetic towards psychological research and dubious of his professor's main claim to psychiatric fame – the classification of mental illness – which, in company with many other psychiatrists and neurologists, he regarded as being based more on conjecture than objective evidence. Even this early in his medical career he saw his knowledge and expertise in anatomy and histology as being central to his theoretical and practical approach to mental illness. His was a classical approach to brain structure and function, which in the words of neurologist Oliver Sacks, 'is atomistic, mechanistic and hierarchic. It divides brain function and behaviour into an enormous number of isolated functions or faculties; it lodges each of these in a special unit of some type – a "centre" or "system"; it sees these centres or systems as being integrated by a network of connections . . . and as being disposed at various levels, so that "higher" centres can command or constrain "lower" centres.'[10] This meant not only was there no place in Edmund's universe for a purely psychological problem divorced from some change or malfunction of the underlying physical structure, but where such instances occurred they were best explained by a lack of *nerve* rather than a failure of the *nervous system*. However distressing the consequences might be to the sufferer in terms of deafness, blindness or paralysis, such an outcome did not signify mental illness but moral weakness. There was, for him, nothing metaphysical or non-material about the brain, no ghost in the machine and no aspect of the human mind that could not be reduced to an electro-chemical manifestation. Although he had been confirmed into the Dutch Reform Church at the age of sixteen, Edmund never seems to have expressed any religious beliefs. If asked what his journey into the mind had revealed to him about the soul, one may presume that he would have echoed the response to a similar question by the French mathematician and astronomer Pierre Simon de Laplace: 'Sire, I have no need of that hypothesis.'[11]

Neurology, the medical specialisation to which Edmund had decided to dedicate his professional career, was at that time such a new science that in the year of his birth even the words 'neurology', 'neurological' and 'neurologist' were not in general use by European doctors. A study of dictionaries both general and medical, in English, French and German, shows the neurological field made its appearance only during the mid-1880s. Before then, textbooks dealing with topics in neurology, such as Moriz Benedikt's *Nerve Pathology and Electrotherapy*, published in 1874, used only such terms as 'nerves' and 'nervous'. When one of the founders of 'organic' psychiatry, Wilhelm Romberg, was appointed Professor at the University of Berlin in 1867, he occupied the chair not for Neurology but 'Psychiatry and Nervous Diseases'. Similarly, when Jean Martin Charcot was appointed in 1882 to what was essentially the world's first neurological chair at Paris's Saltpêtrière hospital the speciality was known simply as 'Maladies of the Nervous System'. Only in America were the terms 'neurology' and 'neurologist' in general use from as early as 1872, when Dr William Alexander Hammond at Bellevue Hospital and a group of like-minded medical practitioners united to form the New York Neurological Society. By doing so they took a bold step, because, for most medical practitioners at that time, 'neurology' was considered boring and seemed to offer little opportunity for original research or progress. When, at a meeting of this society in 1883, Hammond expressed his disappointment that 'a speciality so broad and comprehensive should not excite a still greater interest than it had done', a leader article in *Medical Record* responded by suggesting that this 'lack of interest' arose because of a further prejudice in the medical community: 'nearly every practising physician felt himself to be more or less of a neurologist'.[12]

Although the situation had improved somewhat by the time Edmund qualified, neurology was still neither widely recognised nor highly respected. Indeed, it was seen as ranking only slightly higher in status than that most despised of all medical specialisations, psychiatry. In an age when the mentally ill were still locked away in vast and gloomy asylums that were hardly more than warehouses for the insane, psychiatrists (or alienists, as such doctors were often known) were viewed by their colleagues as virtual jailers.

While studying medicine in the 1890s, for example, Ernest Jones overheard one student sarcastically suggesting that at their meetings psychiatrists read each other learned papers on 'an improved variety of Chubb lock'.[13]

Vagueness as to the precise expertise required to be a specialist in nervous disorders reflected centuries of uncertainty about the nature of mental illness itself. During the Middle Ages disorders of the mind were often attributed to demonical possession, and the cure, usually some type of exorcism to cast out the devil, was left in the hands of monks and priests. By the nineteenth century those patients who occupied the no man's land between sanity and total madness were deemed to be suffering from either hysteria or neurasthenia. Offering a rule-of-thumb guide to distinguishing between them, one American neurologist suggested if the patient was tearful and emotional, the physician should diagnose hysteria; if they were depressed and inert, it was clearly neurasthenia. This latter condition, first named by the New York neurologist Charles Beard in 1869, was regarded as being caused by nervous exhaustion resulting from overwork or overindulgence.[14]

If the diagnosis was unscientific and often obscure, the methods of treatment were hardly more sophisticated or reliable. Sedation, in the forms of opiates, 'hyoscine and digitalis'[15], had been used by asylum doctors since the mid-nineteenth century to put the mad to sleep for a while in the hope that, on awaking, they would somehow be cured. One widely used drug was methylene blue, originally developed for use as a commercial dye but later discovered to be a potent sedative in the treatment of the mentally ill.

Apart from drugging their patients, if only to calm down the violently deranged, the only other widely used form of treatment was electrotherapy. By the middle of the nineteenth century the administering of electric shocks was one of the few types of non-invasive physical treatment for nervous disorders, and it was, as a result, strongly advocated and broadly used. As late as the 1880s Freud declared regretfully: 'My therapeutic arsenal contained only two weapons, electrotherapy and hypnotism.'[16] Although the European dedication to electrotherapy stemmed partly from a lack of alternatives, it was also a case of following the well-established medical dictum that even if you have no idea why something works, you should continue using it as long as it does. As we shall see later, during the First World War electric shocks became the treatment of choice for a majority of psychiatrists. However, by then a higher voltage was used, often with the deliberate intent of causing intense pain.

When accepting his appointment at Heidelberg, Edmund had also applied for the post of a junior doctor under Professor Frederick Jolly, who, since 1890, had been Director of the Neurological Clinic at Berlin's prestigious Charité Hospital. Disenchanted with Kraepelin's philosophical approach to psychiatry but with no response from Professor Jolly, Edmund moved to the department of Professor Franz Nissl, a specialist in brain architecture. Today Nissl is remembered for a technique that he devised while still a student in Munich: using aniline dyes to stain brain tissue in order to identify structures within cortical cells. By using this technique, Nissl and his research assistants opened a new era in neuropathology by demonstrating a relationship between mental illnesses and specific changes within the brain and nervous system.

From Heidelberg, Edmund's next career move took him, in May 1904, not to Berlin's Charité as he had hoped, but to the Clinic for Neurology and Mental Illness at Halle University. There he worked as a clinical assistant to the most famous of all his mentors, Professor Carl Wernicke. In his mid-fifties when Edmund first met him, Wernicke enjoyed a formidable international reputation as the author of *The Aphasic Syndrome*, a landmark study of speech disorders that he had published in 1874, at the age of only twenty-six. While he had been out of sympathy with Kraepelin's views on diagnosing mental illness as a result of clinical observation, Edmund found his new professor's opinions far more to his liking. Wernicke regarded neurology and psychiatry as inseparable, and emphasised that even though it might not always be clear what was happening in the brain or nervous system of a mentally ill patient, this was no reason for abandoning a materialistic approach.

Although he enjoyed the stimulation of working with Wernicke, who proved an excellent teacher, Edmund missed the comforts of family life and returned to his parents' home in Strasbourg whenever possible. In April 1905, following one such visit, he wrote wistfully to his father: 'It is still winter here, no leaves on the trees and no flowers. The journey was fine, but I have so few things to do here that I could have stayed longer in Strasbourg. I have obtained some French statistics on psychosis. Wernicke has sprained his ankle and doesn't work in the clinic but is in a good mood.'[17]

However, not all of his trips to see the family were harmonious, and his quick temper and impulsive frankness often led to rows with his younger brother Dirk, who was training to become a lawyer. They usually argued over either women or their different tastes in literature and music. And they were still doing so four years later. In his diary for 24 August 1909, Dirk noted:

Friday evening and the family was sitting in the garden when Edmund, who was staying for a few days or weeks, began talking about my friends. He criticised Ernst Stadler who 'reads Stefan George[18] and writes long and aesthetic letters to the "stupid cow"' [Stadler's unnamed girlfriend]. When I started to defend my friends, he accused me of becoming feeble-minded [*Verblödung*]. This was too much for our parents who insisted that it was either 'facts or silence' [*Tatsachen oder Schwigen*]. I was out of my mind and furious, not only because I am perfectly well aware of his feelings towards Gretchen [Dirk's current girlfriend] but also due to the very malicious way he expresses himself. I do not remember how we settled the argument. The parents were as nice as ever to me, but my relationship with Edmund is disturbed. While his intentions were probably OK his behaviour is too impulsive.[19]

In July that same year there was general rejoicing in the family when Edmund learned that his Habilitation,[20] essential if he were to take up an academic career, had been accepted. His clarity of thought and painstaking attention to detail may be judged from the report on this thesis by one of his two external examiners, Professor Ziehen from the Medical Faculty at the Royal Friedrich-Wilhelms University of Berlin:

> In his extremely extensive and carefully assembled review of the literature, the author sets out to demonstrate, following Wernicke, that 'Anxiety Psychosis' is not in itself a disease. While this proof is neither as complete nor as certain as the author believes it to be he has moved a long way towards resolving the question. It demonstrates that the author is thorough, careful and intellectually critical. The literature review is almost complete and the style is clear and elegant.[21]

After praising Edmund's other research papers and commenting on his skill in a clinical examination, Ziehen concludes that his study of aspects of cell activity within the cerebral cortex opened new perspectives for the teacher of brain function at a cellular level: 'I have no doubt that the author demonstrates enough skill and knowledge to be accepted for Habilitation.'[22]

At Halle, which, like Geneva, Edmund found 'absolutely boring and tasteless', his impetuous nature and outbursts of temper landed him first in a duel and then in prison. Writing about the event to his father, he explained with casual insouciance:

> I was involved in a student's duel in the summer, and although no one was injured the police got to learn about it and we were sentenced to three months in prison. Of course I told Wernicke about it who was very nice and who advised me to sort matters out by taking a holiday. I have therefore taken a four-week

temporary leave of absence from 15 March onwards, as we will probably have our sentences reduced, and will then come to Strasbourg where I will serve my sentence in the Fort. It is boring, but cannot be changed. Maybe I will run out of money, then I will write again and you can send me some more. All the best to everybody, Edmund.[23]

The fact that Edmund was permitted even to take part in a duel is a measure of the progress that this grandson of a wine merchant had made up the strictly hierarchical German social ladder. No gentleman of honour would have demeaned himself by engaging in a duel with a tradesman such as his grandfather; but Edmund had attained the elevated status of an officer and a professional. As a contemporary duelling code puts it: 'He may be considered a gentleman who, be it through birth, through self-acquired social position, or as a result of completed studies, raises himself above the level of the common honourable man and by dint of one of the aforementioned may be treated as an equal with the officer.'[24]

While prohibited under the German Penal Code of 1871, duelling was still widely acknowledged as the only legitimate means whereby an *Ehrenmann* (man of honour) might defend that honour in the face of insult. For the *Ehrenmann*, life was of far less importance than safeguarding one's honour through a physical demonstration of courage, will and moral superiority. In 1907 Maximilian Beseler, the Prussian Minister of Justice, told delegates to Prussia's upper chamber of parliament: 'Our duel rests not only on injured honour but also indirectly on the fact that the masculinity of the injured is attacked and that the offended seeks restoration of his questioned masculinity in the duel. It is impossible to find punishment wherein it would be expressed that the impugned masculinity is once again recognised.'[25] During a 1912 debate about revisions to the archaic duelling code, for example, one commentator exalted in the fact that 'the German people sees in bravery, thank God, the highest purpose of man', while even those in favour of abolition recognised that 'courage is an essential prerequisite of honour. Cowardice is as little compatible these days with the concept of honour as earlier.'[26]

Exactly what led Edmund to be drawn into a duel and whether he was the instigator or recipient of the challenge is not known. However, given his impulsive nature and quick temper, it is possible he offended a colleague by using one of the three categories of insult deemed sufficient to provoke a duel. These ranged from a slight or curse (for instance being called a *Schwachkopf*, or imbecile) to the most serious, involving a blow or slap to the face. Although even this could be symbolic rather than physical: 'The violation of another's physical integrity was considered so reprehensible that even a threatened blow was regarded as an extreme offence,' notes Kevin McAleer in his definitive study of German duelling customs at the turn of the last century. 'Gentlemen would spare themselves the exertion by stating simply: "Consider yourself slapped!"'[27]

Participants and supporters of duelling could be found throughout the professional classes, especially among army officers. In the Kaiser's Germany military officers, such as Edmund and his father before him, were considered the measure of all things. In the words of Isabel Hull, 'the standards of the officer corps were basically the standards of the nobility tightly focused and made more explicit'.[28] As such, provided its codes had been strictly adhered to, duelling was regarded as a perfectly legitimate means of defending the honour of oneself or one's family. This perhaps explains Edmund's light-hearted attitude to his imprisonment. He knew that he would be unlikely to serve more than a month in jail. (Even if he had killed his opponent, the sentence would probably have stretched only to two years, or could have been even more lenient. A few years earlier, a Königsberg lawyer named Ernst Borchert was accidentally jostled by a drunken soldier while attending a masked ball. Borchert insisted on 'satisfaction' and they met at dawn the next day with loaded revolvers. Having each walked twenty-five paces, the two men turned and fired. The soldier, still the worse for drink, missed completely. The lawyer fired off five shots, even though he had killed his opponent with the fourth bullet. Far from being tried for murder, the courts accepted that, while against the law, such conduct was both reasonable and acceptable when it came to matters of honour.)

Edmund's duel had been stopped before it even started: word had reached the authorities and the police arrived before swords could be crossed or scars exchanged. In court, after proudly admitting his involvement, he was sentenced to three months. In the event, he served only two weeks behind bars, a sentence he had clearly anticipated because, as we have seen, he had requested just four weeks' leave of absence from the university.

His time at Halle came to an abrupt end in September 1905 when Wernicke was killed in an accident while cycling in the Thuringian Forest. Within a couple of months of Wernicke's death, however, Edmund's professional prospects brightened considerably when Karl Bonhöffer, the newly appointed Director of Berlin's Charité Nerve Clinic, offered him a post as junior doctor. It was the position he had long been hoping for, and the twenty-seven-year-old accepted without hesitation. Within the month he had moved into hospital-run lodgings at 20–22 Schumannstrasse,[29] which was to be his home for more than a decade. Apart from his military service during the First World War, he worked at the Charité for the next twenty years, rising steadily through the medical hierarchy. From 1918 he was an assistant professor and consultant.

Although by nature a blunt and outspoken individual who could sometimes be overbearing, Edmund, like his father, was a humanitarian who saw it as his duty to restore patients to full health. In pursuit of this goal he could be unorthodox and reckless in the expression of his opinions. As has already been noted, he despised any sign of weakness, in either himself or others, regarding it not simply as a personal failing but as a patriotic disgrace, because it dishonoured both the individual and the German nation. His medical training, family background and personality had combined to shape his approach to treating the hundreds of hysterically disabled soldiers he dealt with during the war. A genuine mental illness, he had come to believe, must always be caused by some kind of physical changes to the patient's brain and/or nervous system. From this it inevitably followed that hysterical patients, no matter how severe or distressing their disability, were either consciously malingering or unconsciously 'simulating', that is, feigning their disability. If the former, they were cowards who must be dealt with swiftly and severely; if the latter, they were weaklings whose problems arose through a lack of will-power.

Three years before the outbreak of war, Robert Gaupp, one of Germany's foremost psychiatrists, described will-power as 'the highest achievement of health and strength',[30] embodying such sublime and essential masculine virtues as stoicism, calmness, discipline and self-control. Gaupp believed these qualities were found only in the truly heroic and virile Aryan males, and were entirely absent in women, children, effeminate men and the uneducated masses. By asserting the supremacy of German will-power, however, he was doing no more than reflecting a widely held national belief in the nation's intellectual superiority. As he fully endorsed these views, it is not hard to see why Edmund regarded hysterical disorders as clear evidence of a failure of the individual's will-power, and their successful treatment as representing the will of the doctor triumphing over that of the patient.

With a majority of the hundreds of hysterically disabled soldiers he treated during the First World War, this approach was surprisingly successful. When he applied it to Adolf Hitler in 1918, however, the consequences would prove disastrous.

Chapter Seven
HITLER GOES TO WAR

A vast devastated area of four years of trench warfare. As far as the eye can see truly a piteous spectacle. Trees standing dead, stark and bare, the remains of woods, shell-holes innumerable, pill-boxes rent by shell-fire . . . debris of all sorts, munitions, rifles, equipment, bodies alas of Germans horribly battered, and of our Belgian allies.

Diary of Robert Wilson[1]

At this distance in time and with our terrible knowledge of the slaughterhouse that the battlefields of the First World War so rapidly became, it is hard enough to imagine, let alone understand, the euphoria with which its outbreak, in August 1914, was greeted throughout Europe. In Germany the patriotic fervour was so ecstatic and obsessively delusional that some psychiatrists regarded 'mobilisation psychosis' (*Mobilmachungspsychose*) as a mental illness.[2] Nor was such irrational exuberance confined to Germany. In Chatham Barracks, England, twenty-seven-year-old Rupert Brooke, a newly commissioned sub-lieutenant in the newly formed Royal Naval Division, expressed his nation's mood in a sonnet entitled 'Peace'; although, as his biographer Nigel Jones points out, the title 'War' would have better expressed its sentiments. In it, comments Jones, Brooke 'gave expression to the spirit of stern resolution, and also relief that a peace that had stagnated into corruption had been broken by the thunderclap of war'.[3] 'Now, God be thanked who has matched us with His hour,/And caught our youth, and wakened us from sleeping,' enthused the one-time atheist, before describing his fellow warriors as 'swimmers into cleanness leaping . . . Glad from a world grown old and cold and weary', a world that Brooke decried as being filled with 'sick hearts that honour could not move./And half-men, and their dirty songs and dreary'.[4] In a letter to a friend, the actress Cathleen Nesbitt, Brooke later proclaimed, 'The central purpose of my life, the aim and end of it, now, the thing God wants of me, is to get good at beating Germans.' With these words he voiced the sentiments of millions of young men.[5]

On music-hall stages recruiting sergeants took their places alongside female vocalists as they exhorted the young men in the audience: 'We don't want to lose you, but we think you ought to go,/For your King and your Country both need you so.'[6] Not that the young men of Britain and the rest of Europe required any such bidding. Inspired by romantic notions of the vitality and glory of heroic combat, they queued in their hundreds of thousands to volunteer. Such was the enthusiasm to enlist that within twenty days of Kitchener's famous appeal – 'Your King and Country Need You' – being authorised by Parliament, all of the hundred thousand men deemed necessary had joined up.[7]

In Germany, psychiatrist Robert Sommer, head of the Clinic for Nervous Disorders at Giessen University, voiced similarly patriotic sentiments in his anthem 'I Am a German', which included the lines: 'The German Reich, for which our fathers died, is alive . . . We wish only to shield it from the wrath of our foes . . . The old spirit of '70 is renewed . . . Hail Kaiser, Reich and Land/It unites us, the German people band'.[8]

On 4 August 1914, the day German forces invaded their country, the Belgian royal family processed sedately along the rue Royal to Parliament amid tumultuous acclaim. King Albert, wearing military uniform, was mounted on his horse, while Queen Elisabeth, a Bavarian, and their three children rode in an open carriage. Buildings on either side of the broad avenue were decked with flags and flowers, pavements overflowed with a joyous throng that cheered wildly and congratulated one another on the outbreak of war: 'Strangers shook each other's hands, laughing and crying,' each man feeling, as one recalled, 'united to his fellow by a common bond of love and hate'. Wave on wave of cheers reached out to the King as if the people in one universal emotion were trying to say he was the symbol of their country and of their will.[9]

Even the most humane and rational observers seemed incapable of preventing themselves from becoming caught up in a feeding frenzy of rejoicing. Historian Friedrich Meinecke recalled with pride how an 'exaltation of spirit' had created in him 'one of the most precious, unforgettable memories' and how it had seemed that 'a kind angel might lead the German people back to the right path'.[10]

To express anything other than a fanatical zeal for war in those months of irrational exuberance risked inviting not merely disdain but death. The French poet and socialist, forty-one-year-old Charles Péguy,[11] who was killed in September 1914 at the First Battle of the Marne, had earlier called for the death of Jean Jaurès, the pacifist socialist leader whom he accused of being a traitor to France and a stooge of Imperial Germany.[12] Jaurès was promptly assassinated by a fanatical young nationalist.

Central to this fervent support for the war was a belief, common to all sides, that the ensuing hostilities would be brief, the combat chivalrous and the outcome an easy victory for their own country. 'You will be home before the leaves have fallen from the trees,' the Kaiser assured his departing troops during the first week of August, while an officer leaving for the Western Front promised friends he would be breakfasting at the Café de la Paix in Paris on Sedan Day (2 September).[13] In Russia soldiers and civilians alike anticipated their triumphant entry into Berlin, with an Imperial Guard officer enquiring of the Tsar's physician whether it would be better to take his full-dress uniform, which he would need for the victory procession, with him on to the battlefield or should arrange for a courier to bring it to the front in a few days' time. 'The question', comments

Barbara Tuchman in *August 1914*, 'was not whether the Russians could win but whether it would take them two months or three; pessimists who suggested six months were considered defeatist.'[14]

A major reason for such optimism in Germany and among Austro-Hungarian allies was their faith in the Schlieffen Plan. In the years leading up to 1914 successive chiefs of the German General Staff had foreseen that if Germany were forced to wage war on two fronts, against Russia in the east and France in the west, defeat was almost certain, since the combined strength of their two enemies ensured numerical superiority. To avoid such a disaster, Alfred Graf von Schlieffen, Chief of the German General Staff between 1891 and 1905, devised a battle plan designed to ensure rapid victory in the west, with the conquest of France scheduled to take just forty-three days. He calculated that Russia's immense size, combined with a woefully inadequate railway system and inefficient bureaucracy, meant it would require at least six weeks from the outbreak of hostilities to mobilise its army. Schlieffen intended to take advantage of this by maintaining minimal troops on the Eastern Front and sending the majority of the German Army to strike at France. To avoid massive fortifications along the French frontier, the Germans would invade neutral Belgium, enabling the right wing of their forces to enter France near Lille and continue wheeling westward until they reached the English Channel. Once at the coast they would turn south, cutting off the French Army's line of retreat, while the outermost arc of a vast swath of troops captured Paris and so ensured a swift and humiliating defeat. As soon as the Western Front was secured, Germany would then turn its full attention to Russia.

While the plan initially appeared to be working perfectly in 1914, it was confounded by the Anglo-French victory at the Battle of the Marne. Thereafter, the conflict rapidly became a war of attrition that the Germans and their allies were obliged to fight in both the west and east – the very scenario Schlieffen's masterplan had been intended to avoid.

*　　*　　*

In Flanders that autumn twenty-five-year-old Adolf Hitler, newly recruited as a private in the 16th Bavarian Reserve Infantry Regiment, was just one of millions of insignificant players in a slowly but bloodily unfolding German military disaster. By now his enthusiasm and eagerness to get to grips with the enemy seem as sincere and fervent as could be seen in any number of his comrades. But it had been a different story earlier in the year, when Hitler did not project the image of an ardent patriot but rather that of an artful draft-dodger. While in *Mein Kampf* he claims to have left Vienna in 1913 'primarily for political reasons',[15] he had in reality done so to avoid conscription into the Austro-Hungarian Army. On arriving in Munich with just eighty Crowns in his pocket and a dismal history of failure, indecision and poverty in his immediate past, Hitler walked up the Schleissheimerstrasse, one of the long, narrow streets leading from the station. Spotting a handwritten notice offering a room for rent to a 'respectable gentleman' in a ground-floor window at number 34, he climbed the stairs and knocked on the door of Josef Popp, a tailor. Popp and his wife owned an apartment on the second floor of the sombre greystone building, and rented rooms on the floor above. Since Hitler liked the room and Popp considered him suitably 'respectable', a deal was struck. He would spend much of the next twelve months alone in his room, sketching, writing and reading. One of the first topics to absorb him in his modest room would have concerned a scandal that gripped the German-speaking world in the late spring of 1913. On the same day that Hitler's train had conveyed him from Vienna to Munich, five stunned and outraged Austrian Army intelligence officers had confronted one of their most respected colleagues, Colonel Alfred Redl, in a private dining room at Vienna's Klomser Hotel. A former head of the Austro-Hungarian Kundschaftsstelle (counter-intelligence organisation) and, more recently, Chief of Staff to the 8th Army Corps in Prague, Redl was also, unfortunately for the Austrians, a homosexual spy who, for more than a decade, had been energetically and profitably betraying his country's secrets to the Russians. His treason, which was purely financially motivated, arose from his urgent need for cash, to pay not only for extravagant luxuries, such as a Daimler limousine valued at sixteen thousand Crowns, but for sexual adventures. A Russian nobleman, who was also a high-ranking officer in the Tsar's intelligence service, had provided Redl with access to all the funds he needed in exchange for high-level military intelligence.

When his treachery was finally exposed, through a combination of astute counter-intelligence by the authorities and carelessness on Redl's own part, a deputation of five officers, headed by General von Hötzendorf, the Austro-Hungarian Commander-in-Chief, had called on him at his hotel in the hope of avoiding a scandal by inducing him to confess. Redl agreed and asked for a revolver with which to end his life. None of the five men had one, but finally a Browning was obtained and left with him. With a man placed outside the door, the officers retired to a nearby café, where they smoked and drank coffee until 5 a.m. the following day, when a messenger arrived to say that the colonel had finally taken the honourable way out. But if the military had expected to keep a lid on the episode, this hope was rapidly dashed. The story reached the front pages of the Austrian and German press on 29 May, and for several days afterwards journalists unearthed a host of sensational details about Redl's treachery and his homosexual lifestyle. For Hitler, in his new lodgings, the story confirmed his long-held belief in the corruption and decadence of the Austro-Hungarian Army.

Soon, however, Hitler was concentrating on weightier topics than were to be found in the scandal-sheets. Frau Popp, interviewed during the 1930s, recalled that 'Whole weeks would go by without Hitler so much as budging out of the house. He just camped in his room like a hermit with his nose stuck in those thick, heavy books and worked and studied from morning to night. I can't call to mind that he ever had a visitor. Only once in a while did he ever get a letter – from his sister [actually his half-sister Angela], who was married and lived in Vienna.'[16]

If, by his abrupt departure from Vienna and hermit-like existence in Munich, Hitler had hoped to escape the notice of the Austrian authorities, he was to be disappointed. On 29 December the Vienna police sent a letter to the Munich authorities asking about his whereabouts. The local police traced him without difficulty because Hitler, as he was legally obliged to do, had registered with them shortly after his arrival. They quickly replied to Vienna, enclosing his address. Eight days later Hitler received a summons to report to Linz for military service. This command came as a disagreeable shock, as he had been greatly enjoying himself in the Bavarian capital. He was earning about a hundred Marks a month from the sale of pictures, which, given his modest outgoings, provided a more than adequate income. His friendly and obliging landlords had taken a liking to their strange, lonely, young lodger and charged him only twenty Marks a month in rent, so, after paying for his food, he was left with around thirty Marks to spend on books and music. But there was no evading a police summons, and on 19 January 1914 Hitler, accompanied by a Munich police officer, called at the Austro-Hungarian Consulate, where he made a statement asking to be excused from military service on the grounds of ill-health.

Still pale and thin in spite of his new, comfortable lifestyle, Hitler evidently aroused the sympathy of the consular official, who wrote to the Linz authorities:

From the observations made by the police and the impression gained in this office, it would seem that the excuses put forward in the enclosed letter are entirely in accord with the truth. It would also seem that this man is suffering from a complaint which renders him unfit for service ... As Hietler [sic] seems very deserving of considerate treatment, we shall provisionally refrain from handing him over as requested and have instructed him to report on 25 January without fail to the

Special Conscription Panel in Linz . . . Hietler will therefore proceed to Linz unless you feel that the circumstances described above and his lack of funds justify his being allowed to report in Salzburg.[17]

Hitler then telegraphed the Linz magistrates, asking them to postpone the date to February. This request was curtly refused and the Austro-Hungarian authorities, obviously angered by his attitude, immediately cabled back: 'Essential you appear'. Their message did not reach him until 21 January, when he replied in writing, enquiring whether, in view of his modest finances, he might be allowed to report in Salzburg, which was closer to Munich. His letter ends: 'I trust I may make so bold as to hope that you will be kind enough not to make things more difficult than necessary for me. I most humbly request that you give my letter your kind consideration and sign myself. Your very humble servant, Adolf Hitler, Artist.[18] This obsequious letter had the effect he hoped for and it was not until 5 February that he was examined by a military doctor at Salzburg and found unfit for military service, 'not strong enough for either combatant or non-combatant duties'.[19]

There can be little doubt that Hitler had been striving to avoid being conscripted into the Austro-Hungarian army which he despised. This was a result of his refusal to serve alongside 'Jews and Czechs', rather than either cowardice or pacifism. His reaction to the outbreak of the war in August 1914 is evidence of that.

On 28 June the Archduke Franz Ferdinand was assassinated by eighteen-year-old Gavrilo Princip, a Bosnian Serb nationalist and student, as he drove slowly through the streets of the Bosnian capital, Sarajevo. Hitler wrote later of his feelings once Europe began to march towards war after that murder:

To me those hours seemed like a release from the painful feelings of my youth. Even today I am not ashamed to say that, overpowered by stormy enthusiasm, I fell down on my knees and thanked Heaven from an overflowing heart for granting me the good fortune of being permitted to live at this time. A fight for freedom had begun, mightier than the earth had ever seen; for once Destiny had begun its course, the conviction dawned on even the broad masses that this time not the fate of Serbia or Austria was involved, but whether the German nation was to be or not to be.[20]

On 2 August he joined thousands of other excited citizens who swarmed around the Feldherrenhalle, the 'Hall of the Warrior Chiefs', in Munich's Odeonplatz, to listen to the declaration of war on Russia. Standing at the window overlooking the square, surveying the jostling crowd through the wire-frame viewfinder of his plate camera, was a young Munich photographer named Heinrich Hoffmann. As the mob cheered their approval for the announcement, Hoffmann pressed his shutter release and preserved the scene for posterity. Some ten years later he was to extract that photograph from his files and carefully study the hundreds of faces with a magnifying glass. By chance, almost in the centre of the shot, where the lens definition was at its best, he found the one man he had eagerly sought: his newly acquired patron and friend, Adolf Hitler, to whom he had become personal photographer. Hoffmann enlarged that portion of the negative and, over the next few years, sold tens of thousands of copies of what was to prove one of the most popular and widely reproduced photographs he ever took. Certainly it is a unique and historic record. Hitler is bare headed and pressed in on all sides by soberly dressed Munich citizens sporting straw hats and bowlers, many waving excitedly. His face, like many in that crowd, is transfixed with excitement. At last he was to be given a chance to prove himself and his fervent German nationalism in battle.

As a boy and a young man I had so often felt the desire to prove at least once by deeds that for me national enthusiasm was no empty whim . . . I had so often sung 'Deutschland über Alles' and shouted '*Heil*' . . . that it seemed to me almost a belated act of grace to be allowed to stand as a witness in the divine court of the eternal judge and proclaim the sincerity of this conviction.[21]

On 3 August he sent a petition to King Ludwig III of Bavaria, asking his permission, as an Austrian, to join a Bavarian regiment. The following day, he claimed, a document arrived by messenger at his lodgings: 'With trembling hands I opened the document – my request had been approved . . . My joy and gratitude knew no bounds.'[22]

A fortnight later Hitler reported for service at the headquarters of the 6th Recruit Replacement Battalion, 16th Bavarian Reserve Infantry Regiment at Munich's Elisabeth School, where he took an oath of allegiance to Kaiser Wilhelm II of Germany and Supreme Commander of the German Army. Once enrolled as *Kriegsfreiwilliger* (volunteer) number 148, he was handed his kit and transferred to the Oberwiesenfeld Barracks for training. There he spent a few weeks drilling, learning to shoot and use a bayonet, and going on long route marches. In late September his regiment was moved to Lechfeld, a town on the confluence of the Lech and Danube some seventy miles from Munich, for a final period of training, and on 21 October embarked by train for the front. As the crowded troop train steamed slowly northwards, carrying thousands of enthusiastic, inexperienced, young soldiers to the war, many saw, for the first time, the subject of their patriotic song 'Wacht am Rhein' ('Watch on the Rhine'). One private recalled dawn on 22 October as the train ran alongside the great German waterway: 'I remember as if it were yesterday, how it just struck us all to see the sun drawing up the mist from the river and unveiling before our dazzled eyes that splendid statue of Germania which looks down from the Niederwald.' Overwhelmed by patriotic fervour, they started to sing: 'Be undismayed, dear country mine/Firm stands and true the watch – the watch on the Rhine.'[23]

The first major battles of the war, the Marne and the Aisne, were over by the time Hitler arrived at the front, Antwerp had fallen and the First Battle of Ypres had ended in the costly stalemate of trench warfare that would last for the next four years. On arrival they were marched straight into trenches between Bapaume and La Barque to relieve the 21st Regiment. Around them on the flat and desolate French countryside were ruined villages with fields pock-marked by craters and littered with the bloated corpses of horses and cattle. The military situation that confronted the 16th Bavarian Reserve as they made their way along the zigzagging lines of fortifications was desperate. Weeks of continuous fighting and bombardment had transformed the 21st Regiment into an army of gaunt and haggard tramps with tattered uniforms and bodies caked with mud and blood. Almost as soon as they arrived at the front line the 16th Regiment received a baptism of fire during the storming of the Wytschaete–Messines Ridge.

Hitler, still a quiet and solitary young man, possessed only one notable characteristic: speed and enthusiasm in obeying every order. In his kitbag he had included a sketching pad, paints and an architect's T-square, so when off-duty he held himself apart from the others painting and drawing. Even in the heat of battle he remained cool enough to observe and record with an artistic eye every moment of the action. For example, in a long and detailed letter written on 27 January 1915 to Ernst Hepp, a Munich lawyer who had advised him over his call-up papers, he captures the scene:

We spent the night in the courtyard of the Bourse, a pretentious building which has not yet been completed . . . the next day we moved into a billet, a huge, glazed hall. There was no shortage of fresh air since nothing was left but the iron ribs. The blast from German shells had shattered the glass to smithereens. At

2 a.m. on the third night we suddenly had an alert and marched off in battle order for the assembly area. No one knew anything for certain, but we thought it might only be a practice. It was a pretty dark night. We had hardly been marching for twenty minutes when we were ordered to move over to the verge so as to let through baggage trains, cavalry, etc . . . morning came at last. We had left Lille far behind. The thunder of the guns was gradually growing louder. Our column moved forward like a gigantic snake.

At 9 a.m. we halted in the grounds of a chateau. At nine in the evening we were given our grub. Unfortunately I couldn't get to sleep. There was a dead horse four feet away from my palliasse, at least a fortnight dead by the look of it. The thing was already half rotten. And on top of that one of our howitzer batteries was in position just behind us and every fifteen minutes a couple of shells went sailing over our heads into the darkness. They made a coughing, whistling noise and then we'd hear, far off, two dull crumps. We all of us listened for them. After all, we'd never heard anything like it before. And while we lay huddled together, talking in whispers and looking up at the stars, a terrible shindig began in the distance and then a *rat-tat-tat* coming nearer and nearer and soon the shell bursts came so thick and fast that they merged into one continuous roar.[24]

In another letter, this time to his former landlords, Herr and Frau Popp, he vividly describes the soldiers' reaction when told by their commanding officer, Major Count Zech, that they would be attacking the English the following day: 'At last! Every man of us was overjoyed.' At six o'clock the following morning, he continues, they joined up with other companies outside an inn. At seven 'the fun began'. Moving by platoons, they passed through a wood and reached a clearing on higher ground where four guns had been dug in.

Out there the first shrapnel was flying over us, bursting at the edge of the woods, and tearing apart the trees like so much brushwood. We had no real idea of the danger. None of us was afraid. Each man was waiting impatiently for the command: 'Forward!' . . . Five or six fellows brown as clay suddenly appeared from the left, and we all broke into a cheer: six Englishmen and a machine-gun!

We shouted to the escort. They were marching proudly behind their catch . . . At last the command rang out: 'Forward!'

We swarmed out and chased across the field to a little farm. To left and right the shrapnel was bursting and in between the English bullets sang. But we paid no attention. We lay there for ten minutes, after which we were again ordered to advance. I was right out in front and no longer with our platoon. Suddenly word went round that Stoever, our platoon commander, had been hit. The captain was leading us. Now we had our first losses. The English brought their machine-guns to bear on us. Again we advanced . . . Shell after shell began to strike the English trenches in front of us. The blokes began swarming out like ants out of an ant-heap and then we charged. We were across the fields in a flash and after some bloody hand-to-hand fighting we cleared one trench after another. A lot of enemy put up their hands. Those that didn't surrender were slaughtered. So it went from trench to trench. Some farm buildings to the left of us were still in enemy hands and we came under ferocious fire. We started going down like ninepins. We'd lost all our officers and most of our NCOs so anyone who still had any gumption turned back in search of reinforcements. When I came back for the second time after rounding up a party of Württembergers, the Major was lying on the ground with a gaping hole in his chest, round him a pile of corpses. Now only one officer was left, his adjutant. We were boiling with rage. 'Lead us into the attack, sir!' we yelled in unison. So we entered the wood on our left. It was impossible to advance up the road. Four times we tried and each time we had to withdraw. Of my whole section only I and one other remained and soon there was only me. My right sleeve was ripped off by a bullet but miraculously I was not even grazed.'[25]

In this skirmish three out of Hitler's eight companions were killed and one was badly wounded. It was the first of many narrow escapes for him. A few weeks later four company commanders arrived at the dug-out where Hitler and some companions were sheltering from the shelling. They ordered the men into the trenches so they could use the bunker for a conference. Hardly had the troops left the bunker than a direct hit destroyed it, killing or wounding all the officers. On another occasion Hitler was sitting in a trench with a group of men when an 'inner voice' warned him to move away. A few moments later a shell landed in the trench, killing or seriously injuring everybody in the group. Once again, Hitler was not even scratched.

On 3 November 1914 Hitler had been promoted to *Gefreiter*, the German equivalent of the British lance-corporal or American private, first class, and was handed his insignia of rank, a small collar button. This was the highest position Hitler reached during four years of almost continuous fighting. His lack of promotion was not due to any shortage of enthusiasm or courage on his part, but rather reflected a belief among his superiors that he did not possess the ability to lead others. As a front-line soldier, Hitler could hardly be faulted, but his officers took his solitary and unsociable personality to indicate that he had no talent for commanding or inspiring men in battle. Instead, they put his dash and daring to the best use they could by making him a *Meldegänger*, or company runner. While in his new job Hitler was sometimes able to sleep in safer and more comfortable billets behind the lines, his work was hardly any less dangerous than that of a front-line fighting soldier.

A photograph of Hitler, taken in 1915, shows him sprinting down a cobbled street carrying a Mauser '98 rifle, the standard infantry weapon. But as a *Meldegänger* his more usual weapon would have been a Luger pistol, which fired eight rounds of 9mm ammunition. It was a short-range weapon intended solely for personal defence, light and convenient for runners whose lives often depended on their speed and mobility. Dispatches were carried in leather belt pouches, each marked with crosses to denote their urgency. A three-cross dispatch had to be delivered in the fastest-possible time, no matter what the risks. Often such messages were sent out with several runners who took different routes in the hope that one would get through. Ignaz Westenkirchner, a fellow *Meldegänger* who knew Hitler at the front, remembered the hazards of their job:

It was no joke this dispatch bearing, especially as Fromelles stood on a bit of a height, and to reach it from the troops in the plains and valleys below we had to toil up the slopes raked by the enemy's machine-gun fire every inch of the way. I can see Hitler before my eyes now, as he used to tumble down back into the dug-out after just such a race with death. He'd squat down in a corner just as if nothing had happened, but he looked a sketch – thin as a rake, hollow-eyed and waxy white.[26]

Hitler continued to ride his luck in this way for the first two years of the war. He believed he was under divine protection and had been singled out for some, as yet unknown, vital mission. Each day in the line from October 1914 to October 1916 would have lent credence to his belief. Each evening Hitler was sent to brigade headquarters at Bapaume through a gauntlet of shell fire and bullets. His route lay between blazing buildings and he would often return to the trench with his clothes singed on his back. 'Our numbers got fewer and fewer,' recalled his fellow runner Ignaz Westenkirchner. 'The stunning din in the air never let up for one moment. All was the wildest uproar of death by shot and shell and cannonade. The thing grew unendurable, not to be believed. It took six runners to get a message through, three pairs set out on the off chance that one man, perhaps, might succeed.'[27] Yet, until October 1916 with men falling around him on all sides, Hitler suffered not so much as a scratch. This belief in his supernatural protection may well have encouraged him to be almost foolhardy in the risks he took. In an affidavit used by him in a libel action in 1932 against a newspaper that had accused him of wartime cowardice, his former commander, Lieutenant-Colonel Engelhardt, described him 'as an exceedingly brave, effective and conscientious soldier'. He then recalled an incident in which Hitler and another soldier risked their lives: 'As our men were storming the wedge-shaped forest (later known as Bayer-Wald), I stepped out of the woods near Wytschaete to get a better view of developments. Hitler and the volunteer Bachmann, another battle orderly belonging to the 16th Regiment, stood before me to protect me with their bodies from the machine-gun fire to which I was exposed.'[28] Other soldiers remembered how he had offered to take on dangerous dispatches to save married men from risking their lives. The authenticity of such stories is somewhat enhanced by the fact that many such statements were made well before he achieved any power in Germany. In 1922, a year before the abortive Munich *Putsch*, for example, Major-General Friedrich Petz, a former commanding officer of the 16th Regiment, wrote that Hitler 'was mentally very much all there and physically fresh, alert and hardy. His pluck was exceptional, as was the reckless courage with which he tackled dangerous situations and the hazards of battle.'[29] Colonel Spatny, another commanding officer, similarly recalled that 'Hitler set a shining example to those around him. His pluck and his exemplary bearing throughout each battle exerted a powerful influence on his comrades and this, combined with his admirable unpretentiousness, earned him the respect of superiors and equals alike.'[30]

The recollections of Hans Raub, one of his fellow soldiers, written at the request of the Nazis' archivist during the late 1930s, cast an intriguing new light on Hitler's life at the front.

I had been Hans, he had been Adolf! Adolf was so fond of jam on rye bread and very grateful when I gave him my jam. Coffee was his favourite drink. Whenever he was on duty next to me waiting on orders and all was quiet . . . Adolf sat there and was reading. Every time he had a book in front of him. When our adjutant called for an orderly I said to Adolf: 'Adolf, get moving!' He knew it meant that he once again had to take an order or else fetch one from someplace. He was a conscientious soldier for the Fatherland ready for duty all the time and went through thick and thin! [One] day, during an attack we had no connection with the front. The telephones would not function because heavy drumfire had torn all cables, the radio did not work and the carrier pigeons were not returning, in short, all was down and so Adolf had to take the risk and he did it endangering his life! We all said: he is not coming back! But he came back and was able to inform us. The same happened on 19 and 20 July [19]16 in the same position, we had been together nearly 18 months in the same position . . . As competent as he was as a soldier, he was a good man in rest too.

I do not know if our dearest Führer still remembers us painting eggs with whitewash in the front garden of Spatny our regimental commander at Easter 1917. Adolf himself placed them into the circular flower bed. Our eggs spelled out Happy Easter 1917. Our commander saw them early in the morning and was very happy about it. Hohenadel and I were given both a glass of schnapps and some cigars by Spatny. If Adolf was given something I do not remember! I hope he did because he had put the finishing touches to our construction art.[31]

Raub's meticulously handwritten testimony, like every other document that describes Hitler's personality and behaviour in the war, portrays him as a dutiful but unassuming lance-corporal known among his fellow soldiers as 'Adi'. While testifying to his courage and fighting zeal, every one of them also confirms his lack of leadership ability and his readiness to obey rather than issue orders.

On 7 October 1916, almost two years after he arrived at the front, Hitler was wounded for the first time. An urgent dispatch had to be taken to an especially dangerous sector of the line, and Hitler, together with another runner – a tall, phlegmatic private named Ernst Schmidt – immediately volunteered. Schmidt, like Hitler, had gained a reputation for coming through the heaviest bombardments unscathed and, since the mission was considered so hazardous, both men were sent with identical messages in the hope that at least one of them would make it through. As they sprinted from cover across a patch of flat land, a British grenade exploded only yards away. The two men flung themselves flat, but on this occasion Hitler was a fraction too slow and splinters ripped into his left thigh. He spent the next two months recovering from his wounds in a hospital at Beelitz, near Berlin, and when discharged on 3 December was ordered to report to the 4th Company, 1st Replacement Battalion of the 16th Regiment in Munich.

To his disgust, he found that civilian morale in the Bavarian capital was poor: 'Anger, discontent, cursing wherever you went,' he noted sourly, 'the general mood was miserable: to be slacker passed almost as a sign of higher wisdom, while loyal steadfastness was considered a symptom of inner weakness and narrow-mindedness.'[32] When wounded he had muttered to Fritz Wiedemann, the regimental adjutant: 'It's not so bad, Lieutenant, sir, right? I can stay with you, with the regiment!' and in January 1917 he telegraphed an urgent appeal to Wiedemann begging to be reclaimed by his regiment before he was sent to another. For Hitler, as Wiedemann would later comment, his regiment was his home. Wiedemann pulled the necessary strings and on 5 March 1917 a relieved Hitler returned to his home with the 3rd Company. According to Ignaz Westenkirchner, he was welcomed back as something of a hero: 'The company cook excelled himself that night and turned out an extra special mess in his honour.

Kartoffelpuffer [fried grated potatoes and apple sauce], bread and jam and tea.'

Apart from a short leave, between 30 September and 17 October 1917, Hitler remained at the front for the rest of the war, seeing action in Flanders, Upper Alsace and Arras, and never seems to have had the slightest doubt that Germany would somehow, against all the odds, emerge victorious. Westenkirchner recalls:

> Towards the end of the war, when to the rest of us the game seemed to be up, he would go wild if anyone expressed doubts about victory. He would stick his hands in his pockets, pace up and down with huge strides, and rage against pessimism. He still believed in victory at the time he was gassed. For him the heavy attack in Flanders by the English in October 1918 was a proof that our submarine campaign was succeeding.[33]

In July 1918 Hitler saved the life of a wounded company commander when he dragged him out of range of an American artillery bombardment. Not long after, he prevented German guns from accidentally firing on their own advancing infantry by carrying a vital message to the rear. On 4 August he was awarded the Iron Cross, First Class. In recommending him for one of Germany's highest military awards, his commander, Lieutenant-Colonel Freiherr von Godin, stated: 'As a runner his coolness and dash in both trench and open warfare have been exemplary, and invariably he has shown himself ready to volunteer for tasks in the most difficult situations and at great danger to himself . . . I consider that he fully deserves to be awarded the Iron Cross, 1st Class.'[34]

In the early hours of 8 August, General Sir Henry Rawlinson's 4th Army joined forces with Foch's attacking French. Supported by five hundred tanks, Australian and Canadian troops broke out of the trenches and retook miles of territory on that first day, creating such panic among the demoralised German troops that sixteen thousand surrendered almost immediately. For Hitler, as for Germany, the

Great War was about to come to an inglorious conclusion, but he still had one piece of luck to come his way.

According to John Godl, in September 1918 an English soldier, twenty-seven-year-old Private Henry Tandey, changed the course of world history when he had Hitler in his rifle sights but decided against shooting him. The incident occurred during the capture of a French village. As the ferocious fighting for the village came to an end, a wounded and battle-weary German soldier limped into Tandey's line of fire, and stared at him without making any attempt to defend himself, as if resigned to the inevitable. 'I took aim but couldn't shoot a wounded man,' Tandey recalled, 'so I let him go.' At the time Tandey thought little more of the incident, and he ended the war as the most decorated private soldier in the British Army, having received a Distinguished Conduct Medal for determined bravery at Vaulx Vraucourt, the Military Medal for heroism at Havrincourt and the Victoria Cross for conspicuous bravery during the battle in which he spared Hitler's life. The fact that he did so only came to light twenty years later during Prime Minister Neville Chamberlain's ill-fated appeasement mission to Berchtesgaden in 1938. On the wall of Hitler's mountaintop home Chamberlain saw a painting depicting Tandey carrying a wounded comrade to the first-aid station at the Menin Crossroads in 1914. A puzzled Chamberlain is said to have asked Hitler about this curious picture,[34] and in reply Hitler pointed out Tandey in the foreground and commented: 'That's the man who nearly shot me. That man came so near to killing me that I thought I should never see Germany again. Providence saved me from such devilishly accurate fire as those English boys were aiming at us.' He then asked Chamberlain to convey his best wishes and gratitude to Tandey.

According to Tandey's nephew, William Whateley, the British Prime Minister did just that. He recalls how the telephone rang one evening, and when his uncle returned from taking the call he told them in a matter-of-fact way that it had been Mr Chamberlain, who had related his conversation with Hitler. 'It wasn't until then that Tandey knew the man he had in his gun sight twenty years earlier was Adolf Hitler,' says John Godl, 'and it came as a great shock. Given the tensions at the time, it wasn't something he felt proud about.'[35]

After the Tandey incident, Hitler may have felt that his luck would hold until the end of the war. If he had, he would have been wrong.[36]

Chapter Eight
FORSTER GOES TO WAR

Psychologists, sociologists and the like had not yet been invented so there was no pernicious jargon to cloud simple issues. Right was right and wrong was wrong and . . . a coward was not someone with a 'complex' . . . but just a despicable creature . . . Frugality, austerity, and self-control were then perfectly acceptable. We believed in honour, patriotism, self-sacrifice and duty.
Ian F.W. Beckett and Keith R. Simpson,
A Nation in Arms[1]

After Kaiser Wilhelm had declared war on his cousin, the Russian Tsar Nicholas, Germany's doctors rejoiced. With the general public, they believed that after a few months' exhilarating action at the front the nation's young men would return not merely victorious but physically and morally renewed by the experience of combat.

Whether Edmund Forster, recently appointed as an associate professor at the Charité Hospital's nerve clinic, found time to leave his post and join the vast and jubilant crowds who swarmed in their thousands along Berlin's Unter den Linden is not known. But even if medical duties prevented his physical presence there can be little doubt that he, like his colleagues, shared the feverish excitement of the masses who gathered in the pouring rain outside the Reichstag. And we may presume that he silently exulted as the Kaiser proclaimed that there were no longer any political parties but 'Only Germans . . . without distinction of party, without distinction of social position or creed, to hold together with me through thick or thin, through need and death.'[2] When he called on the party leaders to step forward and give him 'their hand upon it', all but one of the wildly cheering deputies immediately surged forward. The sole exception was Karl Liebknecht, a member of the Social Democratic Party and a future leader of the German Communist Party.[3] It was, says historian Paul Lerner, a call to arms that resonated through all sectors of German society: 'Intellectuals, artists and students, most notably the rebellious sons of Germany's educated middle class, valorised war as the repudiation of a bourgeois society that they condemned as decadent and overly materialistic; thousands of young men eagerly enlisted and zealously rushed off to the front, romanticizing the danger and "vitality" of combat.'[4]

Both public and professional opinion was united in the belief that there was no better cure for 'nerves dried up and languishing in the dust from years of peace' than the battlefield and the 'mighty healing power of the iron bath [*Stahlbad*]',[5] which, by purging its neuroses, would restore the nation to its former imperial glory. This view was bluntly articulated by Walter Fuchs, a military doctor, when he described war as 'The only means by which we, as a nation, can be saved from physical and psychological lethargy and emasculation which are relentlessly threatening.'[6]

Those advancing this rosy vision of war ranged from the foolishly naive to the ruthlessly calculating. Romantics envisaged the battlefield as a naturally healthy alternative to fetid city living and believed that after a few months of fresh air amid rural surroundings Germany's soldiers would come marching home with their minds purged of 'the damaging effects of modern developments'.[7]

While the romantics were disastrously ignorant of the realities of modern warfare, Social Darwinists knew full well that the conflict would rapidly turn into a bloodbath. But for them this was a point in its favour. War was part of the process of natural selection that, by culling the inferior stock of the urban masses, would ensure Germany emerged from the conflict militarily triumphant and genetically purified. 'Psychiatric critiques of modernity – articulated in medical terms – valorised war as an anti-modern antidote to the "physically damaging" conditions of early twentieth-century German society.'[8]

It was true that, in Prussia alone, urbanisation and industrialisation had been accompanied by a 429 per cent increase in asylum inmates – against a population increase of just 48 per cent – but claims that this demonstrated the nation's moral disintegration and mental degeneration were in the main cynically self-serving. German psychiatrists were merely attempting to establish their profession's pivotal role in the forthcoming conflict. As Berlin neurologist Kurt Singer, who served in a hospital close to the Western Front, put it:

> Will and obedience are ultimately determined by the intactness of the nervous system. Therefore psychiatry plays a major role in the war, next to the main areas of medical activity: surgery, internal medicine and hygiene. It separates the ill from the healthy. It prevents the will of an individual, when led astray, from contaminating those around it. Its task is important because mental disorders, when they remain unrecognised, are dangers for the many, for those fit for combat, and for the basic principle of military organisation, which is discipline.[9]

Such was its cultural potency and perceived central role in safeguarding individual and national health that the concept of will-power permeated every aspect of German military and psychiatric thinking of the period. In 1910 Kaiser Wilhelm had told an audience of officers and cadets at the Naval Academy of Flensburg-Mürwick: 'The next war and the next battle at sea will demand of you healthy nerves. It is through nerves that its outcome will be decided.'[10] Five years later A.A. Friedländer, a noted German psychiatrist, exulted: 'On all fronts, in the field just as at home, German victory sparkles. It is the victory of strong German nerves, German composure, German will and the discipline of German men.'[11] In a similar vein the Hamburg neurologist Alfred Sänger commented:

'If Hindenburg [the German commander-in-chief] is correct when he says the victor in this war will be the one who has the stronger nerves, then that, God be thanked, will be us Germans!'[12]

Edmund Forster, too, strongly espoused such views, and, as we shall see, they greatly influenced his approach to treating hysterical soldiers, including Adolf Hitler. On the day war was declared he immediately reported for military service, regarding it as a doctor's duty to set an example to the nation. He was not alone: between 1914 and 1918 26,300 doctors (out of 33,000) had volunteered for military duties; 1,325 were killed and 2,149 wounded during the course of the fighting.[13]

Within hours of the Kaiser's announcement of war Edmund had packed his bags and boarded a train to Kiel, three hundred miles away on the North Sea coast, to take up his appointment as auxiliary doctor at the Kiel–Wik Naval Hospital. With his previous military training and extensive medical experience, it was only a matter of weeks before thirty-six-year-old Forster was promoted to senior assistant doctor and then, on 14 November, posted to a nearby officers' training school.

For the first few months of war the majority of the patients Forster treated were suffering from injuries to the brain or nervous system; very few presented with psychiatric problems. Indeed, so insignificant was breakdown among front-line soldiers that doctors attached to the 1st Bavarian Army Corps were able to report: 'Astonishingly the percentage of mental disorders in the field army is extraordinarily small and cannot be compared to the numbers observed in other wars and even in other armies.'[14] In January 1915 Berlin neurologist Kurt Mendel agreed: 'It is conspicuous just how few cases of psychoses have arisen in the current war in view of the almost superhuman hardships, excitation and emotional strain that our troops have had to endure . . . The special facilities for mental illness that were considered in the medical ordinances have proved to be unnecessary.'[15]

It even seemed that the optimistic belief that warfare would *benefit* mental health by reversing the 'damaging influences of civilisation' (*Kulturschädlichkeiten*) would be borne out by events. 'The nervous health of our people has proved to be better than many expected,' commented Robert Gaupp in 1915, 'all in all the nervous system of our people in war has shown itself to be strong and good.'[16]

Early in the same year psychiatrist Otto Binswanger recounted how in the year leading up to the outbreak of war he had treated

a whole series of weak-nerved youths . . . anxious, cowardly, irresolute, weak-willed little creatures, whose consciousness and feelings were determined only by their own egos, and who amounted to nothing more than whiners, complaining of physical and mental pain. Then came the war. The illnesses fell away in an instant. They reported to their divisions and – what seems even more remarkable to me – every single one of them, with only one exception, has held up to this day . . . Thus, even among those with sickly dispositions the great purifier war has done its work.[17]

At the Kiel–Wik Forster fretted for action and pleaded with his superiors for a transfer to Flanders. In February 1915 his wish was granted and, with a promotion to marine medical officer, he was posted to Marine *Lazarett* No. 2, based in Bruges in north-western Belgium. Once there he was appointed a consultant in the neurological department. He quickly discovered that the mood of ill-informed optimism still widely prevalent in Germany was fast disappearing among military doctors at the front.

The swift and decisive victory that all sides had so confidently predicted during 1914 had turned into stalemate and stagnation. With the German advance brought to a halt and troops literally bogged down in the mud of the Western Front, it was becoming increasingly apparent to German, French and British doctors alike that mechanised warfare breaks not only bodies but minds. Soldiers, first in their hundreds, then by the thousand, and then in hundreds of thousands, were being crippled without a drop of their blood being spilled.

That war was able to destroy men psychologically as well as physically should not have come as the surprise it did. More than four decades earlier, during the Franco-Prussian War of 1870–71, German military medical officials, including Edmund's father Franz Joseph, had for the first time been required to keep casualty statistics. These showed that even during this year-long campaign more than three hundred soldiers had been diagnosed as suffering from a serious mental disorder. During the Russo-Japanese War of 1904–5 the Russians had, for the first time in any conflict, established a psychiatric hospital to treat mentally ill soldiers. Within a few weeks scores of men were being treated for hysteria, epileptic reactions, alcohol-induced psychosis, nervous exhaustion and what would today be termed post-traumatic stress disorders. Yet, despite such well-documented evidence, the medical establishments on all sides in the conflict were caught unawares by the scale of the mental health disaster unfolding before them. By the winter of 1917 war neuroses had risen to the point of parity with physical injuries, up from 14 per cent of all injuries in 1914 to 45 per cent three years later. 'Their number has grown and grown,' Gaupp reported late in 1917. 'Scarcely is one nerve hospital opened than it fills up and space must be found somewhere else. We've now got to the point where nervous illness represents the most important medical category and in our province the nerve hospitals are practically the only ones that are always full.'[18]

In his clinic Forster was treating an ever-rising number of patients with mental disorders that were as diverse as they were bizarre. Some patients were partially paralysed, lacked all co-ordination or were plagued by constant tics and tremors. There were soldiers whose limbs were contorted by violent seizures, those perpetually bent at an acute angle, others who were blind, deaf or mute, many whose speech was made incomprehensible through stutters and stammers. There were even patients who, incapable of speaking, could give voice only to an eerie, rhythmic barking. Nothing in Forster's training or experience had prepared him for this endless, freakish parade of disabled and disordered men flooding into his wards.

'The experience of the war revolutionized German mental medicine,' comments Paul Lerner. 'Although individual cases of hysteria had been known to occur in men, its widespread appearance among German troops was wholly unprecedented and shattered prevailing assumptions.'[19]

Before they could devise effective treatments, doctors had first to decide exactly what was causing the kaleidoscope of calamity now confronting them. At first, the German medical profession responded as if the soldiers had been the victims of some 'colossal industrial accident' by attributing their disabilities to what was quaintly termed 'railway brain'.[20] This diagnosis had first been made in the 1880s by Germany's most eminent neurologist, Hermann Oppenheim, while he treated the survivors of railway accidents. Although apparently uninjured, some of these people had displayed tremors, tics, stutters and partial paralyses similar to those now being found among the soldiers. Oppenheim had concluded that the force of impact between two speeding trains had caused tiny lesions in the brain or nervous system. He argued that, despite being undetectable, even using a microscope, these minute injuries were still sufficient to account for the disabilities. Once the war had started Oppenheim extended his theory to account for the effects of relentless artillery bombardments, and the explosion of bombs, mines and grenades. These too, he suggested, produced undetectable lesions in the brains and nervous systems of soldiers.

This explanation was eagerly adopted by the medical and military authorities, who were reluctant to accept that their courageous lads could ever suffer a mental breakdown. The phrase used to describe these invisible injuries was 'shell shock', implying that the impact of the exploding ordnance had physically injured the sufferer. In German clinics neurologists and psychiatrists even began distinguishing between simple *Granaterschütterung* (shell explosion), *Granatexplosionslähmung* (shell paralysis) and *Granatfernwirkung* (the indirect effects of an explosion).

Edmund, too, was far more comfortable when dealing with a medical rather than a psychological problem. When he was completing his training at Strasbourg his clinical professors considered labels such as 'neurotic', 'neurasthenic', 'hysterical' and 'hypochondriacal' merely as terms of opprobrium.

Although the total absence of physical evidence had caused doctors on both sides of the conflict to feel uneasy about Oppenheim's theory from the start, it was not until the summer of 1916 that the 'microscopic lesions' theory met its first serious challenge. It came in the form of a study by Dr Harold Wiltshire, a captain in the Royal Army Medical Corps, who had been treating British troops in a French hospital. Early in the war, Wiltshire, an experienced London physician, had been among the many doctors who viewed the hardships and hazards of trench life as in many ways beneficial to the soldier's health. In a letter to the *Lancet* he claimed, 'Moderate cold and exposure tend to improve rather than to diminish physical well-being . . . when the troops are well-fed, exposure and hardship do not predispose them to nervous breakdown.' But he also cautioned that

> The degree to which continued psychic strain will predispose to shell-shock is difficult to estimate. Most of my patients claimed that they had kept perfectly well up to the time of the causative incident, but some admitted that they had felt the strain on their nerves . . . It is certain that continued psychic strain is much more potent as a disposing cause in those of a neuropathic predisposition, and I think that it must also have exerted a similar influence in a large number of those who were unconscious of its action.[21]

Even as his letter was being published, however, Wiltshire's views were undergoing a profound change. After twenty months treating mental breakdowns, and following consultations with other front-line doctors, he published an authoritative report stating that his patients were mentally rather than physically injured. The wide variety of signs and symptoms lumped together under the label 'shell shock' was, he argued, caused by their psychological resistance being gradually exhausted under the stress of war: 'These men were in a position of psychic tension in which they could have been knocked down by the proverbial feather and the effect of the blows was psychic rather than physical,' he noted. 'What finally did for them was a "sudden psychic shock".'[22]

Wiltshire based his controversial conclusion on three persuasive strands of clinical evidence. He had never found symptoms of shell shock among soldiers physically injured by explosions, nor had he ever seen symptoms of concussion among mentally disabled troops. Indeed, many of these had suffered their breakdowns when well behind the lines and far from exploding ordnance. Finally, while wounded soldiers were almost invariably cheerful and optimistic, those diagnosed with shell shock tended to be tearful and morose. Although initially rejected by the military authorities, Wiltshire's conclusions received considerable support from other front-line psychologists, psychiatrists and neurologists. Among those who spoke up in his favour was Charles Meyers, a medically trained psychologist based at a hospital in Boulogne who had, paradoxically, first coined the term 'shell shock'. Meyers, who treated more than two thousand such cases during 1916 alone, later admitted his phrase was 'ill-chosen' and even in some respects a 'singularly harmful one', because so-called shell shock could equally well occur

when the soldier is remote from the exploding missile, provided that he be subjected to an emotional disturbance or mental strain sufficiently severe . . . Moreover in men already worn out or having previously suffered from the disorder, the final cause of the breakdown may be so slight, and its onset so gradual, that its origin hardly deserves the name of 'shock'.

In the vast majority of cases the signs of 'shell-shock' appear traceable to psychic causes, especially, in the early cases, to the emotions of extreme and sudden horror and fright . . . Wartime 'shell-shock' was in fact very similar to peace-time 'hysteria' and 'neurasthenia'.[23]

Oppenheim's theory was finally laid to rest during a heated debate at a session of the German Association for Psychiatry in Munich in September 1916. Forster, who attended the convention, heard a number of psychiatrists, including Karl Bonhöffer, argue that not only must Oppenheim's theory be rejected but that psychiatrists must come to terms with the idea that functional disorders of the type they were now treating in vast numbers represented not a medical but a purely psychological problem. While this opinion eventually prevailed, the psychiatrists present continued to insist that the body rather than the mind remained the chief culprit, and that it worked in conjunction with the individual's psychological disposition to produce the symptoms. This left the door open to treat the mind by treating (or, as we shall see in the next chapter, frequently mistreating) the body. With 'railway brain' consigned to psychiatric history, doctors were left with the two possibilities mentioned by Charles Meyers – neurasthenia and hysteria. Neither of these held much attraction for scientifically orientated neurologists such as Forster, because they were little more than labels applied to a ragbag of widely varying symptoms.

The term 'neurasthenia' (literally meaning nerve weakness) had been coined almost fifty years earlier, independently, by two American doctors. As has been noted in Chapter 6, George M. Beard, a New York neurologist, first used it in a paper of 1869 for the *Boston Medical and Surgical Journal*. In the same year a psychiatrist from Kalamazoo by the name of Van Deusen used it in a different journal. Possibly due to their different social status – big city doctor with a rich private clientele versus a 'hick from the sticks' – it was Beard rather than Deusen who received national and international acclaim for this discovery. Indeed, so famous did the East Coast physician become that in France the condition was commonly referred to as 'la maladie du Beard'. According to Beard, everyone possesses a finite amount of 'nerve force', which is gradually depleted through constant use, just as a battery runs down faster the more its energy is consumed. In two books, *A Practical Treatise on Nervous Exhaustion (Neurasthenia)* and *American Nervousness*, published towards the end of his life, Beard expounded his belief that neurasthenia, which he described as 'the soil from which all mental illnesses spring', resulted from 'the complex agencies of modern life; steam power, the periodic press, the telegraph, the sciences, and the mental activity of women'.[24] Those at greatest risk from this 'disease of civilisation' were, in his opinion, not the poor and socially deprived but the wealthy elite whose miseries he explained had previously remained unstudied and unrelieved:

> Life in the technologically transformed, urbanised, industrial-ised world of the late Nineteenth Century may not have had any discernible effect on the dull-witted or uneducated, but it was enough thoroughly to exhaust the more refined, civilised portion of the population. The disease could thus be a sign of either moral laxity or extreme moral sensitivity.[25]

The symptoms of neurasthenia, which ranged from the mildly inconvenient to the profoundly debilitating, included headaches, insomnia, dizziness, irregular heartbeat, nervous dyspepsia, hypo-chondria, asthma, hay fever, skin rashes, premature baldness, drunk-enness, hot and cold flushes, nervous exhaustion, brain collapse, impotence and incipient insanity. As Tom Lutz points out: 'The wide swathe of symptoms made the diagnosis so widely available, and the theory of exceptional refinement and sensitivity made it so attractive – attractive both to those in elites who felt threatened by cultural change and those upwardly mobile persons who associated nervous feelings with new or desired status positions – that an epidemic was the result.'[26]

Although Beard considered neurasthenia to be an exclusively American disease, his concept of an enfeebled nervous system was warmly received in continental Europe and rapidly taken up by French and German doctors. In France the enthusiasm for his ideas was so great that by the early 1900s one French doctor sarcastically suggested that 'everything could be explained by neurasthenia, suicide, decadent art, dress and adultery'.[27] Only in Britain did doctors remain largely unimpressed and uninterested. During a visit to England in 1880, Beard had come under sustained criticism from several eminent physicians, and the British Medical Association showed no interest in further investigating his findings. Their main objection, also voiced by some American physicians, was that 'neurasthenia' was too vague a term to have any clinical merit and was scarcely more than a way of describing a 'mob of incoherent symptoms borrowed from the most diverse of disorders'.[28]

In Germany, by contrast, this vagueness was considered a benefit rather than a drawback because, as one psychiatrist commented, '[it] managed to explain subjective bodily symptoms in terms of objective physical disease, thus removing any suggestion of the patient's own part in them' and enabling German men to preserve 'an ethos of fortitude'.[29]

For moralists, neurasthenia offered further evidence against all they most disapproved of in modern life, from artistic decadence to masturbation and from the emancipation of women to industrialisation. For social reformers it provided a powerful argument against the inner-city slums and sweatshop factories, which psychiatrists such as Robert Gaupp had warned showed an 'extraordinary fruitfulness' when it came to producing illnesses of all kinds.[30] Finally, because the wealthy were claimed to be at greatest risk, neurasthenia helped to ensure that doctors in private practice enjoyed an endless supply of affluent clients clamouring to have exhausted nervous energy expensively recharged. Not only was Beard's theory swiftly adopted by German psychiatrists, but so too was the standard cure, developed by another North American neurologist, Silas Weir Mitchell, from Philadelphia. For female patients he advised complete rest and a milk diet, while male sufferers were prescribed rest, fresh air or a foreign cruise. The men, apparently, did not need any additional milk!

For military doctors who found the notion of neurasthenia unhelpful when attempting to stem the relentlessly rising tide of mentally disabled soldiers, a second and far more ancient diagnosis was open to them: hysteria. In the Ebers papyrus, an Egyptian medical treatise dating from 1550 BC, one may read a description of emotional disorders among women that physicians of the time attributed to their womb moving from its normal position in the body and so disturbing the natural motions of the mind. The cure was to fumigate the vagina in the hope of luring the vagrant uterus back to its proper anatomical position. The same treatment was advocated many centuries later by physicians in ancient Greece, who named these emotional disturbances 'hysteria', from the Greek *hysteron* (womb). Because the womb, which, according to Democritus, was 'the cause of a thousand ills', has a rich supply of nerves, they believed, as did later doctors, that 'its convulsions (excited by the emotional disturbance transmitted through the nerves) spread by sympathy to the head and chest and arouse a centre of vitality which deprives the other parts of the body of vital force'.[31]

From the eighteenth century onwards hysteria was no longer seen as a disease of the uterus but as an illness of the nerves, and by the early twentieth doctors were using hysteria to explain away any disturbance of bodily function for which no organic cause could be discovered. In France Pierre Janet, a physician whose reputation at that time greatly exceeded Freud's, held it was due to a 'splitting of the mind' in which the conscious and unconscious aspects of personality became dissociated. He based this notion on clinical findings that revealed that, while no hysterics could recall the traumatic events that had produced their symptoms, these usually painful incidents were able to be remembered under hypnosis. Freud took a very different view, arguing in 1895 that hysteria resulted from the suppression of traumatic emotions, memories and experiences buried deep in the unconscious.

A French neurologist named Joseph François Félix Babinski (whom we shall meet again in the next chapter) believed hysteria developed whenever a patient became so convinced that he was suffering from some disorder that he developed its symptoms. All a physician need do to remove the symptoms, he explained, was reverse the psychological process that had given rise to the patient's symptoms in the first place.

Without any clear understanding of the physical basis of either neurasthenia or hysteria, there could be no consensus for how best to treat it. The result was that it was left largely to the inclinations and aptitudes of individual psychiatrists and neurologists to devise their own forms of therapy.

For many German psychiatrists, the cause of hysteria lay in a failure of the will. In 1904 Karlsruhe physician Willy Hellpach described the 'will' as the 'A to Z of hysteria',[32] while neurologist Alfred Goldschieder contended that 'The activity of the will is raised to the highest conceivable level through love of Fatherland, through mutual example and not least through camaraderie, which melds superiors and subordinates into a single mass of will.'[33]

Given such beliefs, it is not surprising that when confronted by disabilities for which they were unable to find any physical cause, German psychiatrists, Edmund Forster among them, attributed them variously to a *Willenssperrung* ('inhibition of the will'), *Willensversagung* ('failure of the will') or *Willenshemmung* ('arrest of the will'). While this perception of the will as a sublimely masculine quality and one which Swiss psychiatrist Otto Binswanger believed to have 'purified and fortified our minds'[34] exerted a baleful influence over the treatment of hysterical soldiers on all sides of the conflict, it proved to be especially potent among German military psychiatrists and neurologists. They saw their duty as patriots, officers and physicians in accordance with the official policy of the German Psychiatric Association, which stated that they should: 'Never forget that we physicians have now put all our work in the service of one mission: to serve our army and our Fatherland.'[35] In pursuit of this policy doctors were given licence to devise and practise virtually any treatment, however extreme, that they believed might remove the hysterical disorder and return the soldier, if not to the battlefield, then to some other form of employment helpful to the war effort, as speedily as possible. In the words of Otto von Schjerning, the German Army's chief sanitary inspector, their only goal must be to 'turn shakers back into human beings and return to them the ability to work and lead a worthwhile life'.[36]

While many of the treatments they devised now appear needlessly brutal and highly unethical, for Edmund Forster and his colleagues they merely reflected a general consensus among European psychiatrists that there was no such medical condition as hysteria. As the eminent French psychiatrist Jean-Martin Charcot cautioned his students: 'Bear well in mind – and this should not exact too great an effort – that the word hysteria means nothing.'[37] (Fifty years later similar views were still being expressed by leading American psychiatrists. 'Much of the patient's behavior makes equal sense if one assumes that his blindness was "malingered",' wrote Hanus J. Grosz and J. Zimmerman in 1965. 'That he deliberately and wilfully manipulated others into believing that he was blind, or, when it suited him, into believing that he was beginning to recover his vision. The suspicion will always be there that the patient is in fact malingering. The final distinction between hysterical blindness and malingering is almost impossible to make.')[38]

As a result, soldiers diagnosed as 'hysterics' were generally viewed not merely as defective individuals with 'inferior nervous systems' or 'inferior and degenerate brains', but as 'antithetical and threatening to national unity' because 'strength of will [had become] increasingly

synonymous with military obedience'. Inevitably such deeply preju-
dicial opinions coloured physicians' views of the patients and exerted
a baleful influence over the environment in which they were treated.
Military discipline in hospitals for the hysterically disordered was as
strict and as rigorously enforced as on the parade ground. As the
doctors freely admitted, the purpose of such a severe regime was
to make hospitals so disagreeable that the injured soldiers would
be encouraged to 'come to their senses' and return to the front
line as soon as possible. 'The soldier must have the feeling that
all in all nowhere is as nice as in the field,' wrote Willy Hellpach
in 1915, 'despite all the dangers and the stresses, and nowhere is
as unpleasant as in the hospital station, in spite of its security and
safety.'[39] 'The patients were not abused,' claimed psychiatrist Karl
Pönitz, 'but their stay in the station was certainly not made into
paradise.'[40]

By 1917, with overcrowding in general hospitals rapidly becoming
unmanageable, the German War Ministry, as was explained in
Chapter 2, authorised the 'creation of special sections for this
type of patient' and opened *Lazarette* in remote areas throughout
Germany. The decisions to keep such places small and, where
possible, to locate them well away from large cities were based
on two considerations, one medical, the other political. Doctors
favoured smaller units because these enabled them to get to know
their patients better and exercise greater control over them than was
possible on the wards of a large general hospital. The emphasis on
rural locations was based on the belief that treatments would be
faster and more effective if administered away from the corrupting
influence of big cities, places many doctors regarded as breeding
grounds for neuroses. In addition, as we have seen, German physicians considered it advisable to segregate mentally and physically
disabled soldiers to prevent the spread of hysterical symptoms. In
this they found common ground with many British psychiatrists,
the most notable and formidable of these being Gordon Holmes,
a psychiatrist based at the National Hospital for the Paralysed and

Epileptic in London. 'Hysteria spreads by suggestion from one person to another,' he claimed, 'and has got to be dealt with in no uncertain fashion. Otherwise the best army in the world finds itself in hospital.'[41]

Holmes, the son of an Anglo-Irish landowner who had studied medicine at Frankfurt University and spoke fluent German, was to an uncanny extent Edmund Forster's doppelgänger. Colleagues described the two men in almost identical terms as 'restless, indefatigable, investigator[s] with . . . practical, down to earth, mind[s] and no interest in the major, metaphysical questions of life'.[42] In personality and character Edmund and Gordon shared a bedside manner that was usually brusque, and they both displayed a tough-minded and authoritarian approach to patients *and* colleagues. Holmes was 'much loved by some students for his warm and impulsive nature, [but] he was terrifying when angry and had been known to lift up an erring student by the scruff of the neck to twist an arm "to emphasise a fault in [a] clinical description" . . . [He had] fought with most of his colleagues and come to blows with some.'[43] One can well imagine Forster behaving in exactly the same way.

For patients, the remoteness of the *Lazarette* meant that it was usually impossible for them to receive visits from family or friends. While this undoubtedly added to the patients' loneliness and misery, such isolation was, as far as the doctors were concerned, highly desirable. As one health official in Württemberg cautioned: 'The attempt to arouse sympathy and pity among the civilian population facilitates the persistence of old hysterical symptoms and the creation of new ones.'[44] The military authorities also preferred to keep what was happening within *Lazarette* well hidden from the civilian population. They worried that the often grotesque spectacle presented by the mentally disordered casualties would undermine national morale. Moreover, if the methods of treatment became widely known, there would be a public outcry. As these included painful electric shocks, prolonged immersion in hot or cold baths, near suffocation and lengthy solitary confinement, they had every right to be concerned. In some instances these treatments were so brutal that soldiers survived the battlefield only to perish at the hands of the doctors charged with restoring them to mental health. Under pressure from the military and their own pejorative belief that hysteria was merely another name for malingering, even well-intentioned physicians such as Edmund Forster conducted themselves in ways that made the years of the First World War among the darkest in modern psychiatric history.

Chapter Nine
BATTLEFIELDS OF THE MIND

If the doctor ordered me: 'Amputate a leg, Brecht!' I would answer, 'Yes, Your Excellency!' and cut off the leg. If I was told: 'Make a trepanning!' I opened the man's skull and tinkered with his brains. I saw how they patched people up in order to ship them back to the front as soon as possible.

Bertolt Brecht[1]

'The Legend of the Dead Soldier', one of Bertolt Brecht's earliest and most popular songs, describes how a German infantryman dies a hero's death and is buried by his comrades. But, 'because the war was still far from done', a group of doctors disinterred his corpse and pronounced the man once again fit for combat. Then they 'filled him up with a fiery schnapps' and burned incense to drive away the graveyard stench, and, as a band played, the soldier marched off, once again to die 'a hero's death'. In a similar vein a bitter cartoon by George Grosz entitled *The Faith Healers* depicts a doctor listening to a skeleton through his stethoscope and pronouncing it *'kriegsverwendbar'* – 'fit for duty'.

Both of these stories reflect the increasing obsession of German doctors, from all specialisations, to serve their fatherland by returning injured soldiers to the battlefields as swiftly as possible, no matter what the cost to either themselves or, more usually, their patients. As a 1917 ordinance from the Prussian War Ministry unequivocally states: 'The primary consideration in treating war neurotics is to help them to the full utilisation of their psychically diminished capacity for work.'[2] By 'work' they meant not a return to their civilian employment but into an occupation, preferably as front-line combatants, that directly contributed to the national war effort. 'In attempting to meet these goals,' argues A. Mendelssohn-Bartholdy, 'they not only borrowed from the methods of efficient industrial production, but dealt increasingly with soldier-patients as objects or resources to be efficiently utilised in an impersonal and mechanised system.'[3]

Most of the treatments they used in this process had been developed before the war, mainly in French hospitals. During the late nineteenth century at La Pitié Hospital in Paris, for example, Felix Babinski,[4] an intimidating giant of a man who ruled staff and patients alike with a rod of iron, had developed specific methods for dealing with hysterical patients. A British doctor who watched Babinski at work described how 'He used various forms of suggestion, especially the painful application of faradic electricity, together with vigorous persuasion [and] gave the patients no explanation of the nature or cause of his symptoms.' Perhaps surprisingly, these 'somewhat crude methods [known as *traitement brusque*] were extremely successful and were ... rarely followed by relapse or development of other hysterical symptoms'.[5] A French doctor of Polish extraction, Babinski insisted that all his male patients appeared for treatment naked (females were allowed to retain their underwear for the sake of propriety). He claimed this was necessary to enable a thorough examination of the limbs to be made and tests carried out to determine whether their disorder was physical or mental in origin. It is also likely that, as was the case with German military psychiatrists who later made the same stipulation, his insistence on nudity was primarily a psychological tactic designed to emphasise the power of the doctor and the vulnerability of his patient.

Babinski's method of 'vigorous persuasion', what German psychiatrists and neurologists later termed 'active therapy', was not the only approach that seemed to yield good results with hysterical patients. Working in another Paris hospital, the Saltpêtrière, a contemporary of Babinski, Jules-Joseph Dejerine, merely talked quietly with his patients, albeit these dialogues took place in the outpatient department before a large and attentive audience of students and colleagues. Patient and physician sat across a table from each other and engaged in a conversation that, according to reports, was so absorbing that the individual 'took not the slightest notice of the audience and willingly discussed every detail of his domestic and other troubles'.[6] During their conversation, according to a speaker at the 1913 Psychiatric Congress, patients were led by Dejerine in a masterly and seductive manner 'from their morbid mentality and made to view themselves and their surroundings in a proper perspective'.[7]

The most benign method used in the treatment of hysteria was hypnosis, the effectiveness of which when dealing with hysterics had first been reported during the 1890s. Doctors working at a clinic in the French provincial town of Nancy claimed considerable clinical success with what they soon came to regard as a powerful and universal therapeutic procedure.

Many German psychiatrists initially refused to accept that any of their soldiers could possibly be capable of anything so *unwürdig* (unworthy) as hysteria. However, this rapidly became an inescapable clinical fact. If the condition itself was undeniable, though, its treatment still aroused controversy. Many German doctors contemptuously dismissed hypnosis as medieval mysticism. One of the most effective of the First World War medical hypnotists was Max Nonne, a Hamburg neurologist who treated more than 1,600 patients in the war and achieved such a high success rate that he gained the reputation of a *Zauberheiler* (magical healer). Yet his decision to attempt hypnosis, which he had learned while studying in Nancy many years earlier, came about more by chance than from any initial faith in the procedure. In October 1914 he was asked to treat a lieutenant, recently evacuated from Flanders, who appeared to have been struck dumb. Suspecting the young officer's muteness was psychological rather than physical in origin but with no clear idea how to proceed, Nonne finally decided to attempt hypnosis, something he had never previously used on a hysterical patient and which he seriously doubted would have much effect. To his astonishment, no sooner had he placed the man in a trance and instructed him to talk than his patient immediately regained the power of speech.[8] This success encouraged Nonne to use hypnosis on a regular basis, usually with equally favourable results. Mindful of his profession's undisguised hostility to the procedure, however, he was reluctant to publicise this form of treatment. Before long, though, his often dramatic successes led him to reconsider this decision and, as word of his accomplishments became more widely known, psychiatrists and neurologists started clamouring to be taught his secrets. While cautioning that not every patient could be cured instantly, and admitting that with some it was necessary to 'slave away for hours', Nonne also insisted that in a majority of cases treatment was both simple and speedy. He even claimed that *Blitzheilung* (split-second) cures frequently occurred.[9]

Nonne soon became much in demand as a speaker and toured Germany addressing psychologists and doctors in Munich, Berlin, Metz and Koblenz. With the instincts of a born showman, his hour-long presentations were part academic clinical lecture and part pure theatre. While demonstrating his skills from the platform, he would not only instantly cure soldiers suffering from paralyses, tics, tremors, stuttering and stammering but, by using hypnotic suggestion, make those previously cured reproduce their original symptoms with 'photographic fidelity'. In 1917 he had a 16mm film made to illustrate his lectures, with previously cured patients being re-hypnotised to exhibit their original symptoms. A copy of this sixteen-minute-long documentary still exists and creates in the modern viewer a sensation of almost surrealistic voyeurism. Under the harsh white glare of the camera lights and against a stark black backdrop we watch as anonymous German soldiers, wearing only underpants, tremble and jerk like grotesque puppets in the flickering silence. Abruptly Max Nonne appears beside them, a tall and ghostly apparition in a long white coat. He places his hands on their shuddering bodies, gently massages the twitching limbs, whispers in their ears or snaps his fingers. Suddenly, as if he had broken an evil spell, the trembling ceases and the terrible twitching stops.

After Nonne had successfully demonstrated his treatment to a group of high-ranking military doctors, the authorities finally accepted the merits of hypnosis, and, for the remainder of the war, scores of doctors from all over Germany were sent to Hamburg to learn his methods. Nonne was convinced that any physician could achieve the same outcomes when using hypnosis provided he possessed 'unfailing self-confidence', was able to inspire 'feelings of obedience' on the part of his patient and created 'an atmosphere of healing'.[10] Unfortunately, it soon became apparent that many German psychiatrists and neurologists either continued to dismiss hypnosis as quackery or were so inept in its administration that, despite Nonne's dramatic demonstrations, the technique proved to be at best unreliable and for the most part useless.

As a result, a majority of German psychiatrists, Edmund Forster among them, preferred to use what were euphemistically termed 'active therapies'. These included the injection of saline placebos, as well as the so-called 'agony shriek', which was, if possible, even more beastly than it sounds. Developed by Otto Muck, an Essen laryngologist, for the treatment of hysterically dumb soldiers, it involved thrusting a one-centimetre-diameter steel ball into the back of the throat and holding it forcefully against the larynx until, feeling himself on the point of suffocation, the patient let out a wild shriek of terror. 'In the moment that the patient was startled, he held his breath for a while, let his tongue go, and let out a shriek. The voice immediately returned,' explained Muck, who claimed a high success rate for his method. He also insisted that, far from being upset by such a violent assault, his patients expressed only great joy and gratitude for what he had done: 'They jumped off the chair, squeezed my hand, tried to hug me, and one caressed my face.'[11]

By far the most widely used form of 'active therapy' involved the use of electricity. As was explained earlier, low-voltage electric current had been widely used to treat a variety of ailments since the nineteenth century. But in 1903, while working at Heidelberg's nerve clinic, a psychiatrist named Fritz Kaufmann had watched in awe as a young girl suffering from hysteria made an immediate and complete recovery after the clinic's director, Wilhelm Erb, subjected her to a 'merciless' ten-minute burst of electric current accompanied by strong verbal commands. Twelve years later in the overcrowded wards of Mannheim's nerve clinic, Kaufmann recalled this experience and decided to try using the same procedure to create an 'assembly-line' method for treating neurotic soldiers. He publicised his method, also known as *Zwangsverfahren* (coercive processes) and *Gewaltsuggestionsmethode* (method of violent suggestion) in a series of lectures and demonstrations, as well as in an influential paper published in the *Münchener Medizinische Wochenschrift* of July 1916. The first step was 'suggestive preparation', during which the patient was assured by all members of the medical staff that his treatment would be completely successful. Once convinced he would soon be cured, the patient moved to step two, which involved the 'application of strong, alternating current with the aid of a great deal of verbal suggestion'.[12] Whenever possible the electric current was applied directly to the affected part of the body, so that a soldier with a paralysed leg, for example, would have the electrodes attached to his thigh or calf. The only exception Kaufmann made was if a soldier was hysterically dumb: he would never attach electrodes to the larynx, for fear of causing injury, but applied them to the lower back instead. The electric current, which was administered in bursts of between two and five minutes for up to two and a half hours, was extremely painful and Kaufmann did not claim that it, in itself, was a cure. Describing his experiences at Kaufmann's hands one patient wrote: 'The current was switched on. At first I had a prickly feeling, which suddenly burst into intense pain . . . I heard someone yelling, "You must listen now," and the doctor kept talking at me, "Only uneducated people suffer from such conditions. How will you cope with your stutter in society?" The appeal was to my self-respect and my sense of honour.'13

Kaufmann insisted that in order for his treatment to be effective strict military discipline must be enforced, with the doctor emphasising his superior military rank and barking out commands as if on the parade ground. As Paul Lerner comments, 'The Kaufmann method – analogous to war itself – was conceived of as a battle of wills between doctor and patient, and in his contest with the doctor, the patient had to understand that he could not win.'14 Once the treatment had started it could end only once the hysterical condition had been completely eliminated. To stop prematurely, Kaufmann warned, ran a risk of convincing the patient he was incurable and so making his condition intractable and permanent.

While Kaufmann claimed a high degree of success for his electric-shock treatment, he also admitted that, although cured, his patients were never fit enough to return to the front line.

As we shall see, although Edmund Forster did not use electric shocks when treating Adolf Hitler, his approach closely followed other aspects of Kaufmann's method, including the emphasis on obeying the orders of a superior officer. For Forster, as for Kaufmann, removing the patient's symptoms was just as much a matter of engaging in a battle of wills as of providing therapy. And it was a battle in which, as far as he was concerned, there were no rules of conduct and all that mattered was to win at any cost.

German psychiatrists were impressed by the speed and effectiveness of the Kaufmann method. With their wards swamped by an ever-increasing flood of hysterical soldiers, they not only enthusiastically adopted the same approach but embellished it with variations of their own devising. In Bonn, for example, neuropsychiatrist Heinrich Bickel modified the amount of electric shock the patient received by increasing both the current used and the time for which it was applied – at treatment number six it lasted for twenty minutes – so that the amount of pain involved grew steadily more intense from one session to the next.

The degree of brutality and degradation such 'therapy' involved may be vividly seen in the following description by another Bonn physician, Max Raether:

I hold the treatment sessions only in the evening, mostly between 6 and 9 p.m. and indeed completely irregularly, in keeping with my mood. Furthermore, none of the untreated knows when his turn will come; I give them the order to follow me into the treatment chamber completely unexpectedly.

Once there, their clothes are removed . . . and they are laid on the electrifying bench. A man holds the feet, two men hold the arms, which are laid next to the head, and one man operates the equipment. No one speaks except the doctor. On a short command the machine begins to hum. I usually wait for a while with a timer in my hand. The patient's expectation reaches its peak. I apply the faradic brush suddenly, and only in cases of high analgesics does it take longer than $1/2$–1 minute for tetanus building to develop on the whole body. Then I reduce the current substantially, begin with forceful verbal suggestion, faradise more or less the whole body with the exception of the head, neck, palms and soles with the weaker current, and have one of the paralysed limbs move on command, have those who were voiceless or with other speech disorders repeat words.[15]

Although the Kaufmann method was directly responsible for the deaths of at least twenty patients, it was not until almost the end of the war that protests and resistance by patients, in one instance leading to a full-blown mutiny, became so widespread and well publicised that electric therapy was finally prohibited by the medical authorities.

Before that happened there were some psychiatrists unwilling on either medical or ethical grounds to administer electric shocks. These doctors devised other forms of treatment which, although less overtly painful, were in their own ways just as brutal. Among these was prolonged immersion in a hot bath, a procedure developed by Frankfurt psychiatrist Rafael Weichbrodt, and based on the pre-war fad for hydrotherapy. Although this procedure was utterly different to that used by Kaufmann or that which Edmund Forster used when he treated Hitler's hysterical blindness, there is a similarity in how Weichbrodt prepared his patients for what was about to happen to them: 'After a thorough examination I explain to the hysteric: "Your disorders indicate a sickness of the will, thus you must make the effort to regain mastery over yourself, which can succeed within the next few days,"' Weichbrodt explained. '"If you are not able to accomplish it by yourself, you will certainly be made healthy in the bath, which through its evenly distributed warmth has very healthy effects."' He claimed that even at this early point in the treatment at least a quarter of his patients abandoned their hysterical symptoms, and by the following day could be discharged as entirely cured. The remainder would be placed in a warm bath – the water heated to 37° Celsius – and informed that there they would stay until completely free of their symptoms. 'The patient must remain in the bath day and night,' Weichbrodt reported, 'he must not be taken out for hours or the success is jeopardised. If he is not fine after twenty-four hours, then he stays in the bath for as long as it takes. I believe it is important not to take the patient out until his disorders have completely disappeared.'[16]

Recalling his experience of this 'treatment' at the Görden Sanitarium in Brandenburg, where warmer water – heated to 40° Celsius – was used, Oskar Maria Graff said:

We were defenceless, lying stark naked in a bath of hot water . . . The room was full of steam and wet and slippery. Three attendants walked to and fro at the window. If one of us tried to get out of the bath, they simply pushed him in again. So we just had to lie still, to lie and wait. We were given our dinner in the bath but were not hungry. We grew weary and then weak, unutterably weak. We heard horrible cries of distress from cell doors on one side: shouts, screams, curses and prayers. It was not until the third day that I was taken out of the bath, utterly exhausted, and put to bed.[17]

There were, however, notable exceptions to the notion of treating hysterical soldiers with these forms of 'active' therapy, although the alternative therapies these psychiatrists employed were similarly disagreeable. Otto Binswanger, who believed any cures effected by electric-shock treatment were only temporary, preferred strict isolation. He ordered his patients to remain completely silent and deprived them of food as a punishment for any breach of this strictly enforced command. Berlin psychiatrist Ewald Stier combined isolation in solitary confinement cubicles in a mental asylum with the threat that, if they did not recover swiftly, he would have them transferred to a ward filled with violently disturbed inmates. If any protested that they were not mentally ill, Stier would retort brusquely: 'He who does not have control over his body belongs in the asylum.'[18]

In all these procedures psychiatrists and neurologists deliberately tried to replicate the terror of the battlefield in order to 'shock' the hysterical soldiers whose minds had been 'knocked off balance' by their experiences at the front back to mental health. At the same time they strove to create an atmosphere of strict military discipline, instant obedience and masculine codes of honour in their clinics in the belief that it was only by adopting an authoritarian approach that doctors could command hysterical soldiers to abandon their symptoms. They became, in the words of Paul Lerner, 'Judge, teacher, and disciplinarian . . . [able] to exercise a decisive influence over the fates of thousands of soldiers . . . they supervised the creation of a set of institutions and facilities over which they had complete control. Doctors used their newly achieved control and authority over the patient to promote medical views of German manhood, which were based on duty, obedience and, most of all, productivity.'[19]

Luckily for them, some patients were treated in a more humane way. Several psychiatrists and neurologists discovered that good results – as good as were achieved by Kaufmann – could be achieved either by using a very low electric current or merely by pretending to apply electricity. The procedures they developed, known collectively as 'awake or alert suggestion' (*Wachsuggestion*), were based on the placebo effect and enabled their cures to be achieved with little or no pain, danger or discomfort. One practitioner described them as being somewhere between 'mystical suggestion' and 'coercion of the will' (*Willenszwang*).[20]

While always based on deception, the precise form of trickery employed varied. 'If we ask ourselves which method we will use in a given case, then it will be decided completely by the particularities of the case, the personality of the doctor and the external circumstances,' explained psychiatrist Kurt Goldstein. 'It depends less on the method than on the skilfulness of the doctor . . . Each doctor will make the most use of the method of whose effectiveness he is convinced.'[21]

In Königsberg, neurologist Max Rothmann offered his patients a 'wonder drug' that he enthusiastically claimed was guaranteed to cure them with just one application. However, since the medication was extremely painful, they could receive it only under a general anaesthetic. When they drowsily awoke from the anaesthetic Rothmann ordered them to prove they were now fully cured by moving a previously paralysed limb. Once this had been done, the patients were sent to a private room to sleep off the effects of the anaesthetic. Needless to say, no 'wonder drug' existed and the only medication the patient received was the anaesthetic that put him under. Even so, thanks to the persuasive power of the placebo effect and Rothmann's confident assurances of a successful outcome, the treatment proved so effective that he claimed fourteen out of sixteen cases had been cured in a single session.[22]

Other psychiatrists augmented the same type of treatment by blindfolding patients and placing them in a darkened room before administering the anaesthetic, used complicated medical equipment, such as X-ray machines, which they claimed possessed amazing curative powers, or administered saline injections into the affected part of the body.

At Giessen University Clinic psychiatrist Robert Sommer developed his special procedure for hysterical deafness and deaf-muteness, which, once again, was somewhat similar to the approach adopted by Forster when he treated Hitler. As Sommer explained to a conference of Central German psychiatrists and neurologists held in Bonn in 1917, the idea was to catch the patient off guard and trick him into reacting to the unexpected sound of a loud bell. At the start of treatment he fastened a strap around the patient's forearm and secured the soldier's middle and index fingers in a device that enabled any movements to be recorded as a trace on moving paper. He used written instructions to tell the patient he must keep his hand completely still as the tracing was made:

> While the man's attention is focused completely on this procedure, suddenly a bell behind his head is rung loudly.
>
> Despite their claims to be stone deaf, this unexpected noise frequently startled the patients with their abrupt finger movements being recorded on the graph. Immediately there occurred a twitching of the forearm, which brought forth the evidence that the patient must have heard the tone. Then through calm encouragement vis-à-vis the curve in front of him, the patient's attention was directed to the fact that there could no longer be the slightest doubt that he could hear. From this moment on in point of fact he could hear clearly and reacted correctly to every acoustic–verbal stimulus.[23]

Astonished and delighted by such clear evidence that they were not, as they had believed, deaf, his patients often reacted with delirious joy. Sommer recalled how one man gasped: '"I can hear again". It was brought to his attention that he also could speak again; he repeated letters and words sporadically with partial phonation. By the end of the speech exercise he was softly singing along to "Deutschland über Alles".'[24]

Finally, there were some psychiatrists and neurologists, Edmund Forster among them, who attempted to persuade their patients to abandon hysterical symptoms without resorting to elaborate equipment or complicated medical procedures. Their high degrees of success were obtained through the power of their authority and forceful verbal suggestion, often aided only by minor forms of trickery.

During his years of military doctoring, Forster had specialised in the treatment of hysterical disorders using methods he readily conceded were sometimes 'draconian', and as a result had gained a reputation for sometimes dealing with his patients in an overbearing manner. In 1916, for instance, a senior consultant described his 'very energetic and lively disposition' and his 'fresh, inspiring and agreeable personality', but then added, 'in some cases he had proceeded a little too roughly, attributing his own will-power to others and imposing it on others'.

When it came to assessing a soldier diagnosed as hysterical, Edmund rapidly reached one of two conclusions: that the patient was either malingering or weak-willed. If judged the former, then he saw it as his military duty to return the man to the battle as swiftly as possible. If he were unconsciously simulating his disorder, it was necessary to strengthen the soldier's will-power sufficiently to overcome what was no more than a self-inflicted disability. In such cases Forster used what he called his 'enlightening technique', which involved talking to the patient like 'whiny children and opportunistic malingerers', explaining they were neither sick nor suffering from any physical complaint and that their behaviour was so unworthy of a German soldier that it made them more deserving of punishment than treatment. Rather than following any single procedure, he preferred to develop his therapeutic script more or less spontaneously as the treatment unfolded, adapting it as necessary to match the patient's personality. With some soldiers he played on their sense of guilt at abandoning comrades to the dangers of the trenches while they shirked in a comfortable hospital bed. With others he threatened punishment for insubordination unless they immediately 'gave up' their disabilities. With most he employed his forceful personality almost literally to bully them back to full health: 'With a little bit of will-power you could perform your duties,' he would admonish his patients sternly. I know only too well that . . . not everyone has the same amount of will-power and that is why you are being treated here for a while. Not because you are poorly, but because you have been badly brought up and have no will-power. This will-power of yours [has] to be strengthened.' In other cases he used physical punishments, usually painful electric shocks, to bring the soldier to his senses: 'Just as one does not treat naughty children as sick people and would not reward them with days off school but punish them if they did not try to improve their conduct.'25

His aggressive verbal assaults often brought about a complete cure, and only as a last resort did he turn to the electric-shock machine. Before switching on the current he would 'Always tell the patient that I wasn't giving them electric shocks because they were poorly. Their supposed suffering was only a bad habit that could easily be got rid of if they wished to do so. By forcing them to endure the pain of the electricity I strengthened their will-power and their determination to return to the front rather than endure painful electric shocks in the hospital.'26

While some of his hospital colleagues viewed these methods as unorthodox, they also admitted that he not only brought about rapid cures but even earned the thanks of his patients into the bargain, with those to whom he had been the most abusive later expressing the greatest gratitude.

In January 1918 Forster returned to Berlin and his work at the Charité Hospital while remaining as a consultant to a number of

Lazarette, including those at Pasewalk. On his fortieth birthday he was discharged from the marines, although he remained an on-call consultant to the military until 15 November, when he once again took up his position as an associate professor in the Charité's nerve clinic.

During the four years he placed his skills and knowledge at the service of his country, Forster displayed a deep respect for military authority. His loyalty was recognised and rewarded with numerous decorations, including the Hanseatic Cross of Hamburg, the Bavarian Military Medal and the Iron Cross, First and Second Class. Now, with his military service behind him, he could start making plans, not only to achieve the same high academic distinction his father had enjoyed, but to marry and raise a family. As he folded away his uniform for the last time and put on his civilian clothes, Edmund Forster must have felt relief that all the threats and dangers were in the past. He could not know that, far from surviving a hurricane, he had only entered the eye of the storm that fifteen years later would annihilate him.

Chapter Ten
GAS ATTACK

Poor devils . . . their eyes bandaged, led along by a man with a string while they try to keep to the duckboards. Some of the after-effects are as extraordinary as they are horrible – the sloughing of the genitals for example.

Dr Harvey Cushing[1]

As was described at the beginning of this book, in mid-October 1918, while stationed near the small Belgian town of Wervicq on the River Lys, Hitler was temporarily blinded during a British gas attack. In the German edition of *Mein Kampf*[2] he requires only 132 words to describe this event. The English translation is eighteen words longer, but it remains concise:

In the night of October 13, the English gas attack on the southern front before Ypres burst loose; they used Yellow-Cross gas, whose effects were still unknown to us as far as personal experience was concerned. In this same night I myself was to become acquainted with it. On a hill south of Wervick [*sic*], we came on the evening of October 13 into several hours of drumfire with gas shells which continued all night more or less violently. As early as midnight, a number of us passed out, a few of our comrades forever. Towards morning I, too, was seized with pain which grew worse with every quarter hour, and at seven in the morning I stumbled and tottered back with burning eyes; taking with me my last report of the War. A few hours later, my eyes had turned into glowing coals; it had grown dark around me.[3]

This succinct description has, for some eighty years,[4] been widely and generally accepted as an accurate version of the events that left Hitler blinded and in pain for almost a month.[5] Yet his account is inaccurate in two respects: one trivial and the other of considerably greater significance. As was mentioned in Chapter 2, Hitler got wrong the date of the attack. This error was probably due to nothing more sinister than a lapse of memory. Given the frenetic conditions under which he had lived during his last few days on the front line, his physical and mental exhaustion prior to the attack and his parlous health immediately after it, such minor confusion is hardly surprising. In the absence of access to his military and medical records, while laboriously two–finger-typing his memoirs in Landsberg Prison, he would have had to rely solely on his recollection.

The much more significant mistake relates to the type of gas, named in his account as 'Yellow-Cross', which he claims the British used in their attack. For it is within this inaccuracy that the clue to Hitler's astonishing transformation from purposeless drifter to single-minded dictator may be found.

By the end of September 1918, the 16th Regiment was dug-in to well-established positions on high ground overlooking the River Lys, south of Ypres, and Hitler's duties as a *Meldegänger* mainly consisted of carrying messages between regimental headquarters and forward trenches on Paul Bucq Hill, one of the highest pieces of ground in the area. To the north-east of Paul Bucq Hill was the gutted town of Wervicq, whose tumbled buildings and rubble-filled streets were dominated by a shell-scarred church spire. In 1914 the pro-German Swedish explorer Sven Hedin had visited Wervicq and described how 'A large part of the population has remained and makes a curious picture in these quaint old streets where German kitchen wagons stand steaming and smoking at quiet street corners.'[6] Four years later the little town, which remained in German hands until the final weeks of the war, had been transformed into a deadly trap for any enemy troops, with concealed machine-gun posts and camouflaged sniper positions at every corner.

Facing the 16th Regiment on the opposite river bank was the British 30th Division, spread out along a ten-mile front and impatiently awaiting their orders to attack. Both sides knew these could not be long in coming. For one thing, the marshy river basin was, in the words of the divisional historian, 'no place to spend the winter'[7] and military planners knew only too well that within a few weeks rains would make any assault across the waterlogged ground and swollen river even more hazardous and costly in lives. Not only that, but the British lines were vulnerable to enemy artillery fire, being 'Overlooked beyond Wervick [sic] church spire by the higher ground south of the River Lys, Paul Bucq hill most obviously but behind again were Roncq and Mont Halluin. Roncq church spire possessing a most valuable and comfortable observation place for the enemy.'[8]

On 13 October, the day before the start of what would become known as the Battle of Courtrai, the intelligence officer of the 6th Brigade Royal Garrison Artillery noted in his diary: 'Six inch batteries carried out BB gas [i.e. mustard gas] concentrations on Busbecqu [east of Wervicq] and battery positions were harassed. At 7.30 p.m. we carried out a gas concentration . . . mustard gas shells were used for the first time.'[9]

Before dawn on the following morning German front-line troops heard the unmistakable sounds of British soldiers assembling for an attack, and one of the messages Hitler carried that night was almost certainly a request from forward officers for an artillery bombardment of the British lines. This was duly carried out, although, because they were firing blind in the darkness, German gunners could only lay down their barrage on positions identified during the day by observers in the spires of Wervicq and Roncq churches. The British, who had noted the fall of shells during the previous days and evacuated the areas concerned, suffered few casualties among the assembling troops. At five-thirty on what was to become a fine, bright day, soldiers from the 90th and 21st infantry brigades swarmed from their trenches and advanced through the early morning mist towards the Lys along a 3,500-yard front. With no cover in the featureless valley floor basin, the artillery barrage that started exactly three minutes before jumping-off time was of vital importance. The official historian of the 30th Division notes:

> It was, for the division, the last big barrage of the war . . . [It] was as good as any under which the division had advanced.
>
> It came down along and in front and behind the Lys with all the cumulative fury of four years of war – machine gun bullets, shrapnel, smoke, gas, thermite and high explosive – the smoke shells from the field guns were particularly blessed by the infantry advancing as close as they could to the curtain they made, for save on the extreme left where it was thinnest, it hid them from what defensive fire the enemy was able to bring to bear.[10]

With a demoralised enemy no longer prepared to sacrifice themselves in what a majority now perceived to be a lost cause, the British troops rapidly gained ground. The first few hours saw hundreds of Germans eagerly surrendering, including one officer who gave himself up fully prepared for captivity with a packed lunch and his servant. Two hours after the attack had started, British forward patrols were entering Wervicq and starting to clear out the snipers and silence machine-gun positions.

With the German forces falling back in disarray, Hitler's final few hours of battle had proved especially hectic and dangerous, and it must have been with considerable relief that, on that morning of 15 October, he and some of his fellow dispatch carriers gathered around a smoky field-kitchen in an abandoned concrete gun emplacement for their first meal of the day. One of the *Meldegänger* present was Ignaz Westenkirchner, who described what happened next:

> Not long after they had started eating artillery fire began and before the men fully realised what was happening blasting grenades mixed with gas grenades were raining down, one gas grenade detonated with the well-known dull thump [*Plomm*] immediately in front of the army kitchen and the old gun-emplacement. The cook screamed 'gas alert' but it was too late. Most of the comrades had already inhaled the devilish mixture of the Yellow Cross grenades [*Gelbkreuzgranate*] and stumbled away coughing and panting.
>
> They hardly made it back to the bombed-out house in whose cellar they had been living when they began to lose their eyesight and the mucous membranes in their mouths and throats became so inflamed that they were unable to speak. Their eyes were terribly painful; it was as if red-hot needles had been stuck into them. On top of that their eyes would no longer open, they had to lift their eyelids by hand only to discover that all they could make out were the outlines of large objects. Six of them, among whom was Adolf Hitler, scrambled to the assembly point for casualties, where they lost contact with one another due to their blindness . . . Hitler ended up in Pasewalk in Pomerania. The war had ended for all of them.[11]

On another occasion, however, Westenkirchner described the same incident very differently:

> We were in the neighbourhood of Commines; dazed and bewildered with the ceaseless flash and thunder of explosives . . . On the night of October 13th–14th the crashing and howling and roaring of the guns was accompanied by something still more deadly than usual. Our Company lay on a little hill near Werwick [*sic*], a bit to the south of Ypres.

All of a sudden the bombardment slackened off and in place of shells came a queer pungent smell. Word flew through the trenches that the English were attacking with chlorine gas. Hitherto [we] hadn't experienced this sort of gas, but now we got a thorough dose of it. About seven next morning Hitler was dispatched with an order to our rear. Drooping with exhaustion, he staggered off . . . His eyes were burning, sore, and smarting – gas – he supposed, or dog weariness. Anyway, they rapidly worsened. The pain was hideous; presently he could see nothing but a fog. Stumbling, and falling over and over again, he made what feeble progress he could . . . The last time, all his failing strength was exhausted in freeing himself from the mask . . . he could struggle up no more . . . his eyes were searing coals . . . Hitler collapsed. Goodness only knows how long it was before the stretcher-bearers found him. They brought him in, though, at last, and took him to the dressing-station. This was on the morning of October 14th, 1918 – just before the end. Two days later Hitler arrived in hospital at Pasewalk, Pomerania.[12]

So there are three contrasting accounts of the same event: Hitler's in *Mein Kampf* and the two Westenkirchner versions. Which is most likely to be correct? Was the gas, as stated by Hitler and confirmed by Westenkirchner in one of his accounts, Yellow-Cross (the German name for mustard gas) or, as Westenkirchner later claimed, was it chlorine?

Certainly, in the account Westenkirchner gave to the pro-Nazi German writer Heinz A. Heinz and which appeared in his *Germany's Hitler*, published in 1934, Hitler's former comrade is mistaken both about the date of the gassing and the time taken to travel between Flanders and Pasewalk. But the much more important question is whether he was correct in identifying the gas used as chlorine rather than Yellow-Cross. This is crucial because, when it comes to determining the true cause of Hitler's blindness, the gas involved is of the utmost significance. If Hitler had been exposed to mustard gas, there could well have been physical damage to his eyes that would have required several weeks of hospital treatment. Indeed, the interval of approximately one month between the attack on 15 October and his full recovery by 19 November is more or less what one would expect in such a case. In an analysis of three hundred patients with moderately severe sight loss due to mustard gas, British doctors found that 72 per cent had regained their sight after a month. If, however, Hitler had been blinded by chlorine, then, depending on the extent of his exposure, the effects might have been expected to disappear in a few hours or, at most, a few days.

Before we examine these conflicting narratives in more detail, it would be helpful to review the different types of gas available to military commanders by October 1918.

The idea of using poison gas to kill, disable or harass the enemy had first been mooted sixty years earlier during the Crimean War. Lord Thomas Cochrane, a young naval officer, devised a plan to produce lethal gas during the siege of Sebastopol, by burning five hundred tons of sulphur and allowing the prevailing wind to suffocate the Russians. The British government rejected his idea on grounds of its inhumanity and because they believed it contravened the laws of civilised warfare, a view later formally endorsed by the Hague Convention of 1907.

In Germany research leading to the first military use of gas was conducted by Fritz Haber, a Jewish chemist employed by Berlin's Kaiser Wilhelm Institute. Despite an explosion in mid-December 1914 that killed his assistant, Dr Otto Sackur, Haber continued his grisly experiments, and by the spring of 1915 had enabled the German Army to launch the first poison-gas attack on the Western Front. It had already been employed against the Russians on the Eastern Front three months earlier, but severe weather conditions had neutralised its effects. The first German gas attack to produce significant casualties and demonstrate the military effectiveness of mankind's first weapon of mass destruction occurred at 5.30 p.m. on 22 April 1915. Observers to the north of Ypres noticed 'two curious greenish yellow clouds on the ground on either side of Langemarck in front of the German line. These clouds spread laterally, joined up, and, moving before a light wind, became a bluish white mist, such as is seen over water meadows on a frosty night.'[13] Wafted by the breeze, the cloud drifted lazily along the ground and, moments later, flooded over and into the enemy trenches. The results were horrific: 'Choking. Coughing, retching, gasping for breath, and half blinded, it is no wonder that the troops were seized with terror at the enemy's expedient and gave ground, stumbling back through heavy shell fire in their efforts to find some escape from the deadly fumes.'[14]

With an estimated 7,000 soldiers injured and 350 killed, two divisions of French troops, from the 45th (Algerian) and 87th (Territorial) divisions, disintegrated, opening a four-mile gap in the lines directly before Ypres, the bottleneck through which Allied communications were obliged to pass. 'In the face of gas, without protection, individuality was annihilated,' comments C.R.M. Cruttwell, 'the soldier in the trench became a mere passive recipient of torture and death. A final stage seemed to be reached in the whole tendency of modern warfare to depress and make of no effect individual bravery, enterprise and skill.'[15]

Gas attacks tended to be made at night or in the early hours of the morning, when atmospheric conditions were most suitable, with the darkness and confusion making it far harder for troops to know when the assault had started. As a result, the psychological impact produced by fear and uncertainty soon became almost as debilitating as the gas itself. Indeed, as the war progressed:

Gas, which had initially been proposed as a means of enabling breakthroughs to be made in the wake of the gas cloud or as a means of retaliation, was being advocated on the grounds that it incapacitated troops, lowered fighting efficiency, caused panic, depressed morale and, by attrition, wore down the enemies' manpower. This applied especially in view of the war weariness and physical exhaustion of the troops.[16]

Once the lethal potency and military advantages of gas warfare had been so dramatically demonstrated, the Allies, while deploring 'Hun frightfulness' in their propaganda, raced to catch up.[17] Germany's lead in gas warfare had come about not because they were less moral than their enemies where its production and employment were concerned, but rather because of higher manufacturing capacity for the industrial dyes on which gas-warfare chemistry is based. Great German chemical works such as the Badische Anilin und Sodafabrik at Ludwigshafen, the Bayer Company at Leverkusen and the Griesheim-Elektron Chemische Fabrik possessed matchless research and development facilities for satisfying military demands. The British, who had neglected their synthetic-dye industry, possessed little or no commercial expertise in producing the precursors of organic poisons. Within a year of the attack at Ypres, however, chemists at a newly opened laboratory at Porton Down in the south-west of England had come up with an array of potentially useful gases.[18] Their efforts were matched by developments in Germany and France, too. The products they created may be placed in one of several categories, according to their medical effects. They include two different types of tear gas – benzyl bromide and xylyl bromide; and nine different lung irritants, including chlorine and phosgene. The Allies identified these different types of gas by means of coloured stars, with Red Star for chlorine, and Yellow Star for a mixture of 70 per cent chlorine and 30 per cent chloropicrin, a combination with the dual advantages of being even more immediately incapacitating and potentially lethal. By far the most widely used, however, was White Star, a powerful lung irritant made up of 50 per cent chlorine and 50 per cent phosgene. By the middle of 1916 this had become what Major General C.H. Foulkes, commander of the Royal Engineers' Special Gas Brigade, called 'the chemical mixture of choice – the "workhorse" gas'.[19] More terrifying than these weapons, however, were the paralysing gases, such as hydrocyanic acid and sulphuretted hydrogen. These acted directly on the nervous system to cause death within seconds. The fourth gas category comprised 'sternutators', so called because they induced sneezing (sternutation is its medical name), as well as an intense burning and aching pain in the eyes, nose, throat and chest, accompanied by nausea and great depression. This was only used by the Germans, and, while effective even in low concentrations, its symptoms rapidly disappeared once the soldier had left the poisoned area.

The final type of gas, and a latecomer on the battlefield, was ßß-dichlor-ethyl-sulphide, a vesicant agent whose properties had first been described by Victor Meyer in 1886. The Germans referred to it as Yellow Cross, from the yellow double- or Lorraine-cross markings they used to identify these shells. The French knew it as Yperite, because it was first used by the Germans at Ypres. The British called it either BB gas, from the first two Greek letters of its chemical name, or colloquially as HS (Hun Stuff). It was probably best known, however, as mustard gas, because of its faint odour, which is reminiscent of either mustard or garlic, depending on its impurities. A vesicant blisters and burns any part of the body it touches, especially the face and hands, because these are usually unprotected by clothing, together with the armpits, groin, genitalia and inner thighs, because these are moist. A unique feature of mustard-gas poisoning, and the one that sets it apart from other battlefield gases, is the slow rate at which its effects develop: 'Only a few of the men who were gassed died at once. Many of the men felt perfectly well after the bombardment [and] marched back with their companions on relief, under the impression that they had got through the affair satisfactorily. Several hours elapsed before they reported sick. The fatal course of the delayed illness was particularly striking.'[20] From between two and forty-eight hours after exposure the symptoms gradually developed and intensified.

Just how horrendous these could be is apparent from the following description in *Official History of the Great War*:

The most important pathological changes to be found in the human body after exposure to mustard gas are those in the respiratory tract ... The destruction of the membrane may have proceeded to such an extent that the whole area of the trachea and the larger bronchi is covered by a loosely adhered false membrane or slough of a yellow colour several millimetres thick.

Occasionally the slough on the trachea and larger bronchi can be separated as a whole and removed giving the appearance of a cast of the bronchial tree. Such a cast has been coughed up during life ... The skin exhibits all stages of burn from the primary erythema, which is the first manifestation of the cutaneous irritation, up to the final stage of deep burn with necrosis and sloughing of tissues. The eyes share in the general inflammation of the skin, and exhibit all the stages of an acute conjunctivitis, from the early chemosis up to an ulcerative keratitis.[21]

Its high boiling point (mustard gas is mostly a liquid at room temperature) makes it highly persistent. Once shelled, an area would remain dangerous for hours or even days as the poisonous fluid either slowly evaporated or was broken down by the elements. In April 1918 it was used so extensively during the shelling of Armentières that the gutters ran with it and no German troops were permitted to enter the town for two weeks. It was a gas completely unlike any other that Allied soldiers had previously experienced:

Up to this date they had been accustomed to associate 'gas' with violent irritating or choking sensations, and many, under the impression that the gas was not strong enough to hurt them, omitted to wear their helmets or keep them on for long enough, nor did they yet grasp that the ground in the vicinity of a burst was heavily contaminated by the poison and continued to be a source of danger long after the bombardment had ceased.[22]

British researchers had first tested this gas in the summer of 1916, but while the Commander-in-Chief, Sir Douglas Haig, had been eager to employ it, the British government refused to permit the use of a substance which, on the basis of the injuries it produced in laboratory animals, they regarded as barbaric. The German military were not as hamstrung by their civilian leaders, and deployed the gas for the first time at Ypres on the night of 12–13 July 1917, fourteen months ahead of it becoming generally available to British troops.[23] However, once the Allies made the decision to supply it to their troops, mustard gas was used so liberally and enthusiastically that between 1 October 1918 and the end of the war on 11 November it resulted in an estimated twelve thousand German casualties. The question is, was Hitler among them?

In March 1918 the Germans had brought to an end the years of trench warfare and, for the first time since 1914, fighting became mobile. More fluid battle lines transformed the use of gas, which now became an important means of taking out enemy artillery, incapacitating machine-gunners and infantry prior to an attack, preventing whole sectors from being reinforced by poisoning large tracts of ground with mustard gas and generally harassing and demoralising opponents by injuring them at times they least expected it.

Following the British 30th Division's successful attack across the River Lys on 14 October, and with the rapid advances into enemy-held territory, it might be imagined that, because mustard gas could put their own soldiers in jeopardy, its use might somewhat decrease. Furthermore, as the countryside around Wervicq still contained many civilian non-combatants, this too might be supposed to have inhibited Allied commanders from its widespread use. Major General Foulkes commented that, as 'The battle zone intruded more and more into areas hitherto behind German lines . . . the presence of great numbers of French civilians remaining in these areas retarded even localized gas activity on the British front.'[24] However, in the view of Matthew Buck, a researcher at Firepower, the Royal Artillery Museum:

> The war was characterised by frequent errors in planning, not necessarily due to indifference or incompetence on the part of the planners but to the very imperfect communications technology available during this period. This made it extremely difficult to provide appropriate or timely responses to constantly evolving battlefield situtions. 'Mustard' was often used on the flanks of attacks precisely because of its persistent nature – flanks which may have changed as the operations developed. It is thus not beyond the bounds of possibility that mustard gas would have been used by the Allies in these attacks, whether appropriate or not. I would even go so far as to suggest that it was a general characteristic of this war, where operations depended so much on fixed plans which often proved inappropriate to the actual development of events that errors were to be expected. Mustard gas was also a relatively new munition as far as the British were concerned, and prized for its effectiveness.[25]

Even if we assume the Allies ceased using mustard gas after their preliminary artillery bombardments on the night of 13–14 October, which indisputably included a large number of such shells, Hitler could still have been exposed to gas fired from much closer range by one of two gas-firing mortars, the Stokes and the Livens. The former, invented by Wilfred Stokes in 1914, was highly mobile, relatively silent and capable of delivering gas at such a rate of fire that up to fifteen projectiles, each delivering as much as two litres of the liquefied gas, might be airborne simultaneously. The Livens mortar, invented by William Howard Livens, an officer in the Royal Engineers, resembled a standard mortar with a three-foot-long mild steel tube attached to a base plate. The bombs could be fired from these mortars from a safe distance by means of an electrical fuse. Projectiles would normally contain thirty pounds of pure phosgene, although almost any combination of gas could be fired over a range of up to fifteen hundred yards. As one military expert observed: 'Improved still further, the Livens projector was capable of dousing large areas with heavy concentrations of gas and was to become one of the most effective delivery systems devised.'[26]

Ignaz Westenkirchner's unequivocal statement that 'chlorine' had been used against him and his comrades might, at first sight, appear to tip the balance of probabilities against the use of mustard gas, from whatever source. Unfortunately, he is not always the most reliable of witnesses. In one account, for example, he claims that the gas attack took place both 'in the early morning' and 'during the evening meal', while his apparent mention of 'chlorine' may simply be a mistranslation from the original German to English.

Hitler's own testimony is similarly flawed. In *Mein Kampf*, as will be recalled, Hitler clearly stated: 'As early as midnight, a number of us passed out, a few of our comrades forever.' Not only do German military records clearly show the British attack occurred early in the morning of 15 October, but Hitler's version is contradicted by the known effects of mustard gas over such a short period of time. Westenkirchner makes a similar error in his other account, claiming that the warning 'gas alert' came 'too late', that the victims were 'coughing and panting' immediately and that they 'hardly made it back to the bombed-out house [before] they began to lose their eyesight . . . [and] were unable to speak'. This description of events, as we have seen, is incompatible with the medical effects of mustard gas. Furthermore, it is unlikely that anyone present, including the cook, would have known if this gas had been used in the attack. Not only is its faint mustard smell typically masked by the more pungent odour of high explosive, but, because it rapidly destroys the victims' sense of smell, troops poisoned in this way rarely had any immediate knowledge of what had just happened to them.

But if it were not mustard gas, what did produce the incapacitating effects that both Hitler and Westenkirchner describe?

The only other gases whose symptoms closely match their descriptions are the lung irritants, and here the most likely candidate, if only because the British used it so freely, is White Star. The odour of this mixture of chlorine and phosgene is, as one might imagine, immediately apparent, and its medical effects are virtually instantaneous: 'Even in concentrations as low as two in a million these gases had an immediate and violently irritating action on the eyes, causing a profuse watering of the eyes and so much pain that it rapidly became impossible to keep them open.'[27] This was accompanied by violent coughing, spasmodic choking and panting with severe irritation of the mouth and throat making speech all but impossible. Exposure may also result in a loss of consciousness and even rapid death through asphyxiation: eight out of ten fatalities occurred within twenty-four hours of exposure. Once removed from the location of the gas, however, many victims quickly recovered, certainly as far as their eye problems were concerned, and except in the most severe cases suffered no serious consequences later in life.

The same cannot be said of exposure to mustard gas sufficient to cause blindness, where, although by no means inevitable, the risk of accompanying respiratory damage is high. Given Hitler's weak lungs that were serious enough to keep him away from school and living in the country in 1904, and that it was probably the same health problem which led to him being declared unfit for military service in 1913, he might have been especially vulnerable. However, his post-war lifestyle clearly demonstrates that he experienced absolutely no respiratory weakness whatsoever. During the 1920s he spent much of his time in Berchtesgaden at an altitude of 1,700 feet on the Untersberg. He seemed to thrive in air so thin and cold that no one suffering from a serious lung weakness could have endured it. 'I lived there like a fighting cock,' he told associates in 1942. 'Every day I went up to the Obersalzberg, which took me two and a half hours walking there and back.'[28] The strength and stamina of his lungs were also evident in his ability to address a large audience in the early days of the Nazi movement, unaided by microphones or loudspeakers.[29]

Thousands of troops on both sides certainly suffered from the appalling effects of mustard gas,[30] but there were many too who were victims of their own vivid imaginations. Post-war analysis of medical records suggested that up to half of all gas casualties came into this category.

> With men trained to believe that a light sniff of gas meant death, and with nerves highly strung by being shelled for long periods and with the presence of not a few who really had been gassed, it is no wonder that a gas alarm went beyond all bounds. It was remarked as a joke that if someone yelled 'gas' everyone in France would put on a mask. Two or three alarms a night was common. Gas shock was as frequent as shellshock.[31]

In 1918, for example, among American troops who had been warned about the dangers of gas without having any direct experience of it in the trenches, significant numbers subsequently complained about having been gassed without presenting any 'symptoms or physical signs suggesting that they had actually inhaled any form of poison gas in amounts sufficient to be harmful'.[32]

This was equally likely to be true in the case of German troops, who were first exposed to mustard gas with the French use of such shells in June 1918. That attack had taken them completely by surprise and spread such consternation that hundreds of casualties, with real and imagined injuries, flooded aid centres, where doctors frequently had great difficulty in correctly identifying those who were alleging or feigning gas poisoning.

After 1917, gas partly usurped the role of high explosive in bringing to a head a natural unfitness for war as poisoning was often: 'an expression of trench fatigue, a menace when the manhood of the nation had been picked over'.[33] So widespread was this problem that doctors were obliged to lay down stringent rules regarding the treatment of those who were deliberately faking their symptoms and others, like Hitler, who – without any conscious attempt to deceive – had developed hysterical blindness. These included clear instructions that all patients alleging gas poisoning were to be observed for between twenty-four and forty-eight hours. This was to be done in the medical inspection rooms of units, bearer companies or field hospitals, or in mild cases in collecting stations, with a view to sending the men back to their units if possible. They were specifically not to be admitted immediately to either a local or a field hospital, nor to a gas casualty station (*Gaskrankenstation*). Only those patients in whom there were unequivocal and objective signs of gas poisoning could be transferred to a gas casualty station, which was staffed by specially trained medical officers and nurses. Hitler, as will be recalled from Chapter 2, was treated like the majority of his comrades: with no suspicion that he was a malingerer. From the aid station at Linselle he was transferred for observation to Oudenaarde. From there, some twenty-four hours later, he was dispatched to Pasewalk.

Hitler's hospital dockets and military records make no mention of a specific gas, simply stating that it was gas poisoning: for example, '*gasvergiftet*' (gas poisoned) from the Oudenaarde doctors, '*Gasvergiftung*' from those at Pasewalk, '*l[eicht] Verwundet-Gasvergiftung*' (lightly wounded, gas poisoning), from the 16th Regiment's casualty list and similarly on many other contemporary documents too numerous to list here.[34]

From where, then, does the widely held and reported but erroneous notion that Hitler was blinded by mustard gas originate? The answer is from his own brief account of the incident in *Mein Kampf*. Was this a deliberate attempt to deceive, to safeguard the truth that, far from being seriously injured in the British attack, he had suffered a mental breakdown?

While this possibility can hardly be excluded, given the duplicity at which he and his propaganda experts were so adept, a more likely explanation is that Hitler sincerely, if mistakenly, believed himself to be suffering from the effects of mustard gas, rather than the unpleasant, but in his case milder, White Star.

Chapter Eleven
THE WAYS OF THE WOLF

It has come! The Führer is appointed Chancellor. He has already been sworn in by the President of the Reich. The final decision has been made . . . All of us are dumb with emotion. Everyone clasps the Führer's hand . . . Outside the Kaiserhof the masses are in a wild uproar . . . The thousands soon become tens of thousands. And endless streams of people flood the Wilhelmstrasse. We set to work at once.

Joseph Goebbels[1]

Shortly before 10 p.m. on Monday, 27 February 1933, Detective Inspector Helmut Heisig of Division 1A of the Berlin Police Department received an agitated phone call from one of his officers reporting that the nineteenth-century Reichstag parliament building was on fire. The officer also announced the arrest of a suspected arsonist: a mentally retarded Dutchman and alleged communist named Marinus van der Lubbe. The following day, in response to this 'outrage', Hitler enacted a decree 'for the protection of the people and the state', which swept away all constitutional protection of political, personal and property rights. He was now well on his way to becoming Germany's undisputed master, with only President von Hindenburg standing between him and absolute power.

What Hitler saw as his divine destiny was about to be realised after fifteen years fraught with risk and marked by violent struggle.

*   *   *

On 19 November 1918 Hitler had left the *Lazarett* and made his way, via Berlin, to Munich, where he presented himself for duty with the 1st Replacement Battalion of the 2nd Bavarian Infantry Regiment. Soon after he arrived in Munich, the socialist government headed by Kurt Eisner, a former journalist, gave way to a soviet republic, and many soldiers in Hitler's regiment began sporting red arm-bands, not as a mark of political allegiance but for personal survival. To be found without one could mean execution without trial at the hands of communist death squads.

To escape from the dangers and chaos of the city, in February 1919 Hitler and a former front-line companion, Ernst Schmidt, volunteered for guard duty at a small prisoner-of-war camp on the Austrian border. There was little guarding to be done because the camp was rapidly being run down as the erstwhile prisoners left for home, so he and Schmidt spent most of their time sorting out old gas masks. When he was not working, Hitler read constantly, being especially interested in the political tracts that were being turned out in vast numbers by a thriving underground press.

By the time he and Schmidt returned to Munich a few weeks later, the soviet republic was collapsing and life had become increasingly desperate for its citizens. Draconian laws were passed in a forlorn attempt to eliminate dissent and bolster the rapidly disintegrating economy. Newspapers had been banned, houses were either being confiscated by government officials or openly looted by gangs of left-wingers, people were snatched off the streets to become hostages, and the daily toll of executions mounted rapidly. Interviewed during the 1930s, Schmidt recalled how:

> Snow lay deep in the streets. Soldiers were streaming back into Munich still, from all the battle-fronts, weary, battered, disorientated men. Coming home to a foundered country where neither food, nor peace, nor work was to be had. There were thirty thousand unemployed hanging around the streets.

Food grew more and more scarce. The people ate anything they could lay their hands upon that was remotely edible. A fallen horse was a godsend. Such a carcass was immediately pounced upon by the starving populace, and in quicker time than it takes to tell every shred of flesh was stripped from the bones.[2]

Many former soldiers had been organised by their disillusioned officers into Freikorps, private armies of ruthless right-wing extremists who had lost everything other than a deep hatred for Jews and Marxists. On Sunday, 13 April 1919 the Freikorps attempted an armed coup and for a time the streets of Munich became battlegrounds. Hitler was stationed at the Maximilian II Barracks in Munich-Oberwiesenfeld when the Freikorps, arriving in search of communists, were greeted with a smattering of small-arms fire. They then stormed the building, either shooting or taking prisoner all those inside, including Hitler. With a group of fellow soldiers, he was then paraded through the streets at gunpoint and locked up in makeshift cells located in the cellars of the local school. On the first day of imprisonment some from Hitler's group were led away and executed by their Freikorps guards.

By a stroke of astonishing good fortune, which Hitler saw as yet more evidence of intervention by divine providence, he was seen by an officer he had known at the front. The officer, who had visited the school only by chance, arranged his immediate release and offered him work on a commission set up to investigate revolutionary activity in the 2nd Infantry Regiment. Hitler eagerly accepted his offer and soon 'produced indictments which threw a merciless light on the unspeakably depraved military betrayals perpetrated by the Jewish dictatorship at the time of the Munich Soviets'.[3]

So enthusiastic and unhesitating was his indictment of fellow soldiers that Captain Karl Mayr, the commission's intelligence officer, offered him another job, this time as a *Vertrauensmann* (undercover agent). Once again he accepted the offer and transferred to a new office based in the so-called Press and News Bureau, in reality the espionage and propaganda unit of District Army Command. Hitler's assignments involved ferreting out all those soldiers and NCOs who had either joined the communists or expressed sympathy for their cause. His unquestioning obedience and the willingness with which he carried out these disagreeable tasks so impressed his superiors that Mayr found him a place on a political-education course at Munich University, which included lectures on German history, economics, domestic and foreign policy. At the end of each lecture, when the topic was opened for general discussion, Hitler invariably spoke, arguing his point so forcefully and persuasively that Mayr, the well-educated son of a magistrate, was impressed. Hitler's ideas may not have been new, but Mayr found the brutal power and absolute conviction with which he expressed them mesmerising. It was as if this otherwise undistinguished former lance-corporal was privy to some great truth, a truth of which everyone else was ignorant but to which, through him, they might ultimately gain access.

'Herr Hitler is a born popular orator,' reported Lorenz Frank, one of his colleagues, 'whose fanaticism combined with the common touch . . . unfailingly compels his audience's attention and commands their sympathy.'[4] Similar views were expressed by his superiors, including Mayr, who was destined to perish in the Buchenwald concentration camp after the Nazis came to power.

However, this assessment of Hitler's skills was not entirely true in the early years of his political career. While Hitler could command the attention and respect of small groups with the passionate intensity of his beliefs, he had never tried to address a large and far more sceptical audience. When that moment arrived a few months later it would prove to be a dismal failure. But, for the time being, Hitler remained in his element. On 12 September 1919 he was instructed to attend a meeting of a group calling itself the Deutsche Arbeiterpartei (German Workers' Party), which had been founded the previous January by Anton Drexler, a tool-maker, and Karl Harrer, a journalist on the

Münchner-Augsburger Abendzeitung. The common belief of all such right-wing groups was hatred for the *Novemberverbrecher* (those men they blamed for stabbing Germany in the back in November 1918), and their common aim the destruction of the Weimar Republic, which, in their view, was *'verjudet'* (full of Jews). Hitler's assignment was to report on their political aims in order that the authorities could determine whether they posed any threat.

The meeting was held in the Sterneckerbräu, one of Munich's smallest and shabbiest beer halls. Hitler, wearing civilian clothes, gave his occupation as 'writer' and took a seat at the rear, where he could observe both the audience and those on the platform. The main speaker was Gottfried Feder, whom Hitler already knew as an instructor on the political-education course that he had attended. Feder's long, uninspiring speech was listened to with indifference by an audience of some forty-five men scattered around the hall. Hitler, who was quickly persuaded that the German Workers' Party posed not the slightest threat to his superiors, seems to have had no intention of speaking, but when the discussion was thrown open to the floor, a Professor Baumann rose to argue that Bavaria should break away from Germany and link up with Austria. Hitler, the fanatical proponent of pan-German nationalism, could not remain silent while such heresy was being advocated. Leaping to his feet, he attacked the professor with such contemptuous sarcasm that Baumann hurried from the hall. Soon after the meeting concluded and, as Hitler made to leave, he was stopped at the exit by Anton Drexler, who congratulated him on his speech and handed him a pamphlet he had written entitled *Mein Politisches Erwachen* (*My Political Awakening*). Thrusting it into his trenchcoat pocket, Hitler trudged back to the barracks and went straight to bed.

Around dawn he was awoken by the sound of mice scrabbling for the breadcrumbs it had become his habit to put down for them each night. Unable to return to sleep, he decided to read the pamphlet in the hope it would provide the basis for his report. In sixteen short chapters Drexler set out his political views and thoughts on the 'Jewish conspiracy'. Although the pamphlet brought together for the first time the words 'National' and 'Socialism', what is more likely to have caught Hitler's eye was Drexler's prayer that a new leader would emerge in this, Germany's most desperate hour of need, to guide the nation to salvation.

On 16 September Hitler received a postcard inviting him to attend a committee meeting with a view to becoming a member of the party. This, after some hesitation, he decided to do, and a few days later he found himself in a dingy back room at the Altes Rosenbad, a beer hall in the Herrenstrasse. Four men sat at a paper-strewn table under the guttering light of a gas flame burning in a broken mantle. The German Workers' Party had no offices, no employees, no printed letterheads and not even a rubber stamp to its name. Its entire property consisted of an old briefcase in which the members kept correspondence and a battered cigar box containing the party's funds: a little over seven marks. It was a little-known, ineffectual party with a membership of less than fifty, and yet, Hitler later acknowledged, it was its obscurity that most attracted him: it was 'only in a party which, like himself, was beginning at the bottom that he had any prospect of playing a leading part and imposing his ideas. In the established parties there was not room for him, he would be a nobody.'[5]

After that first meeting, Hitler reflected for two days before completing his application form, paying his dues and becoming Committee Member Number 7, Party Member Number 555. The membership, however, was considerably less impressive than his number might imply because, in order to increase its apparent importance, the committee had started the numbering at 500.

During his early months of membership, Hitler's philosophical mentor as well as his passport to the elite of Munich society was Dietrich Eckart, a large and jovial bohemian poet, playwright and journalist, who drank heavily, injected himself with morphine on a regular basis and was an active member of the extreme right-wing Thule Society. Eckart had once lived rough on the streets of Berlin and had later been confined to a lunatic asylum, where he wrote and staged plays, using fellow inmates as actors. At the end of the war he had returned to Munich and taken cheap lodgings in the Schwabing district, a quarter much favoured by artists. As a result of his growing literary fame, Eckart had subsequently acquired many wealthy and influential friends. Like Drexler, Eckart had long sought a saviour who would free Germany from Bolshevism and lead his country from the humiliation of defeat into glory. A few months before his first meeting with Hitler, he had written a poem prophesying that the coming Messiah would be a common soldier, a man of the people – yet no ordinary man. He would possess an absolute conviction in his own and Germany's destiny, with blazing eyes and the power to sway the masses to his will. While drinking in a wine cellar, the Brennessel, he expressed this prophetic vision in less poetic terms when he told his friends:

> We need a fellow at the head who can stand the sound of a machine-gun. The rabble need to get fear into their pants. We can't use an officer because the people don't respect them any more. The best would be a worker who knows how to talk . . . He doesn't need much brains . . . He must be a bachelor, then we'll get the women.[6]

Hitler, were he aware of Eckart's prophecy, would certainly have seen it as further evidence of divine providence. Within a few weeks he gradually began to perceive that from this utterly insignificant little party he might create the 'drum' on which to pound out his political messages to the nation. But he also recognised that for this to happen he must first browbeat his cautious and unambitious fellow committee members into transforming and invigorating the moribund organisation. 'After long negotiations I put through the acquisition of three rubber stamps. I also succeeded in having our little invitations to meetings hectographed [an early form of photocopying]. When, in addition to all that, I pressed for larger meetings, Harrer couldn't follow me. He retired and that gave me a free path.'[7]

'Imagine that thundering voice, demanding three rubber stamps,' exclaims Konrad Heiden, one of Hitler's earliest biographers. 'And the speeches on behalf of hectographed invitations!'[8]

Hitler's strategy of distributing publicity announcing their meetings and even expending their scarce funds on newspaper advertisements soon paid off, and attendance at meetings began to rise steadily. In October 1919 Hitler addressed his largest audience to date, a crowd of 111 people, in the Hofbräuhaus Keller. This was the disaster that was mentioned earlier. The oratorical skills that Karl Mayr had found so compelling when Hitler was addressing his class at the university disappeared almost entirely as he rose to his feet. Anxiety and his lack of public-speaking experience left him floundering at the mercy of an increasingly restive and hostile crowd. For Karl Harrer, who watched the ambitious young upstart's humiliation with a certain satisfaction, it served to confirm his initial impression that Hitler had no talent for public speaking.

A man less assured of his destiny might have retreated from the limelight after such a setback and decided to leave the ordeal of addressing large crowds to others from then on. But Hitler merely shrugged off the failure and continued to speak whenever and wherever the opportunity presented itself. Slowly and painfully he began to acquire the techniques of a professional orator. Night after night he was on his feet in the dingy, smoke-filled back rooms of beer cellars arguing his case and honing his public-speaking skills as he learned to cope with every kind of audience reaction, from scornful dismissal to outright hostility. He learned how to 'read' an audience in order to manipulate their emotions and control their responses. Before long he was able, in the words of Dr Hjalmar Schacht, to 'play like a virtuoso on the well-tempered piano of lower-middle-class hearts'.[9]

Among his audience on one occasion was a twenty-three-year-old former pilot and volunteer with Hitler's old 16th Regiment, Rudolf

Hess. Swayed by Hitler's by now forceful rhetoric, Hess became a party member and soon a close friend of Hitler.

Hitler learned his trade as a demagogue in a hard and unrelenting school where violence was an ever-present accompaniment to his words. During the first year his bodyguards, who clubbed and kicked hecklers into silence, remained an ill-organised collection of toughs, most of whom were motivated more by the expectation of a rough house and free beer than by political allegiance. In August 1921, however, these toughs were organised into a disciplined fighting force, initially under the command of Karl Mayr and later under Ernst Röhm. Their real purpose, as bully-boys and street-fighters, was concealed behind the innocuous title of the party's 'Gymnastics and Sports Division' which, a recruiting pamphlet claimed, would 'embody and propagate the military idea of a free nation. It will instil a boundless desire for action in the hearts of our young members, hammer and burn into their brains that history does not make men, but men history.'[10] On 5 October 1921 all such pretence was dropped when the force was given a new name – the Sturmabteilung (Storm Detachment or SA) – and a new commander, Johann Ulrich Klintzsch. The men were fitted out with cheap, sandy-brown, army-surplus shirts, originally intended to be used by troops in Africa, giving rise to the name by which this highly organised and feared people's army soon came to be known – the Brownshirts. Later, to counter the rising power of the SA, Hitler organised a praetorian guard who swore loyalty not to the party but to himself. These men, who wore black ski-caps with silver death's-head buttons on them and black-bordered swastika arm-bands, were the nucleus of the Schutzstaffel (Protection Squads or SS), which officially came into existence on 9 November 1925.

In the early years Hitler certainly needed all the protection these ruthless young men could provide, because the party's meetings invariably deteriorated into mayhem and uproar. Far from deterring Hitler, he relished the violence, the flying beer-mugs, the overturned tables and bloodied heads. When the battle was over and his thugs had finally ejected his political opponents into the night, he would cheerfully resume his speech among the debris of smashed furniture and broken tankards.

A regular member of his audience in those early days was Frau Magdalena Schweyer, who ran a grocery shop across the street from Hitler's lodgings on the second floor of a modest house at 41 Thierschstrasse. Frau Schweyer later vividly recalled a party meeting on 4 November 1921:

A real battle that was. If I hadn't kept my head low over the table that night and folded my arms above it, like all the rest of us women were told to do, sure as fate it would have been knocked clean off my shoulders. We womenfolk were told to get well up in front: it would be safest there far from the doors . . .

Hitler had been speaking for some time when the sign was given. Someone shouted *Freiheit* [the Marxist battle cry – Liberty] and a beer-pot went crash! That was the signal for things to begin. Three, four, five heavy pots flew by within an inch of the speaker's head, the next instant his young guards sprang forward shouting to us women to 'Duck down'. Pandemonium had broken out. One heard nothing but yells, crashing beer mugs, stamping and struggling, the overturning of heavy oaken tables and the smashing of wooden chairs. Hitler stuck to his post. Never got off that table. He made no effort to shield himself at all. He was the target of it all: it's a sheer miracle how he never got hit . . . The room was simply wrecked. There were over four hundred smashed beer-mugs lying about everywhere and piles of broken chairs.[11]

In early 1920 a party manifesto was drawn up by Hitler, Anton Drexler, Gottfried Feder and Dietrich Eckart, who sat arguing passionately around the kitchen table in Drexler's poky apartment. By 6 February they had agreed on twenty-five points, which included the confiscation of all war profits, the unification of Germany, rejection of the Treaty of Versailles, the expulsion of foreigners and the abolition of unearned income. Above all, their manifesto declared open war on: 'Those who work to the injury of the common welfare. Traitors, usurers, profiteers etc. are to be punished with death, regardless of race and creed.'[12] Later, when nervous industrialists and other potential financial backers referred to these demands, Hitler was able to reassure them that Germans need have no fears for their fortunes. His target was solely the capital of Germany's single greatest foe: international Jewry.

Hitler, whom the committee had placed in charge of propaganda, now set about organising their largest and most ambitious meeting to date, at which he would present the new political agenda to the public. This was to be held not in the confines of the Hofbräuhaus's beer cellar, but in its vast and echoing Festsaal (Festival Hall).

On Tuesday, 24 February 1920 Hitler entered the hall to face an audience of around two thousand people. A significant proportion of the crowd had come to make trouble. 'We ourselves were horrified at our boldness,' he recalled later. 'Would one of us be able to speak in this hall? Would he get stage-fright and start to stammer after the tenth sentence, and be shouted and whistled down?'[13] The meeting started inauspiciously with a turgid address by Johannes Dingfelder, a homoeopathic physician. The crowd, who had expected something more radical and arousing, rapidly grew restless so that by the time Hitler rose to speak their mood ranged from amused contempt to undisguised hostility. This, he must have known as he stood gazing out across row upon row of pale faces staring back at him through a haze of cheap tobacco smoke, was his moment of truth. It was a challenge that would either confirm his divinely ordained mission or reveal it as hollow. Even before he started speaking there were shouts of derision, whistles and yells. Within ten minutes interruptions were coming from all sides of the vast hall. There was, he later alleged, so much intimidation that his supporters occasionally had to intervene in order to enable him to continue speaking. A few of them, he conceded, were armed. That is putting it mildly. The Munich District Army Command had sent along a troop of Reichswehr soldiers (according to some sources a company of mine-throwers) to drive opponents from the meeting using whatever means they chose, including cold steel.

Once the political opponents had been driven from the Festsaal Hitler yelled at the crowd: 'If anyone else dares, let him speak up against the programme!' No one did, and the crowd, while undoubtedly terrorised by the violence used to eject the hecklers, was captivated by what was happening on the platform. As Mayr had spotted at the university seminars, it was Hitler's absolute certainty, rather than what he said, that was mesmeric. 'Vehemence, passion and fanaticism,' Hitler wrote in 1923, 'the great magnetic forces which alone attract the great masses; for these masses always respond to the compelling force which emanates from absolute faith in the ideas put forward, combined with an indomitable zest to fight for and defend them.'[14]

At that meeting, the first mass gathering or rally the Nazis had ever organised, the power and passion of Hitler's oratory were such that many of those present felt they were witnessing less the delivery of a familiar political message than the unleashing of some primordial force. It was akin to an elemental power capable of sweeping away rational arguments and intellectual objections with the same ruthless efficiency that the party's bully-boys employed when cleansing the hall of their opponents. Even educated Germans who, before hearing him speak, had dismissed Hitler as a slightly absurd and hysterical rabble-rouser often found themselves persuaded by the sheer force of his passionate self-belief.

After attending a meeting in 1922, Kurt Ludecke, gambler, businessman and adventurer, reported:

When the man stepped forward on the platform, there was almost no applause. He stood silent for a moment. Then he began to speak quietly and ingratiatingly at first. Before long his voice had risen to a hoarse shriek that gave an extraordinary effect of an intensity of feeling. There were many high-pitched rasping notes . . . but despite its strident tone, his diction had a distinctly Austrian turn, softer and more pleasant than the German. Critically I studied this slight, pale man, his dark brown hair parted on one side and falling again and again over his sweating brow. Threatening and beseeching, with small, pleading hands and flaming, steel-blue eyes, he had the look of the fanatic. Presently my critical faculty was swept away. Leaning from the tribune as if he were trying to impel his inner self into the consciousness of all these thousands, he was holding the masses, and me with them, under a hypnotic spell by the sheer force of his conviction.[15]

Numerous reports of the rallies of this period corroborate Ludecke's testimony. Hitler's belief in himself and his divine purpose was absolute, and his passionate oratory had the power to communicate that conviction to others. 'In the *Völkischer Beobachter* [the Nazi Party's newspaper] text these speeches stand before us in all their freshness,' says Konrad Heiden. In each meeting a reporter would minute the speech before taking his copy to the 'print shop that very night, charged with all the power, the hatred, the self-reliance, the factual and grammatical mistakes of an agitated hour'.[16]

By the time Hitler had finished addressing that crowd in the Festsaal of the Hofbräuhaus, he had not only convinced the majority of those who had heard him of his unique abilities as an orator but had even impressed himself with his performance: 'When I finally closed the meeting,' he wrote later, 'we were not alone in feeling that a wolf had been born which was destined to break into the herd of swindlers and misleaders of the people.'[17]

On 1 April 1920 Hitler finally left the army and was able to devote himself to his political career and building up the party. His Munich group was not the only political party calling itself National Socialist. In Austria there was the Deutschsoziale Arbeiterpartei, which combined a working-class movement with pan-German nationalist ideals. In May 1918 this party had changed its name to the German National Socialist Workers' Party (NSDAP) and adopted the Hakenkreuz, or swastika, as its symbol. In August 1920 a delegation from Munich attended a meeting of the NSDAP in Salzburg and, not long afterwards, decided to change its name to the NSDAP and adopt the swastika as its own.

As Hitler strived to expand and consolidate his power base among the masses, he found himself increasingly facing anger and resentment among the other founding members, who believed their party and its aims were being hijacked under their noses. In a leaflet accusing him of a 'lust for power and personal ambition', Anton Drexler thundered: 'It grows more and more clear that his purpose is simply to use the National Socialist Party as a springboard for his own immoral purposes and to seize the leadership in order to force the Party on to a different track at the psychological moment.'[18]

In the early summer of 1921 the committee took advantage of Hitler's six-week absence in Berlin, where he had gone to make speeches and rally support, to stage a revolt against his increasingly dictatorial attitude. Led by Drexler, they proposed returning the party to its founding principles and merging it with a number of other small political groups in order to limit Hitler's freedom of action and bring him back under democratic control. But, as so many others would in the future, they had totally underestimated their opponent. On 11 July a furious Hitler impulsively resigned from the party. The committee, recognising that without his organisational and oratorical abilities the NSDAP would rapidly disintegrate, back-tracked and tried to reach a compromise. In return for agreeing to rejoin the party Hitler made a number of demands including that of being appointed Party Chairman and given unlimited powers. To increase the pressure further he also brought a libel suit against Drexler on the basis of his leaflet. Protest as they might the committee members knew they had no choice but to accept his outrageous terms and, on 26 July, Hitler rejoined the party as member number 3680. Three days later at an extraordinary meeting of the NSDAP'S 554 paid-up members, all his demands were accepted with only one dissenting vote. Anton Drexler was 'promoted' to Honorary President, a position that robbed him of all power and responsibility. From then on the party's public meetings became increasingly stage managed to ensure maximum psychological effect. Hitler always entered the hall only after the crowd had been marshalled into their seats and made to wait just long enough to become expectant with anticipation. Then, at exactly the right psychological moment, flanked by his bodyguards, he would stride down the centre of the hall, looking neither left nor right. Once he had finished speaking he would abruptly leave the hall without inviting either questions or discussion from his audience. His message was not open to question. His statements were not open to debate: they could be either accepted or rejected.

Under his leadership, the party's membership, influence and power started rising swiftly. Within a few months thousands (non-members of the party as well as members) were crowding into major venues such as the auditorium of the Zirkus Krone to hear him speak. Those most attracted to the Nazis were the self-employed, shop staff, office workers and, especially, farmers and teachers. They were, in the words of one commentator, most likely to be middle-class Protestants 'who lived either on an estate or in a small township and had formerly voted for a party of the political centre or for a regional party opposed to the power and influence of big industry and the trade unions'.[19] The National Socialists were, in short, a party whose greatest appeal was to the dispossessed, the disillusioned and the disgruntled; the unskilled and the semi-skilled together with the small businessman struggling to survive as high inflation eroded their savings and high unemployment threatened their livelihoods. It was, above all, a membership that sought the comforting certainty that only a ruthlessly confident leader, with simplistic solutions to complex socio-economic problems, could provide. During the early 1920s there were millions of such people in Germany, but while he played on the fears and frustrations of the masses with consummate skill, Hitler also held them in contempt, branding the majority as the 'undecided, the stand-asiders, the lazy, the cowardly'. When he told a crowd of five thousand, 'Cowardly men choose the most cowardly as their leader so that they will not have to show courage; and they choose the stupidest among the stupid, so that everyone can have the feeling that he is a little better than the leader,'[20] they cheered and exalted his strength of will and determination of purpose, which they believed would make them equally strong.

Outside Germany Hitler and his followers were viewed as more amusing than menacing: 'There is no doubt', commented the London *Daily Telegraph* on 19 November 1922, 'that a group of reactionaries calling themselves National Socialists, fired by the success of the Fascisti movement in Italy, are desirous of emulating its achievements.' On the same day the London *Times* published a brief story under the headline: BAVARIAN FASCISTS' MOTLEY ATTIRE: 'The Bavarian "National Socialists" are beginning to don uniforms consisting of a tam-o'-shanter, a grey blouse, and a black, white and red armband, with the anti-Semitic swastika. Their leader Herr Hittler [*sic*] is said to be desirous of becoming a Bavarian "Mussolini". The Bavarian Socialists are now taking defensive measures.' This item was considered so trivial that none of the other papers carried it and *The Times* too dropped the story from its so-called 'Royal Edition', the last to be printed, so that Their Majesties missed the opportunity of reading the first mention of Adolf Hitler in any British newspaper.

But if few outside Germany had heard of the NSDAP, and those who had refused to take it seriously, the Nazis were a rising force in Bavarian politics. Hitler was proving himself not only a brilliant speaker but a skilled propagandist whose influence extended over every detail of the party's presentation. When it was decided that the party needed a flag, he turned his artistic talents towards designing

Lindwurmstrasse, Munich, where Edmund Forster was born in 1878

An etching of Franz Joseph Forster, Edmund's father

COURTESY ARNE FORSTER AND MECHTHILD MUDRACK

The Forster family in Holland, left to right: Edmund, Dirk, Mina, Gretchen, Arne

COURTESY MARIE ROSE VON WESENDONK

Edmund Forster and his brother
Dirk, about 1890

Edmund's brother Arne

COURTESY PAM FORSTER, FROM THE WORLD CRUISE POSTCARD COLLECTION

Watercolour scenes painted by Edmund during his travels in the Far East on
the *Suevia* in 1902 and sent as postcards to his parents

ACourtesy Arne Forster and Mechthild Mudrack

Edmund Forster taken at Greifswald shortly before his death in September 1933

Mila Forster, about 1905

Courtesy Pam Forster

Mila Forster with her sons Balduin, left, and Ruprecht, photographed by Dirk in Paris in July 1933

Lilly and Dirk Forster

BILDARCHIV PREUSSISCHER KULTURBESITZ/H. HOFFMANN

Hitler (second from right) in France during the First World War

US LIBRARY OF CONGRESS

Line drawing by Hitler done while he was serving with the List Regiment in Flanders

Karl Kroner, the doctor who confirmed the diagnosis of Hitler's hysteria and whose interview with the OSS in 1943 first identified Edmund Forster as the psychiatrist responsible for treating Hitler

Pasewalk railway station as it was in 1918 when Hitler arrived to be treated for hysterical blindness

Hitler's hospital admission chits for Oudenaarde and Pasewalk showing his dates of admission and giving the cause of his injuries as gas poisoning

STADT PASEWALK MUSEUM

The original 'shooting house' converted from hostelry to Lazarett in 1914

BROSE

The open field where the Pasewalk Lazarett once stood

Hitler usually spoke off the cuff using only a brief, handwritten outline to guide his thoughts

Part of Eugen Oklitz's letter of denunciation of Forster sent to Bernhard Rust in August 1933

Charité Nerve Clinic in Berlin where Forster worked prior to leaving for Greifswald

BILDARCHIV DES INSTITUTS FÜR GESCHICHTE DER MEDIZIN DER CHARITÉ, CCM, ZFA SIGN. 723

UAG FOTOSAMMLUNG, NERVENKLINIK DIREKTORWOHNHAUS, FOTOGRAF: G. STELZER 1973

Director's house at Greifswald Nerve Clinic where Forster died

Newspaper notices of Forster's death

The overgrown grave of Edmund Forster photographed in 2002

one, making scores of drawings before he was satisfied with the balance of colour on the banner. Against a blood-red field a black swastika stood out boldly on a white circle. No less dramatic and eye-catching were the posters Hitler designed to announce the party's meetings. Like the banners, they were calculated to stun the senses and arouse the emotions rather than appeal to the intellect or even to common sense.

The ruthless authority of Hitler's oratory held a strong appeal for women, who made up a large proportion of every audience and always crowded to the front of the hall, not just because it was safer there but so they could be closer to their idol.

> Women hung eagerly on every word of his speeches as he made arbitrary assertions and swept away objections with emotionally charged rhetorical arguments until he was finally assured of rapturous approval – an approval which turned into frenzy.
>
> It was sexual excitement which he knew how to kindle, especially among his female listeners, just as it was an erotic affinity with all the elements of passion and ecstasy which characterised his relationship with the masses – whom he in any case identified with womankind.[21]

Hitler was well aware of his power over women and their value to the party. In 1923 he told his Harvard-educated friend Ernst 'Putzi' Hanfstaengl:

> Do you know the audience at a circus is just like a woman? Someone who does not understand the intrinsically feminine character of the masses will never be an effective speaker. Ask yourself: What does a woman expect from a man? Clearness, decision, power and action. What we want is to get the masses to act. Like a woman the masses fluctuate between extremes. The crowd is not only like a woman, but women constitute the most important element in an audience. The women usually

lead, then follow the children, and at last, when I have already won over the whole family, follow the fathers.[22]

Hitler's public manner, part carefully rehearsed – he would practise his gestures before a mirror – part spontaneous brilliance, projected barely suppressed violence as much as political extremism. It was this sense of latent danger that made him, despite his lack of any obvious sex appeal, the target for hysterical adulation throughout his public career. Emil Maurice, his chauffeur, remembered how teenage girls would try to hurl themselves under his Mercedes in the hope of being injured and attracting his attention. His fan mail after 1924 came largely from women of all ages, who included locks of hair, photographs, proposals of marriage and pleas that he should be the man to take their virginity. Often these letters were sent with gifts, ranging from works of art and hand-embroidered cushions inscribed with such slogans as 'eternal devotion' to tasteless erotica. Later, when he'd assumed power, doctors reported that female patients frequently invoked his name just before they were anaesthetised for an operation while others cried 'Heil Hitler' as they gave birth and insisted their newly born infants immediately be held up to a picture of the Führer.

Among several wealthy and influential women Hitler knew in the 1920s was Frau Helene Bechstein, wife of the millionaire piano manufacturer. The Bechsteins were early and generous financial contributors to the party, and helped the Nazi cause by introducing Hitler to potential patrons. Not long after their first meeting, Helene invited Hitler to dinner in her suite at Munich's luxurious Four Seasons Hotel. He turned up in a shabby blue suit to find the Bechsteins in full evening dress. Later he told Putzi Hanfstaengl that he had been somewhat embarrassed by his faux pas and overawed by the majestic surroundings: 'The servants were all in livery and we drank nothing but champagne before the meal,' he told his friend, before adding with some awe: 'And you should have seen the bathroom, you can even regulate the heat of the water.'[23]

Carl Bechstein's Mercedes was also frequently used to transport illicit arms, ammunition and explosives for the SA, with Hitler correctly judging that the Munich police would never dare to stop and search such an opulent limousine. Not that the shipments were without their risks. Bechstein's chauffeur was an erratic driver and Hitler was terrified he would have an accident and blow them all to pieces. The piano millionaire explained they had to use the man because he was too stupid to ask questions or even understand what was going on. As Hitler recalled in 1942, Bechstein commented fatalistically, 'If he runs into another car it cannot be helped; up in the air we'll go.'[24]

After much searching, the Nazis had found a room to serve as headquarters that was within their financial reach. A vaulted hall in a beer house on the Serneckergasse, it had once been an elegantly panelled council chamber, but by the time the NSDAP moved in those days were long gone. The room was not only damp and draughty but so dark that gas lights had to be kept burning even on summer days. Hitler had the room festooned with Nazi banners, but even these garish drapes did little to relieve the prevailing gloom. Their landlord allowed them to use two old sideboards for storing pamphlets. These, plus an ancient desk and a few chairs, were the only furnishings. However, as funds started to flow in they were able to equip the office better and Hitler was no longer obliged to scrounge a typewriter from his old regiment's barrack office.

The party was also starting to attract more attention outside Germany, although much of the reporting was dismissive or inaccurate, and frequently both. On 15 December 1922 a story appeared in the London *Evening Standard* noting that 'Herr Adolf Hitler addressed ten different meetings last night called by the National Socialist Workers' Party. Herr Hitler's bodyguard, a curious mixture of hooligans and ex-officers, accompanied him at all meetings. He is especially bitter against Jews, capitalism and speculation, and also advocates control of the stock exchange.' A torrent of increasingly outlandish and wildly inaccurate stories then began to appear in the

British and American popular press. Several gave Hitler a glorious military history that he would have envied, although his reported age – forty-eight – may not have pleased him so much.

In November 1923 the party moved again, this time to a former coffee house in the working-class Corneliusstrasse, where they had a window in which to display their posters, a large room in which members could pay their dues and prospective members complete application forms, and two small rooms, one of which served Hitler as an office.

The month before Hitler had gone to Bayreuth to deliver a speech and was invited to Wahnfried, the Wagner family home. There he met Cosima Wagner – 'the mistress of Bayreuth' and widow of the late 'master of all masters', Richard Wagner – Siegfried, the late composer's son and Siegfried's English-born wife Winifred. (After Siegfried's death in 1939, Hitler became so intimately involved with Winifred Wagner that many of his associates thought they would marry. Hitler too felt it might be a suitable match: the greatest man in Germany joining blood with the daughter-in-law of Germany's greatest musician.) Also present was the disabled philosopher Houston Stewart Chamberlain, who had married Wagner's daughter Eva. Born in Portsmouth in 1855, the son of a British admiral, Chamberlain was brought up in France and later went to live in Germany. In 1897 he had published *Die Grundlagen des 19. Jahrhunderts* (*The Foundations of the 19th Century*), a philosophical work that had made him internationally famous. He was invited to court, the Kaiser declaring that God must have sent him to the German nation. Chamberlain believed fervently in the concept of a master race, which he designated as Aryan and to which the German people belonged. 'Physically and spiritually', he wrote, 'the Aryans stand out among all men; hence they are by right the lords of the world.'[25] Like so many others in Germany Chamberlain was looking for a leader who would arise from the masses to strike down the corrupt façade of democracy and restore Germany to the supremacy that was an Aryan nation's birthright. He was so convinced he had found this new Messiah that, on his death bed in 1927, he summoned the strength to write Hitler a long letter in which he compared himself to John the Baptist and Hitler to Christ: 'At one blow you have transformed the state of my soul. Now at last I am able to sleep peacefully again.'[26] The acclaim of such a man can have only confirmed Hitler's belief in his own destiny.

It is not known what was discussed at Hitler's first meeting with Chamberlain, but soon after he returned from Bayreuth he took a dramatic step. Only two years after attending his first party meeting, Adolf Hitler had not only reinvented the Nazi Party in his own image but risen to become its undisputed master. It must have seemed to him then that his destiny was coming to fruition more rapidly and with greater ease than he could have believed possible. Then, at 6.30 p.m. on 8 November 1923, he committed what seemed to be, at least initially, the greatest political blunder of his career. He attempted to seize power by means of armed revolt and failed miserably. Perhaps he had expected to emulate his hero Mussolini's easy victory in October of the previous year when he had marched on Rome and, without a shot being fired, King Victor Emmanuel III had bowed to pressure and appointed him Prime Minister. Hitler was far less fortunate.

Gustav Ritter von Kahr, head of the Bavarian government, had called a meeting for three thousand officials of the government in the Bürgerbräukeller on Rosenheimerstrasse. Hitler suspected, wrongly as it turned out, that Kahr intended announcing Bavaria's secession from the rest of Germany and the restoration of the monarchy. For as passionate a pan-nationalist as Hitler, this was a threat he could not allow to let pass unchallenged, so he decided to pre-empt such treachery by starting a revolution of his own. He calculated that the mood of the country and the strength of his movement were such that a bold and decisive action could not fail. The police and army, he believed, would not dare to stand in his way or fight back; especially given the secret weapon he had up his sleeve – the support and physical presence of one of the nation's greatest and most revered generals, Erich Ludendorff.

For Ludendorff to have aligned himself with Hitler was at first sight astonishing. A military hero on both the Western and Eastern fronts during the First World War and Chief-of-Staff to Hindenburg, Ludendorff was considered a god by a majority of his officers. He was also the man who had, to all intents and purposes, deposed the Kaiser. Yet here he was falling in line behind a former NCO. However, Ludendorff had his own agenda: he was prepared to march with the Nazis because he regarded himself as Germany's next great leader in waiting. He viewed Hitler, whom he had first met in 1921, simply as the means by which supreme power might be achieved. While the lance-corporal was undoubtedly a gifted speaker and propagandist, Ludendorff believed he was a nonentity who could rapidly be disposed of in the event of success; and just as easily disowned in the event of failure.

What Ludendorff didn't realise until it was too late was that, in Hitler, he was dealing with an 'abysmal force that was ... to send forth a whirlwind engulfing all traditional greatness.'[27] The old general was merely the first of many who underestimated Adolf Hitler.

The attempted *Putsch* began with the stark drama of a Hollywood gangster movie, progressed rapidly from melodrama to farce, and ended in tragedy. When Kahr rose to speak at 8.30 p.m., the beer hall was filled with civil servants in tailcoats and top hats. Before he had uttered more than a few preliminary words, there was a commotion in the street outside. Hitler had roared up in a bright red Mercedes-Benz open tourer surrounded by a bodyguard of SA men, some of whom carried sub-machine-guns. As his men fanned out around the room, Hitler jumped on to the platform and fired two shots into the ceiling, bringing down several large chunks of plaster. 'The national revolution has begun,' he announced. 'The hall is surrounded by six hundred heavily armed men and no one may leave. The Bavarian government and the Reich government have been deposed and a provisional Reich government will be formed.' Kahr allowed himself to be hustled into a back room, where Hitler, putting the pistol to his own head, screamed: 'If I am not victorious by tomorrow afternoon, I shall be a dead man!'

Returning to the main hall, he removed his trenchcoat to reveal a shoddy black tailcoat, which, one witness later observed, made him look like a bridegroom at a provincial wedding. 'I want now to fulfil the vow I made to myself five years ago when I was a blind cripple in a military hospital,' he told the bemused officials, 'to know neither rest nor peace until . . . there should have arisen once more a Germany of power and greatness.'[28]

The following morning was bleak, with leaden skies and flurries of snow. Soon after eleven o'clock, Hitler marched at the head of some two thousand supporters towards the War Ministry. Once there it was his intention to join up with a small group of SA men under the command of Ernst Röhm who had taken up their positions the previous evening. Accompanying Hitler were his political adviser Max von Scheubner-Richter, Hermann Göring, Rudolf Hess, his bodyguard Ulrich Graf . . . and General Ludendorff.

The first obstacle the marchers encountered was a group of armed police who had positioned themselves across the Ludwig Bridge spanning the River Isar. Ordered to halt, Hitler and Ludendorff ignored the command and continued advancing confidently across the bridge. Seemingly unnerved by the presence of the great general, the police lowered their weapons and allowed the procession across. To reach the Feldherrnhalle, the Nazi columns now had to march along a narrow and arcaded street, the Residenz-Strasse. It was there that a group of greatly outnumbered Bavarian state police, armed with carbines, was waiting. If the procession was to be stopped, then this had to be done before the marchers emerged into the Odeonsplatz. The police raised their weapons but the line of marchers came on unhesitatingly. Suddenly Ulrich Graf ran forward shouting: 'Do not shoot, His Excellency Ludendorff is coming.' Hitler began yelling, 'Surrender! Surrender!' but at that moment Julius Streicher, the burly anti-Semitic rabble-rouser from Nürnberg, attempted to wrestle the carbine from one of the policemen. Immediately his fellow officers opened fire, and in the brief exchange of shots that followed sixteen marchers and four policemen were killed and around a hundred Nazis injured.

In an attempt to minimise casualties the police had deliberately aimed low, with the intention of injuring rather than killing the advancing crowd. But this intended humane action produced exactly the opposite effect as bullets tore into the cobblestones and sent shards of granite ripping into the massed ranks. Max von Scheubner-Richter was killed outright, Graf hit several times, Göring fell with shards of granite lodged in his groin, while Hitler – who, with the instincts of an old soldier, had flung himself to the ground as the shooting started – badly dislocated his shoulder. Ludendorff, secure in the knowledge that no German would dare to fire at him, strode calmly on, passing uninjured through the police lines and into the wide Odeonsplatz beyond.

In the confusion Hitler managed to escape into a side street, where a yellow Fiat, driven by a party doctor, was standing by with the engine running. He was immediately taken to Ernst Hanfstaengl's house in the village of Uffing, where Hanfstaengl's wife tended his injury. When he arrived, Hitler was hysterical and, brandishing his revolver, threatened to shoot himself if 'those swine' tried to arrest him.[29] He hid in the attic for the next two days before an informer, most likely Hanfstaengl's gardener, tipped off the police. Arriving in strength to arrest him, they found Hitler cowering in his hosts' wardrobe. He allowed himself to be taken into custody without putting up any resistance.

On 16 February 1924 his trial began, along with those of other leading National Socialists, in Munich's Infantry School on the Blütenburgstrasse. If the revolution had been a tragi-comedy, then the trial before a trio of third-rate judges was a travesty and proved little more than a soapbox from which Hitler, with the connivance of the Bavarian Minister of Justice, Dr Franz Gürnter, displayed his oratory.

He was permitted to attack witnesses, air his political views and make a long speech in his defence from the dock. 'Hitler gave the impression of a man exulting in his destiny and genius. When he spoke, it was as though a furnace door had opened and the flames roared out . . . His speeches from the dock were manifestos and revolutionary tracts.'[30]

Finally, the judges handed down their verdicts: General Erich Ludendorff was freed immediately, Hitler was jailed for five years to be served in the fortress prison of Landsberg-am-Lech.

The German press responded angrily to the leniency of Hitler's sentence, with the *Berliner Tageblatt* of 30 March commenting under a headline BANKRUPT JUSTICE that

The verdict that was passed down today in the Infantry School in Munich and which exceeded the direst expectations of sceptical critics is tantamount to a declaration of bankruptcy of Bavarian justice. It is a verdict without example in a time when so many errors of justice are being committed daily in political trials . . . never before has a court more openly defied the foundation on which it rests, upon which every modern state is built.

In London *The Times* commented sourly on 2 April that if the trial had proved nothing else it had shown that plotting against the constitution of the Reich was not regarded as a serious offence in Bavaria. But the consensus among most foreign journalists was that the bungled *Putsch* had put an end to the brief and faintly comical career of a tiresome rabble-rouser.

For a while Hitler appears to have shared this opinion, refusing to leave his cell and passing the time by reading and eating vast quantities of sweet cakes and cream pastries. Within a few months he had put on several pounds, and the lean features of his immediate post-war years were lost behind a plumper profile that would eventually become familiar to millions.

At first the prison warders viewed Hitler and his fellow Nazis with nervous hostility, certain he would either attempt to escape or his followers would storm the prison to free him. As a result, they regularly rehearsed such an event. It was during one such mock alert that Dietrich Eckart died from a heart attack. Before long, however, Hitler's confidence returned and he immediately set about transforming Landsberg into a National Socialist stronghold, with himself as the undisputed leader. Using his considerable personal charm, he converted first the wife of the prison governor and shortly afterwards her husband Oberregierungsrat Leybold to the Nazi cause. (Hitler would later reward Leybold by placing him in overall command of German prisons.) With their superior's conversion to National Socialism, all apprehension on the warders' parts quickly disappeared and they were careful to salute Hitler on entering his cell. The National Socialists imprisoned with him, including Rudolf Hess, addressed him as *Führer* (Leader) and at meals he sat at the head of the table, under a swastika banner, with the others standing at attention until he had taken his seat. During the day he read or wrote his political autobiography, *Mein Kampf*, laboriously picking out every word of the manuscript using two fingers on an ancient prison typewriter. He also found time to dream up the idea of the Autobahn and sketch out his design for the Volkswagen!

Hitler's female admirers did not forget or neglect him. Frau Bechstein and Frau Wagner were regular visitors, while well-wishers sent him so many flowers, chocolates, books, wine and cakes that an adjoining cell had to be turned into a storeroom to house them.

At ten o'clock on 20 December 1924, having served less than a year of his sentence, Hitler was released on parole and met at the prison gates by Adolf Müller, a wealthy friend whose firm published the Nazi newspaper *Völkischer Beobachter*. Also there to greet him was Heinrich Hoffmann, the Munich press photographer whom he had first met three years earlier, when a news agency had commissioned Hoffmann to photograph the Nazi leader. At that time Hitler was refusing to allow the taking of any pictures, and when Hoffmann tried to snatch one his bodyguard grabbed the camera and destroyed the negative. While this was due in part to concern for his personal safety, it also displayed his desire for anonymity. Hitler, who was going under the pseudonym of Herr Wolf, revelled in holding in rapture a vast audience one day and then walking among them, virtually unrecognised, the next. He also relished those occasions when an unsuspecting stranger would engage him in conversation about the mysterious Adolf Hitler. Now, newly released from prison, he was only too eager for all the publicity he could get and willingly posed outside Landsberg's town gate, with a background so grim and fortress-like that many believed it to be the prison's exterior. The failed *Putsch* and highly publicised trial had made his name and face well known throughout Germany and the rest of Europe. He now intended to build on and exploit that notoriety.

As he was driven back to Munich, Hitler knew he had a momentous task of reconstruction on his hands. The party had splintered after the failed *Putsch*, with many prominent National Socialists, including Göring and Hanfstaengl, forced into exile, while others remained behind bars. Those remaining at liberty were disorganised and disillusioned, with many blaming Hitler for the bloody fiasco in Munich. But Hitler's faith in himself and his destiny was as strong as ever. He still believed providence had a use for him, but he made the decision to use different tactics to achieve his goals: from now on he would utilise political rather than military means. Which is not to say he ruled out the use of force, far from it, but such intimidation would be cloaked in secrecy and concealed behind soft words. The masses would be persuaded through the power of his oratory and the Weimar Republic replaced by a National Socialist government not through a victory of arms but by a triumph of his will.

He was no longer the anonymous and mysterious Herr Wolf prowling in the shadows but a figure of national significance and influence. The years of the wolf were dead and gone. The frenetic Adolf Hitler of the pre-*Putsch* days lay buried alongside

Dietrich Eckart in the grounds of Landsberg Prison and a harder and if possible even more dangerous man had walked to freedom through the fortress's heavy oaken doors. All that remained of the man who'd been incarcerated there was an unshaken belief that every step he took was being guided by a higher authority. 'As the Reds were laying waste to Germany in November 1918, I lay blind in a military hospital,' he screamed at a political opponent a few years later, 'I became seeing then. I go my way to the last.'[31]

When he arrived at his modest lodgings in the Thierschstrasse, friends were holding a welcome-home party. This was to be the extent of his audience for the time being, because the conditions of his parole restricted his movements and prohibited him from speaking in public. Nor did he dare flout these constraints because, as an Austrian citizen, he lived in dread of rearrest and deportation.

On 4 January 1925 he obtained an audience with Dr Heinrich Held, the Minister President of Bavaria, to plead for the public-speaking prohibition to be removed. Despite grave doubts, Held agreed to lift the ban on the NSDAP from 16 February, warning that it would be immediately reimposed were Hitler to espouse extremist views. On 27 February the National Socialist Party was officially reconstituted in the Bürgerbräukeller. Hours before Hitler was scheduled to speak the hall was crowded with more than three thousand party faithful, as well as non-members, while outside the police struggled to hold back an excited throng. Hitler's arrival on the platform was greeted with wild applause and he spoke for more than two hours on the theme of Germany's and the party's future. He warned party members that internal squabbles must cease immediately and that they should regard him as their absolute leader. He then launched into a vicious attack on Marxists and Jews: 'Either the enemy goes over our dead bodies or we go over his,' he screamed. 'Just as in the war the English allegedly conducted the fight against the German Kaiser and militarism, so we will in future certainly conduct our fight against person and object, namely against the Jew as person and Marxism as object.'[32]

This was too much for the Bavarian authorities, concerned about the damaging effects that Nazi anti-Semitism was having on their tourist trade, to tolerate for long. On 2 August the previous year the Munich Tourist Association had written to the Ministry of the Interior complaining that not only were Jews no longer visiting Bavaria but that other visitors were staying away too because they feared violence. Hotels in Munich, Nürnberg and other towns that depended on tourism were suffering a significant decrease in bookings due to the poor image Bavaria now had internationally as a result of 'the political attitude of certain sections of the population here and the rowdy manner in which political attitudes are displayed in public'.[33] Heinrich Held once again banned the NSDAP and reimposed the prohibition on Hitler's public speaking. Over the next few months similar bans were enforced in many other German states, including Prussia, Saxony, Baden, Hamburg and Lübeck.

There followed several years of stagnation for the Nazi Party, which was torn apart by internal disputes and driven almost to bankruptcy as disillusioned financial backers withdrew their support. The initial excitement generated by Hitler's release from prison rapidly faded with his name appearing decreasingly in the press. 'There was in any case, little general interest in extremist solutions in Bavaria,' notes Geoffrey Pridham. 'The NSDAP was a party associated with an abortive attempt to seize power by force, and was not likely to appeal to a population whose main concern was the enjoyment of a quiet life.'[34]

Life in Germany was returning to normal, the unemployment figures were declining and middle-class Germans were becoming more affluent with every month that passed. As a result the Nazis, like the communists, were increasingly seen as a nightmare from the immediate post-war period with little relevance to the real issues facing the nation. Sales of *Mein Kampf*, which had sold ten thousand copies within a few weeks of publication in 1925, slumped and the ban on Hitler's public speaking meant that the Nazis' most potent weapon had been defused.[35]

All Hitler could do was curb his impatience while building up an efficient party machine and courting industrialists who might give the Nazis financial support. A considerable amount of his time was also spent trying to heal divisions within the NSDAP. Despite his rallying call for unity during the 1925 speech, his leadership was by no means unchallenged. To gain support from the landowning aristocracy, Hitler had proposed the restoration of state-appropriated property and lands to the German princes when the Nazis came to power. Many in the party, such as Gregor Strasser, who headed a small but vocal branch of the NSDAP in north Germany, were horrified by this betrayal of socialist principles. In January 1926 Strasser called a conference to discuss this proposal. Hitler refused to attend, anticipating that it would be highly critical. He was right. One of the fiercest attacks on him came from a club-footed Rhinelander named Joseph Goebbels, who labelled Hitler petty bourgeois and called for his expulsion from the party. Impressed by the little man's aggressive oratory, Hitler made a determined effort to win him over, and Goebbels soon realised where the real power within the party lay. More than that, he was personally captivated by Hitler's charismatic personality. On 23 July 1926 he wrote in his diary:

> He is the creative instrument of Fate and Destiny. I stand by him, deeply shaken. That is how he is. Good and kind, but also clever and shrewd and again at times great and gigantic. What a person. What a man . . . He seems like a prophet of old. And in the sky a big, white cloud almost seems to shape itself into the form of a swastika. Glittering light all over the sky . . . Is that a sign from Fate?[36]

Following the April 1926 elections Hitler stepped up the campaign to have his speaking ban lifted: WHY MAY NOT THE FRONT SOL-DIER ADOLF HITLER SPEAK? demanded a headline in the *Völkischer Beobachter*. Posters of Hitler, his mouth covered with sticking plaster, appeared on walls and trees throughout Bavaria: 'He alone of 2,000 million people on earth may not speak in Germany,' thundered the slogan. Germans were constantly reminded in *Beobachter* editorials and the speeches of other NSDAP members that Hitler had been a courageous soldier ready to die for Germany.[37]

The Bavarian authorities, well aware of the risk of removing the ban, resisted all such attempts, preferring Hitler to be seen as a patriotic martyr than heard as a virulent rabble-rouser. It was not until 1927 that the authorities finally yielded to the intense pressure and lifted the prohibition, albeit with stringent conditions. The NSDAP had to guarantee that it would 'not employ illegal means for achieving its aims' and that the SA and SS would not break the law.

On 6 March Hitler made his first public speech in two years, when he was allowed to address a crowd in a provincial town, and on 9 March he spoke to nearly five thousand people at the Zirkus Krone in Munich. His speech was moderate and his supporters kept on a tight rein. Before the meeting started Hitler had warned his followers: 'Those who harass the police officials or try to stir up the masses are serving the enemies of our movement . . . resistance to the forces of the state and their lawful regulations is forbidden in all circumstances.'[38]

The Reichstag Election in 1928 confirmed the move by the electorate away from extremism. The Social Democratic Party (SPD), which largely supported the Weimar Republic, increased its support, and an SPD member was made Reich Chancellor. All the right-wing parties suffered severe reverses at the ballot box, with the NSDAP winning only 12 seats in the Reichstag against the SPD's 152.

All this changed dramatically in the weeks and months following the Wall Street Crash of October 1929 and the onset of the Great Depression. Germany, which was more dependent on foreign loans than any other Western nation, was worst affected. As slump turned into recession, factories closed, banks collapsed, middle-class incomes were destroyed by inflation and unemployment figures soared. It was the economic disaster for which the Nazis had long been praying and from 1929 onwards the popularity of the NSDAP exactly paralleled the unemployment figures. During that year, with 1,320,000 people out of work, the National Socialists had 176,426 members and were attracting only 800,000 voters. By 1932, when unemployment had risen to six million, NSDAP membership was over a million and six million voters supported them at the ballot box.

Greater financial support from the major industrialists began to show itself in ever larger rallies and increasingly opulent offices. On 1 January 1931 the Nazis moved into their new headquarters in the Brown House, the former Barlow Palace, overlooking Munich's elegant Königsplatz, purchased for 500,000 marks and refurbished at a similar cost to party funds. Hitler had a lavish office on the first floor panelled in oak, lit by Venetian glass chandeliers and dominated by a vast desk, behind which hung a giant oil painting of Frederick the Great.

On 26 February 1932 Hitler was made a German citizen and the following month achieved 30 per cent of the votes in the first round of the Reich elections, a proportion that rose to 37 per cent during the second round, making the Nazis the strongest party within the Reichstag. At the end of January 1933 he was finally appointed Chancellor of a national-conservative cabinet.

With supreme power so nearly in his grasp, Hitler became strangely indolent. He worked only when it was absolutely necessary, preferring to spend his time studying architectural plans, reading or, when in Munich, drinking tea and chatting with his cronies in his favourite haunts.

He was biding his time, awaiting the one cataclysmic event which, he was confident, would enable him to attain his divine destiny. On 27 February, with that telephone call to Detective Inspector Helmut Heisig reporting that the Reichstag was ablaze, his moment finally arrived.

Chapter Twelve
BEFORE THE DELUGE

It was on a dreary night of November that I beheld the wretch – the miserable monster I had created . . . I saw the dull yellow eye of the creature open; it breathed hard, and a convulsive motion agitated its limbs.

Mary Wollstonecraft Shelley, Frankenstein[1]

Although Hitler received considerable coverage in the German press from the early 1920s onwards, it is doubtful that in those years Edmund Forster paid much attention to his former patient's political career. As with so many of his class and background he viewed the right-wing rabble rouser's growing prominence with a calm and superior indifference. Only after Hitler's release from prison in 1924, when his power and influence grew, did Forster become increasingly nervous and guilty about the catastrophic outcome of his treatment. Nevertheless, throughout the 1920s, Forster concentrated on his own professional and personal ambitions, and must have been well satisfied with what he achieved in both.

As soon as he was freed from military duties and obligations, Forster devoted much of his time and attention to research and clinical activities at the Charité. He continued with investigations begun before the war, on the pathology of brain tumours and the effects of syphilis spirochete on the nervous system. On the busy wards, his department had 240 psychiatric and neurological beds and was staffed by some 36 doctors; he was the senior neurological consultant and often acted as locum for the Director, Karl Bonhöffer. Although he did not publish widely in the academic field, Forster did contribute chapters to two major textbooks and, more importantly as far as professional advancement was concerned, spent much time lecturing and conducting demonstrations at gatherings of the Berlin Neurological Society, a highly influential organisation described as the 'meeting place for outstanding experts'.[2] 'On the whole the atmosphere in the clinic was especially clinical and cold, without unnecessary gossip or chatter, with colleagues although on friendly terms at work never developing any deeper friendships away from it,'[3] recalls Hanns Schwarz, who worked there during Forster's time. It was also highly competitive. Erwin Gohrbandt, another doctor, commented that under Bonhöffer: 'Only those who had the talent and intelligence to become high flyers could hope to survive for long, with any who failed to make the grade soon being told to leave.'[4] It was here that Forster's experience and eloquence as a lecturer proved to be a significant advantage, because, by proving himself such an effective advocate, he advanced both his own and the Nerve Clinic's reputations. As a colleague, he was considered an independent-minded, if sometimes overly dogmatic, researcher whose volatile personality and quick temper sometimes made him difficult to work with. But few would have disagreed with Bonhöffer's appraisal that he was a 'caring doctor and a very good human being'.[5]

Meanwhile, Forster's personal circumstances had undergone significant changes. Before the war he had become friendly with Marie Pauline Bretschneider, known to family and friends as Mila, a slender woman with reddish-brown hair who was seven years his junior. Both her parents had died when she was young and, as the eldest daughter, she had the responsibility for bringing up her siblings. The friendship between Edmund and Mila developed into romance, but by the time they decided to marry the war had started, and they both agreed to delay the wedding until after it was over.

When Mila and Edmund had first met she had been keeping house for her brother Paul, a Roman Catholic priest, but in 1914 she started to work for Matthias Erzberger, an eminent politician and statesman. Although she began as his secretary, Mila was soon promoted to the role of personal assistant, and assisted him in running his company, the Deutsche Farm-Plantgen-und-Handelsgesellschaft (German Farming, Plantations and Trading Company).

The son of a craftsman, born in the Black Forest in 1875, Erzberger had worked as a journalist with the centrist newspaper *Deutsches Volksblatt* before turning to politics. In 1903 he had been elected to the Reichstag and gradually established himself as the leader of the Roman Catholic Zentrum Party's left wing. Although initially in favour of the war, by 1917 he was deeply involved in working towards a negotiated peace. In his book *Der Völkerbund* (1918), he had supported the idea of a League of Nations and in November 1918 led the German deputation to Compiègne, in France, where on the 11th he signed the Armistice. In the view of the German right wing this was an act of treason for which they never forgave him and which ultimately led to his assassination. After the war Erzberger served in Germany's first republican government, in which he vigorously supported acceptance of the Treaty of Versailles, and as Vice-Chancellor and Finance Minister proposed economic reforms that were bitterly opposed by right wingers. They launched a campaign accusing him of political corruption that reached such a pitch that he was finally forced to sue for defamation. Although the courts found in his favour, only nominal damages were awarded and, with no support from his party, he was forced to resign from his ministry. In 1921, while holidaying in the Black Forest, he was shot dead by members of an extreme right-wing nationalist organisation.[6]

On Thursday, 12 September 1918, with German defeat imminent, Edmund, having just been discharged from the marines, and Mila showed their faith in the future by marrying. He then moved out of the hospital accommodation that had been his home since he started working at the Charité and, with Mila, rented an elegant apartment on the third floor of a modern building at 8 Boznerstrasse (literally 'high-status street') in Berlin's Schröneberg district. Their first son, Balduin Konrad, was born on 20 February 1920, and on 6 August the following year a second boy, Ruprecht, arrived to complete Edmund's family.

The Berlin into which these children were born was a city of extraordinary contrasts: of great wealth living shoulder-to-shoulder with desperate poverty; of bright lights, persistent strikes and appalling violence. The violence was largely centred on the merciless street fighting between communist gangs who had declared, 'There can be only one salvation for the German people. The red flag must wave victoriously over the whole of Germany,'7 and the right-wing Freikorps. 'Anyone who falls into our hands first gets the rifle butt and then is finished off with a bullet,' one Freikorps youth wrote to his family. 'We even shot ten Red Cross nurses on sight because they were carrying pistols. We shot those little ladies with pleasure – how they cried and pleaded with us to save their lives. Nothing doing! Anyone with a gun is our enemy.'8 Except for the wealthy, who could afford extortionist black market prices, desperate shortages of virtually every consumer item meant a majority of Berliners survived on ersatz everything. Ilya Ehrenburg, an émigré Russian writer who visited the city in 1921, noted that the men's clothing shops offered pink and blue dickies as substitutes for shirts; cakes sold in the Josty Café were made from frostbitten potatoes; while cigars with Havana labels comprised cabbage leaves steeped in nicotine. One evening Ehrenburg was accosted by a man offering to take him to an interesting night spot. He reported in his journal where his acceptance of the offer led him:

We travelled by underground . . . and finally found ourselves in a respectable flat. On the walls hung portraits of members of the family in officer's uniform and a painting of a sunset. We were given champagne – lemonade laced with spirits. Then the host's two daughters appeared – naked – and began to dance. One of them talked . . . [about] Dostoevsky's novels.

The mother hopefully eyed the foreign guests: perhaps they would be tempted by her daughters and would pay: in dollars of course.'[9]

And then there was inflation. In January 1923 the exchange rate was 7,000 Marks to the dollar. Then the French invaded the Ruhr, the heartland of German heavy industry, and by July the Mark had sunk to 160,000 against the dollar. A month later a single dollar would net one million Marks. A sort of desperate madness seized those still in work as they raced to exchange their vast, worthless, wages for something – anything – that might conceivably be bartered for something – anything – else. Billions of Marks would be paid for shoes that didn't fit, unwanted clothes and trashy trinkets, which, only months earlier, would have cost no more than loose change. After giving a concert, the pianist Artur Schnabel had to ask a fellow musician to help him carry his numerically enormous fee home. Passing a delicatessen he eased the burden on his helper by spending half of the mountain of Marks on two sausages. By the following morning prices had increased to such an extent that he was unable to purchase even a single sausage with the other half of his earnings.

With his secure and well-paid job at the Charité and private consultancy work, Forster managed to keep his family well fed and comfortably housed throughout those grim years, but working at the Charité made it impossible for him to escape the appalling reality of life in Berlin. One visitor was told by the doctor who showed him around the children's ward:

'You think this is a kindergarten for the little ones. No, these are children of seven and eight years. Tiny faces, with large dull eyes, overshadowed by huge, puffed, rickety foreheads, their small arms just skin and bones, and above the crooked legs with their dislocated joints the swollen, pointed stomachs of the hunger oedema. You see this child here,' the physician in charge explained. 'He consumed an incredible amount of bread, and yet he did not get any stronger. I found out that he hid all the bread he received under his straw mattress. The fear of hunger was so deeply rooted in the child that he collected the stores instead of eating the food: a misguided animal instinct made the dread of hunger worse than the actual pangs.'[10]

On 12 February 1921 there was another Forster family wedding in Berlin when Dirk Forster married Lilly Bredow, a beautiful and accomplished woman whom he had met at a wartime ball. Edmund and Dirk had always fought over girls when they were growing up, with Edmund usually the victor. The family subsequently saw Dirk's capture of Lilly as his final revenge against his brother. Lilly's Jewish grandmother, who belonged to the wealthy family which owned the Nivea cream company, had been a friend of Brahms, with whom she had made music, and Lilly had inherited her talents. A gifted musician and painter who had studied under the eminent German artist Lovis Corinth,[11] Lilly counted many eminent musicians, artists and writers among her close friends. It was rumoured that she had an affair with the celebrated conductor Wilhelm Furtwängler and urged him to promote the career of another of her friends, a gifted Austrian conductor named Herbert von Karajan.

In April the newly married couple moved to Paris, where Dirk was to take up an appointment as an embassy councillor. This was his latest step on the diplomatic career ladder that had seen him in Amsterdam at the outbreak of war, then in the Foreign Office in Berlin to 1916, and latterly and as a consul general in Budapest. It was not an easy time to be a German in Paris, where hostility still ran high and many Parisians refused to rent out accommodation, provide services or even speak to their former invaders.

In 1926 Dirk and Lilly returned to Berlin for five years before he was posted again to Paris. In Berlin they enjoyed a life which, according to their daughter Margot, was filled with 'painters, musicians, home concerts, cheerful fiestas with friends and artists.

Money was scarce. As soon as the guests had arrived, the carpet at the entrance was moved to the dining room, and, when the guests had left, moved back to the entrance hall. Although he never owned a car, Ehni [Dirk] loved to travel all his life. But with Edmund's "Opel-Popel" [the nickname the Forsters gave to their family car] travelling was easy. When the airship *Graf Zeppelin* made its maiden voyage Dirk was a passenger.'[12]

If Edmund Forster had put all thoughts of Adolf Hitler from his mind, he was forcefully reminded of his hysterically blind patient on opening his newspaper on Monday, 12 November 1923. The headline story concerned an unsuccessful coup in Munich during which the National Socialists had attempted to overthrow the government and seize power. A few days later came news of his former patient's arrest and forthcoming trial for treason. Over the subsequent weeks Forster followed the news with a mixture of fascination and dismay. That the man who had been so ineffectual at Pasewalk should have been responsible for such an action seemed astonishing. That Forster had played an unintentional role in this transformation was harrowing.

Soon after the trial ended there was another Forster family gathering in Berlin, this time on the occasion of Arne's funeral. Edmund's brother had never recovered from damage caused to his lungs by gas poisoning during the war (he'd served as a lieutenant on the Western Front), and in March 1924 he went down with pleurisy and died a few days later, aged just forty-three.

The following year Edmund Forster decided the time had come to further his career and applied for the post of Director of the Neurological Clinic at Greifswald University. The vacancy had come about when Paul Schröder,[13] a popular and effective director who had headed the clinic since 1912, moved to Leipzig. Greifswald lies on the flat plains to the north of Berlin in Mecklenburg – West Pomerania. The university,[14] which was founded in 1456, is situated on the western side of the thirteenth-century town on the

River Ryck. Greifswald itself appealed to Forster not so much for its architectural treasures, although these included several medieval churches, but because of its close proximity to the Baltic, which would enable him to indulge his passion for sailing. Forster's first impressions were that: 'The clinic is very beautiful but small and with only a few students.'[15]

The reference provided by his boss at the Charité is better described as warm rather than glowing: 'Forster can be depended on to run the neurological department,' Karl Bonhöffer informed his Greifswald colleagues. 'He possesses an independent mind which is not swayed from any course of action that he believes to be correct. His research into the neurological and mental consequences of brain injuries is outstanding.' He ended with a note of caution that some of Forster's theories, especially those on the causes and treatment of hysterical disabilities, had been severely criticised.

The Greifswald Medical Faculty appointments board included among its members the departing Director, Paul Schröder; Friedrich Pels-Leusden, Director of the Surgical Clinic and Dean of the Faculty; and Willi Vorkastner, a consultant in the Neurological Clinic for many years. Three years earlier Vorkastner had been made Director of the Law Medical Institute and – somewhat bizarrely, given his role on the interview panel – had also applied for the Director of the Nerve Clinic job. In addition there were two lecturers in psychiatry and neurology, who had been given the task of drawing up a list of suitable candidates. Based purely on his scientific accomplishments, they had placed Forster in third place behind Richard Henneberg (one of Forster's colleagues at the Charité) and Vorkastner. The board concluded that Forster's 'work shows independence and boldness when tackling major problems and his teaching is highly praised', but they warned: 'The Faculty is aware of certain "difficulties" in Dr Forster's personality, but do not consider these sufficiently serious when weighed against his considerable scientific achievements, especially since such incidents have become increasingly rare over the past few years. We therefore hope that Dr

Forster, should he be appointed, will prove a harmonious member of the department both now and in the future.'[16] The board offered the post to Henneberg, who turned it down. Then they tried another candidate – Martin Reichardt from Münster University. He turned it down, too. Next, rather than going with a sure bet – Vorkastner – they plumped for Edmund Forster. Happily for the board, he accepted.

On 13 April 1925 Forster was notified that he had been awarded the Chair of Psychiatry and his appointment was subsequently officially confirmed in a letter from the Minister for Science, Art and Education of the People on behalf of the Prussian State Ministry. At the same time he became Orderly Professor at the Medical Faculty, as well as Director of the Psychiatric and Nerve Clinic. At the end of April he and his family moved into the rather gloomy four-storey Director's house located adjacent to the only slightly less forbidding Nerve Clinic. This appointment gave Forster everything he had ever hoped to achieve in his career: a status equal to that of his father, interesting work and, perhaps most important of all, the opportunity to transform what he considered a moribund institution into one with an international reputation for clinical and research excellence. But even before he started work, there was an undercurrent of resentment within the clinic from the failed candidate Willi Vorkastner. In 1927 this escalated into a bitter row. Impulsive and quick tempered as ever, Forster took comments in a report by Vorkastner as a personal insult and wrote to the university's Curator: 'I would like to inform you obediently that Professor Dr Vorkastner in his position as a leading medical doctor offended me in a most vulgar manner.'[17] The argument rumbled on thereafter.

Soon Forster also became involved in a bitter turf war with another faculty member, Friedrich Pels-Leusden. From the start Forster had thrown himself wholeheartedly into the task of restructuring the clinic into a leading centre of science, culture and the arts. One of his first actions was to create a less institutional atmosphere on the wards. He replaced the drab hospital uniforms women patients had been forced to wear with attractively designed and colourful clothes. The psychiatric and neurological wards, which had not seen a coat of paint since the building had been opened some twenty years earlier, were redecorated in bright colours. In order to get these changes past the university's finance department, he claimed to be introducing them as part of 'therapeutic trials', designed to study the effect of different colours on patients. The findings from this 'study' were, unsurprisingly, never published.

More controversially, he also purchased several works of art, including paintings, sculptures and furniture, because he believed that being surrounded by art speeded recovery. There was nothing new in this idea: Florence Nightingale had also extolled the importance of art and colours in aiding convalescence. And studies in our own time have 'for the first time . . . established physical and biological evidence for the influence of art on healthcare'.[18] However, in the 1920s Forster's ideas were viewed with grave suspicion by his colleagues, and he quickly gained a reputation for eccentricity, a trait that did little to endear him to the extremely conservative Greifswald faculty. Although his motives were well intentioned, these purchases would later be produced as evidence against him in an internal investigation conducted by the university authorities once the Nazis had come to power. It was not just that he had spent considerable sums of their money on what was condemned as worthless and morally degenerate art, but that he had made these purchases from Konrad Lattner.[19] Although long neglected (the last entry for him in the *Directory of German Artists* was in 1956), Lattner was in his day an artist and sculptor of some standing. Between 1921 and the early 1930s he held regular one-man exhibitions in Greifswald. He became a close friend of Forster, and the clinic was one of his most enthusiastic patrons. After September 1933 most of Lattner's '*entartete Kunst*' (degenerate art) was destroyed.

Another, and far more costly, project was the creation of a self-contained neurosurgical unit that could perform brain surgery to the highest possible international standards. Forster was a great admirer of pioneering work being done in America by Harvey Williams Cushing, a specialist in the removal of brain tumours and widely regarded as the world's foremost neurosurgeon.[20] This ambition brought Forster into conflict with Friedrich Pels-Leusden, Director of the Surgical Clinic, and his team of general surgeons, who believed all operations should come within their remit and feared a specialist unit would undermine their status and authority. From the start they vehemently opposed and resisted all of Forster's attempts to develop the unit, and in 1929 matters came to a head. The trigger for the dispute was Forster's decision to transfer a patient in need of the urgent removal of a brain tumour to the Charité in Berlin. Not only was Pels-Leusden deeply and personally affronted by his colleague's lack of confidence, but he was concerned that, without patients to observe in surgery, his ability to instruct medical students would be seriously compromised. Forster, in his typically blunt and confrontational way, refused to back down or find a compromise. Instead, he correctly, if tactlessly, pointed out that operating skills and procedures at the Charité were infinitely superior to those at Greifswald, and that his patient's chances of recovery would therefore be significantly enhanced by transferral. When Pels-Leusden continued to resist, Forster forced through the appointment of a brilliant young neurosurgeon, Friedrich Wilhelm Kroll, to head his new unit.

Kroll, who had trained under Otfried Foerster (then considered Germany's top neurosurgeon) at Bredau, was a specialist in the surgical removal of brain tumours. He soon gained such a good reputation that an increasing number of neighbouring clinics and hospitals began sending their patients to Greifswald for treatment. Between 1932, when the neurosurgical unit was finally opened, and 1934 Kroll performed more than seventy successful operations. Pels-Leusden then challenged Kroll's qualifications and denied there was any need for a specialised neurosurgical unit. In a letter to the Education Ministry he described the work done as mere 'dilettantism' and insisted that many of the operations were not only unnecessary but carried out too hastily. As a result of his scheming, the unit was disbanded and Kroll dismissed.

Another major project in which Forster was closely involved was the construction of a new X-ray building, directly accessible from the Nerve Clinic. Up to that time the X-ray department had been in temporary accommodation, with plates being developed in a makeshift darkroom in the cellar.

In the clinic Edmund cultivated a relaxed atmosphere of mutual trust and co-operation among his medical staff at all levels. Although welcomed by most, this aroused the antagonism of some of the older and more hidebound traditionalists, who favoured a formal and hierarchical command structure. What Edmund regarded as a friendly attitude towards junior doctors and nurses they considered over-familiarity. As with his other attitudes and practices, this helped to foster an undercurrent of disapproval towards him at the university.

The main emphasis of his research, as it had been at the Charité, was into the effect of syphilis on the central nervous system, especially in relation to the progressive paralyses that occur during the final stages of the disease. He was also engaged in an investigation of cell structure and function, especially with respect to brain tumours, as well as developing new diagnostic laboratory techniques. While at the Charité, he had succeeded in demonstrating the existence of the syphilitic pathogen within the brain by using a syringe to extract cells from the brains of living but paralysed patients. At Greifswald he continued these studies with the aim of growing the pathogen in a culture, this time mostly using animals in his experiments. Although his findings were not of any great scientific interest, of far greater importance was his development of a simple method for preparing cells from the cerebrospinal fluid for microscopic examination. His success here represented a significant technical breakthrough that provided a valuable new diagnostic tool.

With his assistants Konrad Zucker and Julius Zádor he also researched the effects of mescaline on the brain. By taking the drug himself, Forster confirmed that hallucinations were due to an individual's inability to distinguish between events in the outside world and what was going on inside their head.

Even more controversial, and ultimately damaging to his reputation, leading to charges of tormenting patients, was the encouragement Forster gave to Zádor in what became known as the *Kipptischversuche* or 'tilting-table' experiments. These involved placing volunteers (in many cases brain-injured patients) on a specially designed platform that could be tilted in any direction. The subjects – naked if male; in pants and a bra if female – were placed in a starting position, for example seated, lying on their stomach or back, or on all fours, and then filmed as the platform wobbled backwards, forwards and from side to side. Their responses were then compared with those of patients suffering from a variety of neurological disorders. In a paper presented to the Paris Neurological Conference in May 1933, Zádor explained: 'If you put a normal person on the table and then tilt it first left and then right it is possible to observe certain consistent reactions through which he or she strives to maintain their balance and original position.' But when it came to patients suffering from various diseases of the central nervous system 'the balance reactions when they were tilted to the left were absent whereas when they were tilted to the right the reactions, even when slightly inhibited, were clearly present. This indicates severe damage to the balance mechanisms on the left side of the body.'[21]

At the time, many were shocked by these experiments, but in the days before CAT and MRI scans could be used to pinpoint the location of brain injuries, Zádor's research was of potential value as a diagnostic aid.

At Greifswald, as in Berlin, Forster chose his friends not from among his colleagues but in artistic, writing and showbusiness circles. As a result, he became increasingly isolated within the clinic, where he appears to have had only one close friend. Ironically, this man was a former Nazi Party member. Thirty-eight-year-old Rudolf Degkwitz, married with four children, was a paediatrician who joined the university in the same year as Forster. In 1918 he had belonged to the extreme right-wing Freikorps Oberland. Later he joined the Nazis and in 1923 even marched alongside Hitler during the 9 November Munich *Putsch*. For reasons now not known, he fell out with his former friends and was dismissed from the party. Perhaps out of resentment for this treatment, he abruptly switched from being one of Hitler's most fanatical supporters to a sworn enemy of the Nazis. He was the only member of staff who supported Forster when the university decided to rid itself of his assistants, Julius Zádor and Konrad Zucker, purely because they were Jews.

In January 1933 Forster tried, without success, to save Zádor's job. His involvement may even have been counterproductive, such was the antagonism towards him from certain sectors of the Medical Faculty. Forster, however, refused to accept the university's decision, and after Zádor's dismissal allowed him to continue with his research until May 1933, when they left together for the Paris conference at which Zádor gave his presentation on his tilting-table experiments.

Forster's defence of Konrad Zucker may well have been more ambivalent because, during 1926, they had both had affairs with the same woman.

Fräulein Rietzkow was employed as a laboratory assistant, and Forster, who always had something of a roving eye, appears to have been infatuated with her, at least for a short time. What he did not realise was that this tall, dark-haired Jewess was also involved with Zucker, visiting him in his rooms at the clinic while Forster was lecturing. Inevitably, given the narrow and claustrophobic atmosphere within the clinic, the clandestine triangle soon became common knowledge. When Mila found out what had happened she was hurt and angry, but would not countenance a divorce. After visiting his brother in December 1926, Dirk wrote to Lilly: 'I was not happy about Edmund, as I am afraid he is no longer happy at home. I can only hope things will work themselves out.'[22] In the event this hope was partly realised and domestic peace was restored, although it seems likely Mila never entirely forgave Edmund's infidelity.

From the end of the 1920s Edmund's life had settled into a routine. He spent much of his time away from home attending conferences, presenting papers or taking leaves of absence, sometimes with his family, but often alone. He loved driving and criss-crossed Europe in Opel-Popel, thinking nothing of motoring the hundreds of miles between Greifswald and Munich on trips to see his mother.

He was either unaware of or unconcerned by having made more enemies than friends at the clinic. Nor did it seem to trouble him that the university authorities were becoming increasingly scandalised by his noisy parties and bohemian friends. Never one to keep his opinions to himself, Forster made little attempt to conceal his contempt for Hitler and the Nazis, but these comments were uttered with such a combination of irony and earnestness that less sophisticated members of staff sometimes failed to understand the point he was making. Those who did were appalled at his recklessness began to avoid any conversation with him for fear of being damned by association.

The dangers of such comments are illustrated by a joke that circulated in Germany during the early 1930s:

Two men are fishing from a bridge. The man standing on the right is continually catching fish, while the one on the left catches none.

At last, infuriated by his lack of success, he demands, 'How is it you get all the luck?'

'Why, look at the badge you are wearing,' his friend replies. 'The fish are not fools. When they come up and see that swastika they know better than to open their mouths.'

One day, while speeding through Greifswald in Opel-Popel Edmund was stopped by a policeman.

'Anyone who drives as fast as you do has to be crazy!' the officer told him.

'*I* decide who is crazy around here!' Forster snapped back.[23]

The flippant riposte may have struck him as a good joke at the time. But like the Frankenstein monster he had inadvertently created in Pasewalk, it would all too soon come back to haunt him.

Precisely *how* he had created that monster would not be revealed to the world until 1963, many years after both the scientist and his monster were dead. Even then, few would believe it. But that was hardly surprising, because the book that outlined in detail how Forster cured Hitler was, ostensibly, a work of fiction.

Chapter Thirteen
VISION AT PASEWALK

We dredged him up, for killed, until he whined,
'O sir – my eyes, – I'm blind, – I'm blind, – I'm blind!'
Coaxing, I held a flame against his lids
And said if he could see the least blurred light.
He was not blind; in time they'd get all right.
                    Wilfred Owen, 'The Sentry'[1]

Back in October 1918, for the first time in his medical career
Edmund Forster had been baffled. During four years as a military
psychiatrist and neurologist he had never come across a patient
quite like Adolf Hitler. While every other hysterical soldier he had
treated had used their disability to escape from the war, the ferocious
lance-corporal was only too eager to rejoin it. The man's excellent
military record and his Iron Cross, First Class, combined with
an unrelenting belligerency towards the enemy, rapidly convinced
Forster that here was no malingerer but a soldier desperate to return
and assist his comrades at the front. All of which presented Forster
with a unique psychiatric problem. Hysteria, he had always asserted,
was due either to deliberate malingering or unconscious simulation
of a physical disorder, and, as a consequence, must always be dealt
with using the 'draconian' means that were described in Chapter 9.
In adopting his approach Edmund did not consider himself to be
either heartless or unfeeling but as acting entirely in the patient's
best interests. In one article he had explained: 'If we reproach them

about their actions in a tentative or mild manner, they feel they are in the right, because they believe their whole personality has been misunderstood and that nobody can see through them or see them as they really are.'2

But where Hitler was concerned, Edmund realised his usual tactics would be inappropriate and ineffective. How could he persuade the lance-corporal that it was only his lack of will-power that prevented him from doing his patriotic duty when the man's greatest desire was to do just that?

Undecided as to what approach would work, Forster decided to do nothing for a week or so except interview Hitler, observe his behaviour on the wards and ask for reports from the other medical staff. Before long, he had formed in his mind the picture of an extreme nationalist, deeply despairing of Germany's fate and bitterly resentful of the fact that the deaths of so many had been squandered and that so many brave men had been betrayed. At night, unable to sleep, Hitler prowled the wards, and in a harsh yet oddly compelling voice told anyone prepared to listen how Germany's military setbacks were entirely due to the treachery of Jews and Marxists, and how the nation needed a heroic leader cast in the Wagnerian mould to guide them from the humiliation of defeat to military and political glory.3

It is very likely, given Hitler's interest in German folk history, that he had heard of and may even have regaled his fellow patients with the tale of a fifteenth-century shepherd lad who suddenly discovered that he possessed a remarkable gift for oratory. Everywhere he went, peasants and artisans flocked to hear him harangue the social system, attack established authority and preach a fierce gospel of violent rebellion. He became known as the Trommler (Drummer) because of the insistent and compelling drumbeat of his words. Instinctively, the Trommler knew how to exploit the bitterness of the downtrodden and impoverished, who were soon gathering in their hundreds to hear a man capable of finding the words to express their darkest dreams and deepest resentments. He claimed to have been sent by God to guide, comfort and lead them out of the darkness and into the light. Before long his fame was such that he provoked mass hysteria wherever he appeared, and guards were needed to protect him from the enthusiasm of his own followers. His clothes became sacred relics and his home town of Niklashausen, in the Tauber valley, a holy city to supporters. Finally, his influence grew so powerful and so dangerous that the ruling princes sent their armies against him. Captured, he was arraigned before an ecclesiastical court on charges of sorcery and heresy and, in 1476, burned at the stake. His ashes were scattered in the River Tauber to prevent the grave from becoming a shrine. Before he died, he prophesied that when his nation's despair was greatest another such as he would emerge from the masses and lead his nation to glory by giving voice to the secret yearnings of the ordinary German people.

It was a story with powerful emotional appeal for a fervent nationalist such as Adolf Hitler, and may well have been in Edmund Forster's mind when he devised an unorthodox method for treating his awkward and unusual patient.

By the first week of November 1918 he was ready to put this treatment into action. That evening he summoned Hitler to his consulting room, ostensibly for yet another eye examination. The blinds had been drawn and the only light came from two candles on the desk. After carefully studying each eye, Forster replaced his ophthalmoscope in its case and snuffed out the candles. He told Hitler that, despite his earlier doubts, he now knew for certain that mustard gas had caused serious burns to his eyes. The 'thick white layer' of dead tissue across both corneas meant that he would never see again. This was, of course, completely untrue. Hitler's only trauma was caused by his constant rubbing of his eyes in a self-defeating effort to reduce the irritation. But Forster had come to the conclusion that progress would be made only if Hitler believed himself the victim of a physical, and therefore, to his way of thinking, honourable, injury. 'I should never have assumed that a pure German, a good soldier with an Iron Cross, First Class, would lie or deceive,' Forster explained apologetically. 'Everyone has to accept their lot. The individual is powerless where fate is concerned. Miracles do not happen any more.'[4] He paused to let this hopeless news sink in before moving to the second part of his plan. In this he would offer a faint hope by explaining that, while it was true that any 'ordinary' individual would be condemned to lifelong blindness by such injuries, there remained the possibility that someone extraordinary, a man of destiny chosen by a higher power for some divine purpose, might overcome even an obstacle as great as this. If he really were a reincarnation of the Trommler, then God would send Hitler a sign by restoring his sight.

'But that goes only for the average person,' Forster continued thoughtfully. 'Miracles still frequently happen to chosen people. There have to be miracles and great people before whom nature bows, don't you agree?'

'If you say so, Doctor,' Hitler responded.

'I am no charlatan, no miracle worker,' Forster went on. 'I am a simple doctor but maybe you yourself have the rare power that only occurs once every thousand years to perform a miracle. Jesus did this, Mohammed, the saints.'

Hitler made no reply but in the darkness Edmund could hear him breathing heavily.

'I could show you the method by which you can see again, despite the fact your eyes have been damaged by mustard gas. With your symptoms an ordinary person would be blind for life. But for a person with exceptional strength of will-power and spiritual energy there are no limits, scientific assumptions do not apply to that person, the spirit removes any such barrier – in your case the thick white layer on your cornea. But maybe you do not possess this power to perform miracles.'

'How can I tell?' Hitler demanded. 'You as a doctor must tell me if I can do so!'

'Do you trust yourself to my will-power?' Forster enquired and when Hitler remained silent, continued: 'Then try to open your eyes wide. I will light my candle with a match. Did you see the sparks?'

'I don't know. Not a light but a kind of white, round shimmer.'

'That's not enough. That does not suffice. You must have absolute faith in yourself, then you will stop being blind. You are young, it would be a tragedy if you remained blind. You know that Germany now needs people who have energy and faith in themselves. Austria has not got a chance, but Germany does.'

'I know that,' Hitler said, but his voice had totally changed. He stood up and held on to the edge of the table, trembling.

'Listen,' Edmund Forster said firmly, 'I have two candles here, one on the left and one on the right. You must see! Do you see them?'

'I am beginning to see,' he said, 'if only it were possible!'

'For you anything is possible!' Forster said loudly and firmly. 'God will help you, if you help yourself! In every human being is a part of God. That is the will, the energy! Gather all your strength. More, more, more! Good! Now it is enough! What do you see now?'

'I see your face, your beard, your hand and the signet ring, your white coat, the newspaper on the table and the notes about me.'

'Sit down,' Edmund said, 'and take a rest. You have been cured. You have made yourself see. You behaved like a man and you managed to put light into your eyes because of your will-power.'

Forster smiled contentedly. Everything he had hoped would occur had happened. He had played Fate, played God and restored sight and sleep to a blind insomniac.[5]

This remarkable exchange does not feature in a contemporaneous report of the treatment but may be found in a novel entitled *Der Augenzeuge* (*The Eyewitness*), written twenty years after the event it describes by an award-winning Czech author named Ernst Weiss. Purportedly a work of fiction, *The Eyewitness* is in fact an accurate account of the treatment Edmund Forster employed, based directly on the notes that the doctor made in Hitler's medical file. Although in his novel Weiss calls the patient 'A.H.' and the clinic simply 'P', there is no doubt that he was referring to Adolf Hitler and Pasewalk, or that the psychiatrist who narrates the story is, in the words of Rudolph Binion:

> Pure Forster in everything germane to Forster's encounter with Hitler. He is an innovator in brain surgery apart from his special interest in hysteria. He holds hysteria to be all-out simulation that fools the simulator himself. Of A.H. he remarks: 'In his lying he believed he was telling the truth' – which matches Forster's 'These hysterics talk of their love of country and their courage until they are carried away with themselves like the actor who, in playing Hamlet, takes himself for the Prince of Denmark.'[6]

Other similarities abound. Like Edmund Forster, Weiss has his psychiatrist narrator born in Munich, practising medicine on the Western Front, serving in a military hospital, and even earning the Iron Cross, First Class.

But how could a Czech novelist come to know so much about Edmund Forster and the method by which he had successfully cured Hitler's hysterical blindness? The answer is that Edmund Forster had not only described his treatment in great detail, but even handed over to Weiss and some other German émigré writers a copy of the Pasewalk records.

At the end of May 1933, Forster left Griefswald with Julius Zádor to attend the conference at which his recently dismissed colleague would deliver his tilting-table lecture.[7] Offering Zádor a lift in the Opel-Popel was just the latest example of the support Forster had given to the young Jewish doctor, in spite of the risks that such actions created for himself in the increasingly anti-Semitic climate of Nazi Germany.

At the conference Forster met Dr Alfred Döblin, a fellow neurologist, who had specialised in treating nervous disorders before finding literary fame with a bestselling novel, *Berlin Alexanderplatz*. Earlier that year, Nazi persecution had forced him into exile in Zurich, although his aim was to settle in Paris. For him, the conference was an opportunity to meet old colleagues and gather information about work prospects in France. Forster, who of course was widely read in French, Dutch and English as well as German, and enjoyed the company of writers, had undoubtedly heard of Döblin and probably went out of his way to arrange a meeting. The two neurologists talked shop, gossiped and exchanged notes on interesting medical cases.

During this conversation Forster, perhaps encouraged by Zádor, who naturally had no love for the Nazis, began to disclose some details of Hitler's hysterical blindness and the method he had adopted to treat it. Döblin, always a fierce opponent of fascism, had particular reasons for feeling especially bitter at that moment. Two weeks before the conference, he had learned that a group of Nazis had ransacked his former home in Germany and burned all his books. He was therefore especially intrigued by Forster's account, and, realising the enormous political damage it would cause Hitler (still only a few months into his chancellorship at this point), pleaded with him to reveal all he knew to a wider public. Such entreaties would have gained a sympathetic hearing from Forster, who had many Jewish colleagues and friends, and made no secret of his contempt for Hitler and all he stood for. He may also have felt some responsibility for the monster his treatment had inadvertently helped to create and whose destruction he would dearly like to engineer. He would have been well aware of the damage his revelations could do to a leader who was constantly emphasising his 'exceptional strength of will'. Where the German public was concerned, hysterical disorders reflected a 'weakness of the will' caused by either an 'inferior nervous system' or a 'degenerate brain'.[8] Indeed, so contemptuous were the Nazis of hysterics that their infamous laboratory for 'race biology' would later extol the bombing of congested cities on the grounds that 'The person whose nervous system is deficient will not be able to survive the shock. In this way, bombing will help us discover the hysterics in our community and remove them from social life.'

But Forster would have been under few illusions about the risk to himself and his family in the course of action that Döblin was now urging. Since early 1933 it had been an offence punishable by imprisonment even to question the cause of Hitler's wartime blindness which would have been seen as tantamount to defaming the Nazi leader, and to provide medical proof of hysteria was likely to invite an even harsher response. At the conclusion of a subsequent meeting with émigré Jewish writers in July that year, Forster would give every indication of fearing for his own safety.[10]

While naturally anxious over the possible consequences, Forster's reluctance to speak out probably owed as much to concerns over medical ethics as to fears for his personal safety. On graduating from medical school he, like every other student, had sworn a Hippocratic Oath which included the promise that: 'What I may see or hear in the course of the treatment or even outside of the treatment in regard to the life of men, which on no account one must spread abroad, I will keep to myself, holding such things shameful to be spoken about.' Throughout his medical career he had held this oath to be sacrosanct, but now he was confronted by the fact that the only way he might bring to an end the career of a man whose opinions he despised was by violating it. Following his meeting with Döblin, however, Forster believed he had found a way of resolving his ethical dilemma *and* safeguarding himself. There was, he concluded, nothing unethical in handing over a copy of Hitler's *Krankenblatt* (hospital file) to a fellow neurologist, such as Döblin. What his colleague chose to do with this confidential information would then be a matter for his and not Forster's conscience. Furthermore, if the information was released in Paris by an anti-Nazi with a background in neurology, Forster's role in the affair might never be suspected by the authorities. In retrospect, this may seem like a hopelessly naive conclusion, but for Forster it must have appeared the only way to resolve his crisis of conscience.

So his plans were laid: on returning to Greifswald he intended to prepare three copies of Hitler's medical notes. The first he was to place in a Swiss safety-deposit box for security and the others he would hand over to Döblin in Paris towards the middle of July. While there he would also have a meeting with some other leading anti-Nazi German writers, to whom he intended disclosing medical information about two other senior members of Hitler's party. The first concerned his treatment of Hermann Göring for morphine addiction and the second details of a report he had prepared on Bernhard Rust, now Prussian Minister of Education, at the request of the criminal courts, about which more will be said in Chapter 14. Because both of these stories had already received mentions in the foreign press, Forster believed this would not involve a significant breach of patient confidentiality. As a cover for this meeting, he would arrange to travel home via Paris after attending his mother's eightieth birthday party.

When the neurology conference finished, Forster drove Zádor home to Budapest and from there, on 9 June, wrote to his brother Dirk,[11] suggesting that the celebrations for their mother's birthday on 16 July should be held in the small town of Lindau, on Lake Constance, rather than at her home in Deisenhofen. Although Wilhelmina seems to have liked the house she had built in the 1920s, the rest of the family considered it badly designed, shoddily constructed and located near an uninteresting and impoverished village. From Edmund's point of view, though, the main advantage of Lindau was its proximity to Basle in Switzerland, where he intended to conceal Hitler's medical file. The family agreed to his suggestion and, only a few weeks after his return to Greifswald,[12] Forster applied to the Rector for a month-long leave of absence, commencing on Wednesday 12 July, in order to attend his mother's birthday party. It is likely that he asked Dirk's wife Lilly to make contact with some suitable Jewish writers who would be interested in meeting him, since she had a wide range of friends among émigré writers, artists and musicians. Nor was this talented and self-possessed woman likely to have been deterred by any risks involved in setting up the meeting. Lilly's ability to react coolly and calmly in a crisis is illustrated by an incident at a high-society tea party she hosted in the German Embassy in Paris. As she stood up to pour tea, her sheer silk trousers slid suddenly down her legs to form a pink puddle around the ankles. Without showing the slightest sign of surprise or embarrassment, Lilly continued pouring the tea with one hand while deftly retrieving her trousers with the other.[13]

Early on 12 July Edmund and Mila loaded Opel-Popel with the luggage necessary for a four-week motoring holiday and set off with Balduin and Ruprecht on their drive to Lake Constance. They arrived three days later for what proved to be a large and exuberant party, with all the extended Forster clan gathering to toast Wilhelmina's health. When Edmund and his family finally departed it was with the promise to pay another visit before the end of summer. In the event Wilhelmina would never see her son again.

Their first overnight stop was in Basle, where Edmund deposited a copy of Hitler's *Krankenblatt* in a bank vault.[14] They then continued with their drive to Paris, arriving at Dirk and Lilly's comfortable apartment, not far from the German Embassy at 78 rue de Lille, late on a Friday afternoon. The following morning, Edmund strolled in the warm summer sunshine to the Royal Café,[15] in the Place du Théâtre Français, where the meeting was to take place. In addition to Alfred Döblin, the group included Walter Mehring,[16] a poet, novelist and playwright, and Leopold Schwarzschild, journalist and co-editor of *Das neue Tage-Buch (The New Diary)*, an influential anti-Nazi journal.[17]

Also present was Ernst Weiss, a surgeon turned novelist who lived in Prague. Weiss, a German-speaking Czech Jew, had done his medical training in Prague and Vienna, where he had later attended lectures by Sigmund Freud. In 1910 he had worked as assistant to

Emil Theodore Kocher, Berne's most distinguished surgeon and winner, in that same year, of the Nobel Prize for Medicine. Kocher expected his assistants to write detailed reports on each case and it may well have been these tasks that first awakened Ernst Weiss's interest in authorship.

Two years later, Weiss went down with a lung ailment and, deciding his health would benefit from the sea air, signed on as ship's doctor with an Austrian cruise liner. Over the next twelve months he journeyed to China, India and the Caribbean, occupying his time by writing his first novel, *Die Galeere* (*The Galley*), published in 1913. The warm reception both this and his subsequent book *Der Kampf* (*The Struggle*), published three years later, received from critics and the public had encouraged him to continue with his spare-time literary career. During the First World War he had served as a regimental surgeon with the Austro-Hungarian Army on the Eastern Front, but in 1920 had abandoned surgery to become a professional author. By the time he met Edmund Forster, Weiss had published twenty-three books and plays and won two prestigious literary awards.[18]

Although Forster's original plan had been to provide details about Hitler only to medical colleagues, it seems that, having overcome his reluctance to speak, he talked openly to all present. In 1951, Walter Mehring referred in his book *The Lost Library* to what he called that 'creepy Parisian exile episode' when Forster 'treasonably revealed the ominous Pasewalk hospital documents to the collaborators of *Das neue Tage-Buch*: Leopold Schwarzschild, Ernst Weiss and myself'.[19] Mehring later confirmed that Forster had spent three days with them and handed over two copies of the *Krankenblatt* for safe keeping.[20]

This evidence notwithstanding, some historians still question whether these clinical notes would have existed fifteen years after the Pasewalk *Lazarett* was closed. Others argue that if such documents had survived, they would have been filed away in some official repository rather than remaining in the hands of Edmund Forster.

Both objections miss the point that as a part-time consultant, Forster would have kept copies of all his patient files at the Charité Hospital in order to refer to the relevant notes prior to each visit. A distinction must also be made between official records, entered on hospital forms, and the personal notes a psychiatrist would keep not only for subsequent treatment sessions, but to provide material for reports, lectures and academic publications. Hysteria, as we know, was of great professional interest to Forster. He had published one paper on the topic in 1917 and in 1922 included details in a chapter for a textbook on neurology.[21] As he considered Hitler's case unusual and his treatment unique, it seems reasonable to suppose he would have retained the notes on file.

Forster's naive and overly optimistic expectations – that if highly publicised his revelations would effectively end Hitler's political ambitions – were dashed when the weeks passed with nothing appearing in *Das neue Tage-Buch*. Although a courageous and independent-minded journalist, considered by many to be one of Nazism's most eloquent opponents, Leopold Schwarzschild knew that to publish Hitler's hospital notes could be tantamount to suicide. Even though there was little love lost between the French and German governments, such a virulent and well-substantiated attack on a nation's leader was bound to result in tremendous political pressure for retribution. He may have feared that this would lead to *Das neue Tage-Buch* being shut down by the Paris authorities, possibly followed by his deportation to Germany, where certain imprisonment and likely execution would have awaited. Even if he avoided such a fate, there remained the very real additional danger of assassination by one of the many German agents operating in France or a French Nazi sympathiser. As a result, instead of publishing the documents, he passed the files to Ernst Weiss for safe keeping.

Forster's amateurish attempt to cover up his meeting with the émigré writers was probably doomed from the start. His brother Dirk was already under suspicion through his marriage to a half-Jew, and almost from the moment Hitler came to power his diplomatic career ground to a halt, never to recover. Even if Dirk were not under surveillance, it is probable that his wife's links with many Jewish and anti-Nazi friends among the exiled German community were well known in Berlin. It is equally likely that Nazi intelligence agents and their French sympathisers were keeping a watchful eye on an anti-fascist journalist of Leopold Schwarzschild's eminence and influence. All of which suggests that Berlin would have been aware of Forster's meeting and what was discussed before he and his family had even left for home.

Given the political pressure on the émigré writers not to step out of line, it seems unlikely that any details of Hitler's Pasewalk *Krankenblatt* would have become public knowledge but for the curious circumstance of Ernst Weiss's desperate need for money. After his meeting with Forster, Weiss returned to Prague to care for his sick and elderly mother. Following her death in September, he rented a room at the city's Praga Hotel, where he stayed until 7 February 1934. During this time he published *Der Gefängnisarzt oder die Vaterlosen* (*The Prison Doctor or the Orphans*) and started writing his next novel, *Der arme Verschwender (The Poor Squanderer)*.

In the summer of 1936 he moved to Paris, and during the autumn of that year a mutual friend introduced him to a young German-Jewish couple, Mona and Fred Wollheim. Fred, a lawyer, worked at the Institut de Droit Comparé while Mona, a philologist who had studied at the Sorbonne, supplemented their income by giving private lessons in German, French and English. A few months after their meeting Weiss wrote to ask Mona if she would be willing to type the manuscript of a new novella. She agreed and, as a result, Weiss and Mona started seeing far more of each other. He was in his fifties; she, thirty years his junior.

Although not conventionally handsome (Mona once described Weiss as 'stocky with a bony face'), Weiss soon captivated Mona with his intellect, humour and casual talk of such literary friends as Franz Kafka, Thomas Mann and Stefan Zweig. Before long she began writing him poetry and soon after that they became lovers. Their affair lasted until 1938, when Mona rejected Weiss's ultimatum that she must leave her husband. Despite this abrupt parting, Mona remained friendly with him, and when, later that year, he pleaded poverty and begged her to type one final manuscript free of charge, she agreed. Had she refused, it seems unlikely that *The Eyewitness* would ever have seen the light of day.

By early 1938 Weiss, like many exiled Jewish writers, had fallen on hard times. France's policy of appeasement meant it was all but impossible to find a publisher willing to take the risk of bringing out their novels. Even if they did, few readers showed any interest in them. 'They had left behind their readers, their publishers, the magazines and newspapers that had published their works,' says Klaus-Peter Hinze, 'and thus they lost their source of income.'[22]

Weiss, ill with a stomach ulcer, was living alone in a small back bedroom on the fifth floor of the Hôtel Trianon at 3 rue de Vaugirard, close to the Place de la Sorbonne on the left bank of the Seine. His financial situation, although precarious, would have been even more desperate but for the kindness of Thomas Mann and Stefan Zweig, who had arranged for the New York-based American Guild for German Cultural Freedom to make him a stipend of thirty dollars a month. In the summer of 1938 Weiss read an article in the German emigrant newspaper *Pariser Tageszeitung* that appeared to offer an escape from his penurious and increasingly precarious existence in Paris: the same guild that paid his stipend was offering a literary award for the best German novel by an exiled writer. The American firm Little, Brown and Co. was to give the award as an advance payment for the American edition of the prizewinning novel. The judges would include Thomas Mann, Rudolf Olden and Bruno Frank, entries had to be written under a pseudonym and the competition was solely for works of fiction.

Like many novelists, Weiss regularly wove factual events and real people into his narratives, but when he disguised Forster's case notes as a work of fiction it was simply to meet this stipulation. Despite the 1 October deadline being less than a couple of months away, Weiss decided to attempt to submit an entry, not only in the hope of winning the cash prize but to improve his chances of gaining a US visa. While searching for a suitable plot, he recalled his meeting five years earlier with Edmund Forster and decided to use the *Krankenblatt* dossier as the basis for his novel, which he would enter using the pen-name Gottfried von Kaiser. He started immediately, writing feverishly and barely sleeping or eating until the manuscript had been completed and Mona had finished typing the clean copy. The novel was a first-person account of a psychiatrist's involvement 'in the life of one of those people who after World War I created such massive changes and immeasurable suffering in Europe'.[23]

During the First World War, while serving in a military hospital, the narrator is ordered to treat 'a corporal of the Bavarian regiment, an orderly in the regimental staff – A.H.'. He learns that the man has been 'gassed by a grenade that the English had shot off during his last patrol; his eyes had burned like glowing coals; he had staggered back to the regimental staff with his report'. A.H. is immediately sent for treatment, although 'not in one of the field hospitals with others who had been gassed, whose eyes had been seriously damaged by poison gas, mustard gas and chlorine gas, but he was among the emotionally disturbed'.

After curing A.H.'s blindness, the narrator describes his post-war life as a doctor in private practice, his marriage to a Jewess named Victoria and the birth of his two children. Once the Nazis come to power he finds himself in grave danger. One night his father, a fanatical Nazi, calls with an urgent warning: 'He wasted no words. He told me he knew from the best sources that shortly there would be a thorough search of my house ... "You are supposed to have papers about the Führer? I can't believe it. You are much too intelligent to keep something compromising, and it would be madness to take them along to Switzerland, for you know very well that our arm reaches far".'

Trusting his father's promise that Victoria and their two children will soon be able to join him, he flees to exile in Switzerland, taking A.H.'s medical records with him. For safety, he deposits these in the vault of a Berne bank.

When his wife is arrested by the SS, he returns to try to secure her release. Arrested, he is sent to the Dachau concentration camp and brutally beaten. 'They had turned the whips around so that they could use the gristly end ... they no longer struck only the upper part of my body but also my legs and the soles of my feet. There must have been fifty to sixty blows. I did not count them.'

An SS guard, whose child's life he once saved, tells him the electrified fence and perimeter lights will be turned off for five minutes during the night while the generator is serviced. Using this knowledge, he escapes and is reunited with his family in Switzerland. After recovering from the injuries inflicted by his torturers, they move to France and settle, as did Weiss, in Paris.[24]

With the typing complete, Mona helped Weiss parcel up the manuscript of *Der Augenzeuge* and mail it to the United States, where it was added to a pile of 239 other competition entries from hopeful émigré authors. Weiss failed to win the competition, with the prize going instead to thirty-six-year-old Arnold Siegfried Bender, a minor novelist who wrote under the pseudonym Mark Philippi. However, by sending his manuscript out of France Weiss saved it from certain destruction by the Nazis. In June 1940 German troops raided Mona's flat. Later she recalled how her apartment was emptied of all her books and papers: 'Among the documents taken away were Weiss's diaries as well as novels by Thomas Mann and Stefan Zweig containing handwritten dedications to Weiss by the authors.'[25] Mona managed to escape from France and start a new life for herself in New York, but her husband Fred was arrested and later perished in a French internment camp.

What proof is there that *Der Augenzeuge*, despite being presented as a work of fiction, provides an accurate account of the way Edmund Forster treated Hitler's blindness?

Its truth or falsity clearly depends on an ability to establish three crucial points: that Hitler was suffering from hysterical blindness rather than physical injury to the eyes caused by mustard gas; that he was treated by Edmund Forster; and that Forster's treatment involved persuading Hitler that the restoration of his sight would be a sign both of his superior will and divinely ordered destiny.

Although the absence of Edmund Forster's clinical notes means that the evidence on all three points is circumstantial, it is nevertheless compelling. We should start by reviewing what we know about the likely cause of Hitler's blindness.

As was explained in Chapter 10, while Hitler and his companions *were* victims of a gas attack on the morning of 15 October, both the symptoms described by Ignaz Westenkirchner and especially the speed with which these appeared strongly suggest not *mustard* gas but White Star, the phosgene and chlorine 'workhorse gas' in such widespread use by the British Army. Provided exposure to White Star was limited, any blindness it caused, through swelling of the eyelids and profuse lachrymation, would be only temporary and easily treated. Yet, according to Westenkirchner's account, while the other soldiers went for treatment to a hospital outside Brussels, Hitler was transported some six hundred miles to a special *Lazarett* at Pasewalk. As was explained in Chapter 2, the doctors at Oudenaarde had no choice but to transfer him to a clinic specialising in nervous disorders if they concluded that his blindness was due to hysteria.

The identification of Edmund Forster as the neuropsychiatrist who treated Hitler at Pasewalk in 1918 first became public knowledge with the declassification of Karl Kroner's statement to US Naval Intelligence made while he was living as a refugee in Iceland in 1943. This document not only names Forster, but states that Hitler's blindness was hysterical in origin.[26]

Individually, each of these pieces of evidence might appear suggestive rather than persuasive. Taken together, however, they seem to establish beyond reasonable doubt both that Hitler's blindness was psychological rather than physical in origin and that Edmund Forster treated him for a hysterical disorder.

Accepting, then, that he was one of the hundreds of thousands of soldiers treated by German psychiatrists and neurologists during the First World War, what proof exists that Forster's treatment was anything like that described in *The Eyewitness*?

We may start with the fact that it is entirely consistent with all that is known about Forster's approach to the condition. In the words of Dr Jürg Zutt, a colleague at the Charité, he 'took hysteria to be mostly humbug and treated hysterics accordingly'.[27] Second, if Weiss's specialisation had been psychiatry, it would be reasonable to assume that he was describing his own method of treating such disorders. But Weiss had been a surgeon, so he would have had no experience of dealing with mentally disturbed patients. It is therefore far more probable that he based his account on Hitler's *Krankenblatt*, which Forster had handed over to the émigrés in Paris. Furthermore, it seems unlikely that Weiss would have had any compunction about incorporating real people into his work of 'fiction'. During the summer of 1937, for example, he and Mona had met two Austrian women during a holiday in Lyons-la-Fôret. These women had told them a touching anecdote about a child. A few months later, while typing the manuscript of Weiss's novel *Verführer (Seducer)*. Mona found he had included this anecdote verbatim, as well describing many other details and individuals she immediately recognised.

Hitler, although couching his experiences at Pasewalk in mystical terms, certainly saw his time in the *Lazarett* as a turning point in his life. In their seminal books on leadership, Warren Bennis and Robert Thomas claim that every leader passes through at least one intense, transformational experience that they call a 'crucible'.[28] This is the event that either makes or breaks them. For Hitler, that 'crucible' experience occurred at the Pasewalk *Lazarett* in October and November 1918.

Stories that Hitler had experienced some form of 'divine revelation' were circulating in Germany long before the Nazis assumed power. On 9 January 1923, for example, the *Münchner Post* published an article in which it described how after the war:

> He lay injured in a military hospital. It is said he was stricken by a kind of blindness. And he was freed from this blindness by an inner ecstasy, which showed him the way to free the pan-German [*Großdeutsche*] people from the materialistic enslavement by Marxism and capitalism. He, Hitler, sees it as his duty to free his people. The whole will of this man is determined by the belief in his Messianic mission.

In which case it may be fairly asked why Dr Forster managed to create only one rather than dozens of Hitlers during his career as a military psychiatrist. The answer is that Hitler's case was unique and, as such, demanded of Forster a unique psychological approach. Hitler was not a malingerer; he desperately wanted to regain his sight so that he could return to the front line. As a result Forster's normal tactic of pulling rank on the unfortunate soldier and lambasting his lack of will-power clearly would not work on Hitler. So he needed a new strategy, and he found one: he convinced Hitler that his 'divine mission' depended on him seeing again. Hitler, as we have seen, remained convinced of this throughout the turbulent 1920s, never doubting that he would eventually achieve the power that finally came his way in January 1933.

For more than twenty years Weiss's manuscript lay gathering dust in a filing cabinet until, in the early 1960s, it was discovered by Paul Gordon, a publisher of play scripts. Realising its merit and historical importance, Gordon offered it, unsuccessfully, to a number of West German newspapers and publishing houses. At last, in 1963, a young publisher named Hermann Kreisselmeier agreed to its publication, but insisted that the book should be judged purely as a literary work drawn from the author's imagination and inspiration, without any reference being made to its factual origin. It was a decision that was to doom the book's chances of commercial success, and of the five thousand copies printed in 1964, less than half had been sold a decade later.

Ernst Weiss had once written despairingly: 'With the years going by, emptiness is growing around me. I am still living, feeling, having desires and hopes. I do not fear death itself, but I dread the hour, when, out of exhaustion, there is no hope left within me for anything.'[29]

On Friday, 14 June 1940 that hour arrived.

During the morning a disconsolate Weiss had watched as German troops tramped down the Champs-Elysées, witnessed the swastika raised over the Arc de Triomphe and seen it fluttering above the Eiffel Tower. Returning to his shabby little room, he sat at his desk in the gathering dusk. Below he could hear the clatter of rifles and stamp of jackboots as German soldiers paraded in the Place de la Sorbonne. He knew that in America Eleanor Roosevelt and Thomas Mann had been working tirelessly to secure him safe passage across the Atlantic, but the months had slipped by without any word and now, ill and exhausted, he abandoned all hope. Taking out his pen, he wrote a farewell note to his friends that ended with the words: '*Vive la France quand-même*' (Long live France all the same). Then, going into the bathroom he ran a bath, swallowed some sleeping pills and, lying down naked in the warm water, he slashed open his wrists with a cut-throat razor. But in his distress this once skilful surgeon bungled the job. Rather than the swift and painless end he had sought, his death was, from all accounts, slow and agonising.

It was also desperately ironic. Awaiting him at the American Embassy were the US visa and the liner ticket he had longed to receive.

Chapter Fourteen
DECLINE AND FALL

There will be no mercy now. Anyone who stands in our way will be cut down. The German people will not tolerate leniency.
Adolf Hitler, February 1933[1]

It all began with a letter.

On Tuesday, 22 August 1933 Bernhard Rust, the recently appointed Prussian Minister for Science, Art and Public Education, received a disjointed, three-page, handwritten letter from a Berlin student named Eugen Oklitz. Dated 21 August, it denounced Professor Edmund Forster in ringing terms as an amoral Marxist, crook and pro-Semite. Instead of being consigned to the nearest waste bin or deposited in the 'Mentally Deranged' file, his bizarre allegations were carefully studied and treated with the utmost seriousness. In the light of its crucial role in Edmund Forster's demise, Oklitz's letter is reproduced in full:

> The Director of the Greifswald Nerve Clinic, Professor Forster is a Jew-lover, and, of course, as everyone knows, makes no secret of his anti-National Socialistic views, continues to try to ridicule the national government and even now talks confidently of the '4th Reich'.
>
> It seems outrageous that this prominent Marxist, who obtained his position at the Nerve Clinic in Greifswald by devious means, is still around and even his friends are

surprised that this Jewish amoral parasite is still in charge of his sexually perverted and contaminated clinic where, at night, doctors climb in and out of the nurses' windows, it is absolutely typical of the place that those involved do not even bother to deny what is happening.

Forster is supposedly married to the ex-private secretary of Erzberger (it seems that this was the reason why Forster was made Director of Greifswald) and he appears to regard it as good manners, when in company, if he disappears upstairs with some lovely lady, and to emerge from a bedroom with the woman clad only in pyjamas. His female employees are victims of his alcoholic excesses and thanks to his powerful position he forces his attentions on them in the way I have just mentioned, as an example one can mention the farewell party for the Jew doctor Zadow [*sic*].

Because of this it is hardly surprising that the matron is not permitted to discipline her nurses or her employees/co-workers as all these ladies are having affairs with the doctors. The perverted conversations which can be heard in the clinic are enough to make every decent person blush with shame. A particularly amoral type is the Czech Dr Woider, a very close friend of the Hungarian Jew Dr Zadow who will be mentioned later in this letter.

This Czech sends a daily, detailed, report to Dr Zadow in Paris, which proves Woider is guilty of sabotage and spreading negative news about Germany (horror news!). This Czech, despite the general unemployment and against the lawful regulations is still in work, receives free board and even a salary! Furthermore this cheeky foreigner and hater of Germans boasts about his filthy 'goings on' and believes it is permissible, when surrounded by people with opposing views, to read his foreign newspaper in a provocative manner and speak in negative terms about the national government!

It is also interesting that Dr Forster has delayed, for as long as possible, the lawful dismissal of this previously mentioned Jew Dr Zadow in order to purchase with taxpayers' money a photographic table, which is just a joke against the German government since this table costs 6000 RM. Zadow gains a personal financial advantage in this purchase since Zadow receives 15% for each one supplied.

Furthermore, several thousand metres of film have been wasted by this foreign Jew, we estimate it is about 30,000 metres. All this happened after 30 January and particularly after 1 April 1933.

The scientific loot from these films Zadow, with the help of his boss Professor Forster, took in Forster's private car, with Forster, to Paris, where Forster's brother, Embassy Councillor Forster, did everything for his friend, the parasite Dr Zadow, who now very cynically says he hopes to return here very soon. This trip to Paris is said to have been done on expenses and like everything else which has been claimed as business trips seems very suspicious indeed. These 'business trips' were fairly regular events in Forster's clinic. On one of these business trips in his own car to his brother in Paris, Forster took with him an assistant Miss R. (now dismissed), she returned with <u>three ball gowns</u>! Miss R. was later dismissed at the same time as Dr Z. when it became known that she was betraying Forster and had enjoyed a relationship with this Dr Z, liaisons which had taken place while Forster was lecturing. After this female assistant had been dismissed, negatives and prints of Miss R. and Director Professor Forster were found, which showed they had been <u>photographed in the 'nude'</u>!

Furthermore Forster only listens to Paris on the radio and claims it is the only way to hear the truth and that the <u>speeches of Hitler are only for lunatics and the mentally insane</u>.

When Forster at the beginning of April (or May) was in Berlin, and was asked by a colleague how he had liked the speech of our people's chancellor and this colleague had spoken enthusiastically about our Führer, all Forster could do was to speak negatively about Hitler's speech.

It is also a fact that the Nerve Clinic has been embellished with particularly charming pictures (beautiful women's breasts etc.), which are the works of a painter who at the time was employed out of friendship and an enthusiasm for this kind of kitsch 'art': approximately four of these repulsive paintings had to be removed because they were causing a public outrage! This is how institute monies were wasted!

It wasn't enough that one X-ray department was constructed at a cost of 85,000 RM, plus a further 35,000 RM to equip it. One asks oneself who obviously lined his pockets there!!! It should therefore be strongly recommended that a commission with powers to carry out a detailed check of the account books is set up, especially as in the past such checks have uncovered wasteful practices by the clinic: although without discovering the person responsible for these dishonesties! It is an indisputable fact that certain amounts were spent without justification! To mention just one other small detail. Very recently, allegedly for a business trip to his home town, the foreign Jew Dr Zadow was paid 55 RM, as can be seen in the account!

For this foreign Jew large amounts of money are available, for an unemployed party member however there wasn't even any lunch!

Professor Forster is supposed to have packed his suitcases just in case anything is discovered so that he can disappear across the border to Paris 'on a business trip'.

The letter was signed simply 'Oklitz'.[2]

Although Eugen Oklitz, a fanatical young Nazi, was a student in Berlin rather than Greifswald, he had at family links with the latter university. His father had been Bursar since 1925, and his sister Louise had been employed as a laboratory assistant in the

Nerve Clinic. In passing on the letter to the Curator at Greifswald, Rust instructed him to take the matter seriously and treat it as a matter of priority because it was from 'a reliable and well-informed individual'.[3] This endorsement seems to have been based on the facts that Eugen Oklitz enjoyed a high reputation within the Nazi Party and his sister had worked under Forster at the clinic until very recently.

Allegations against Louise Oklitz, also a member of the Nazi Party, had earlier been made by Johanna Rätz, Forster's secretary, and Klar Korth, a shorthand–typist in his office. These centred on two alleged blackmail attempts by her, the first of which had occurred in the summer of 1931. A part-time worker, Louise had applied for a full-time post and dropped a hint that if she didn't get the job, she would pass on some scandalous information about Forster to her father, adding menacingly that 'he had already managed to cost another professor his position'.[4] When, about a year later, Forster learned of this threat, his first impulse was to dismiss Louise immediately, but he was persuaded not to do so after Louise flatly denied ever having made it.

In June 1933 Louise left the clinic but, according to Johanna Rätz, appeared in Rätz's office a few weeks later (while Forster was attending his mother's birthday party) and instructed her to warn Forster about a recently dismissed staff member who was in a position to cause serious problems for him. When Rätz refused to do this, Louise informed her bad things would start happening at the clinic unless she was immediately re-employed by Forster, and at a higher salary. Rätz claimed she again refused to pass on this threat, at which point Louise left.

It later transpired that Eugen and Louise Oklitz had tried to obtain information from the medical files about the brother of a Greifswald lecturer named Hermann Brüske who had been treated in the clinic. Their purpose was to try to find some dirt on Brüske, a prominent Greifswald Nazi, to use against him in a power struggle taking place within the local National Socialist Party office.

Exactly what motivated Eugen Oklitz to write such a letter can never be fully established. At the time, Forster's colleagues believed he had probably done so at the urging of Louise, but it is equally likely that he was merely following orders from high within the party, from either Bernhard Rust himself or even Hermann Göring. To appreciate why these Nazi officials were so eager to have Forster disgraced and dismissed, we need to take a step back to earlier in the year and consider how the Nazis were consolidating their grip on power.

On 4 February Wilhelm Kähler, the Prussian Minister for Science, Art and Education, was replaced by fifty-year-old Bernhard Rust, the former secondary schoolteacher on whom Edmund had previously prepared a psychiatric report. Rust, a fanatical Nazi, was in every way the last person who ought to have been given such a position. 'Dr Rust preached the Nazi gospel with the zeal of a Goebbels and the fuzziness of a Rosenberg,' commented William Shirer. 'He boasted that he had succeeded overnight in "liquidating the school as an institution of intellectual acrobatics".'[5]

After studying philosophy at Berlin and Munich, Rust had become a secondary schoolteacher and fought with distinction as a lieutenant during the First World War, receiving the Iron Cross, First and Second Class, for gallantry. Invalided out with a serious head wound that he later claimed affected his mental stability, he returned to teaching. In 1922 he joined the Nazis. Three years later he was made Gauleiter of Hanover-North and in 1928 Gauleiter of South-Hanover-Brunswick, a post he held until 1940. However, in 1930 he was dismissed from teaching after being accused of an indecent assault on one of his female students. Forster, perhaps out of sympathy for a courageous ex-soldier, prepared a report stating Rust's actions were caused by his head injury, and the case was dropped. The diagnosis proved no obstacle to a political career, however, and Rust was elected to the Reichstag later that same year.

Early in his chancellorship, Hitler had informed the Reichstag that at the same time as 'purifying' all aspects of public life – that is *expelling* all Jews, Marxists and indeed anyone else suspected of not offering the Nazis unwavering loyalty – his government would be undertaking a thorough 'moral purging' of the body corporate of the nation, including the educational system.

Bernhard Rust was to be the instrument of that 'purification'. No sooner had he assumed office than he began enthusiastically purging the Prussian education system of all those teachers and lecturers less than wholeheartedly committed to Nazi ideology. That of course included all Jews and anyone espousing left-wing views or raising a dissenting opinion. In the space of a few months more than a thousand educators were sacked, arrested, imprisoned or forced into exile, including the physicists Albert Einstein and James Franck, and the chemists Fritz Haber, Otto Warburg and Richard Willstätter.

However, 1933 saw another and even more dangerous former patient achieve high office in Germany, a man whose brutality and ruthlessness had gained him the nickname '*der Eiserne,*' the 'iron man': Hermann Göring. 'Göring is the personification of direct force and, if need be, insensate brutality,' commented one observer. 'He is never subtle or aloof. He has none of the hysteria of a Hitler or the deliberate calculation of a Goebbels. He has no fixed principles. He is an opportunist, ready to embark on any course of action that will make Germany strong. Eighteen stone of geniality or brutality as the occasion may warrant.'[6]

A professional soldier turned wartime aviator, Göring had, by 1917, shot down his twentieth enemy aircraft and received the Pour le Mérite, Imperial Germany's highest award for valour. Demobilised with the rank of captain, he travelled to Sweden, where he earned his living as a commercial pilot, mechanic and shopkeeper before meeting his wife-to-be, the wealthy and well-connected Karin von Kantzow. She persuaded him to return to Germany, and in Munich he met Hitler and fell under his spell. He offered to reorganise the Storm Troopers, and, using his wife's money and contacts, assist the struggling party financially and bring Hitler to the attention of their many wealthy and influential friends. Badly injured with wounds to the groin during the Munich *Putsch*, he avoided arrest only by fleeing to Austria, where he spent six weeks in an Innsbruck hospital. The liberal use of morphine by his doctors when treating his wounds led to addiction and in 1925, having returned to Sweden, he was committed by the courts to Långbro Sanatorium.

Following Hitler's release from prison and the general amnesty given to Nazi Party members, Göring returned to Munich and within five years had become a member of the Reichstag and Hitler's deputy. The death of his wife in October 1931 may have been the trigger for a resumption of his morphine addiction, for which he sought treatment from Edmund Forster. Göring neverthess worked energetically, using all his considerable wealth and influence to smooth Hitler's appointment as Chancellor. As soon as he became Prussian Minister of the Interior he began a ruthless campaign to eliminate all of the Nazis' opponents. Every official who did not wholeheartedly support the party was dismissed, forced to resign or, as in the case of Robert Kempner, the legal adviser to the Prussian police and future war crimes prosecutor whom we met in Chapter 1, arrested.

As part of his internal political battle with SS Chief Heinrich Himmler, Göring established a new and independent force in the form of Abteiling IA of the Prussian political police. On 26 April 1933 he officially named this new force the Geheimes Staatspolizeiamt (Secret State Police). Not long afterwards, an anonymous postal official who had been given the task of designing a franking stamp for the new department abbreviated it to Gestapo, a word that soon became one of the most sinister in the German language. Göring housed his new department in a disused arts and crafts school on Prinz-Albrecht Strasse, not far from his own office in the Leipzigerstrasse, and appointed thirty-three-year-old Dr Rudolf Diels, a civil servant in the political police branch of the Prussian Ministry of the Interior, his personal combination of spy, blackmailer and watchdog.[7] Diels, who had been a member of the extreme right-wing Students' Corps in the Weimar Republic, was clever, subtle, humourless, cynical and highly educated. Although never a card-carrying Nazi, he promised to create for his master an instrument of power the like of which had never previously been seen in the history of Prussia. He was to prove as good as his word.

Under Göring the number of officers employed by the Gestapo increased rapidly from around sixty to almost three hundred. Göring exempted his new authority from the restrictions imposed by Paragraph 14 of the Prussian Administrative Police Law, which stated that the police could carry out their duties only 'within the framework of current laws'. In other words, they had a licence to act outside the law and entirely ignore any notion of human rights. One of Göring's first orders was 'Shoot first and enquire afterwards. If you make mistakes, I'll look after you.'[8] Later, in Dortmund, he added: 'Any mistakes my officials make are my mistakes. The bullets they fire are my bullets.'[9] In Essen he boasted, 'I make a habit of shooting from time to time. If I sometimes make mistakes, at any rate I have shot.'[10] After the Reichstag fire he reintroduced capital punishment by axe, claiming that 'decapitation is an honest old German punishment', and hung a giant executioner's sword in his study, against a wall of flaming red and gold. 'I am not concerned with meting out justice,' he announced. 'My task is to destroy, to exterminate.'[11] Here was a man prepared to eliminate anyone who stood in his way or appeared to pose even the slightest threat to himself, his party or, above all, his beloved Führer.

Given Edmund Forster's professional connection with this powerful, ruthless and murderous man – and of course his earlier, even more significant, link to Hitler – it would have been remarkable if news of his meeting with the anti-Nazi émigrés in Paris had not been brought to Göring's attention. Forster's knowledge of Hitler's hysterical blindness and its treatment meant that it was in his power to discredit the Führer massively in the eyes of Germany and the rest of the world. Under other circumstances it might have been possible to ensure the untrustworthy professor met with an accident, or was even murdered in cold blood. However, such a course of action was risky for two reasons. First, Forster was an eminent, internationally respected academic. Second, and much more importantly, the Nazis did not know the whereabouts of Hitler's *Krankenblatt*. They suspected Forster had taken the opportunity to secrete it abroad, but could not know where, nor whether it would be published on Forster's death. Far better then to ensure he was first dismissed in disgrace from the university. Once isolated from his fellow academics, he would presumably slip into academic obscurity, thereby solving the first problem. Furthermore, if the reasons for his dismissal included charges of mental instability, any further allegations he might make concerning Hitler's hysterical blindness could more easily be laughed off as the ravings of an embittered and emotionally unbalanced man. He could then be more easily arrested, imprisoned and eliminated.

The machinery of Forster's destruction was set in motion over the weekend of 19 and 20 August 1933, when Oklitz's father, probably acting on the orders of Göring,[12] instructed Eugen to write the letter of denunciation. This the young man duly did, making use of information supplied by his sister, who passed on clinic gossip, and his father, who provided him with more substantial details of Zádor's 'tilting-table' experiments and the clinic's finances. His letter was carefully studied and commented upon by various officials within the department when it arrived at the Education Ministry on 22 August: the document reveals copious underlining and marginalia. On the next afternoon, an Education Ministry official identified in the official records as G.M.R. Schnoering telephoned Dr Sommer, Greifswald University's curator and a member of the Nazi Party, ordering him to launch an immediate, urgent and thorough investigation into Oklitz's allegations. He stated that he wanted the whole affair resolved by 20 September.

Sommer wasted little time in implementing these instructions, noting in his diary for Saturday 26 August: 'Sister Braun [the clinic's matron] will give me a list of the witnesses I should question, and I am then to hand over the matter to the police who will decide whether or not to proceed. Regardless of what action the police take, however, my instructions are to suspend Professor Forster with immediate effect.'[13]

The following Monday, the 28th, the internal investigations began in earnest, with interrogations conducted by a senior official from the university's administration department. First to give evidence was the middle-aged matron Edith Braun, whose testimony, running to seven closely typed pages, comprises a series of wild and largely unsubstantiated allegations:

Where politics are concerned I can confirm that Professor Forster often makes outspoken and ill-considered remarks. I have been told that shortly after the Reichstag fire he said, in the hearing of Nurse Thürk, Junior Doctor Goralewski and Sister Elfriede, that only lunatics would believe it to be a case of arson and that in reality the fire had been started by the national government for propaganda purposes ... Professor Forster made these remarks without being prompted to do so by anybody else. I myself did not hear Professor Forster say, [in] the spring of this year with reference to the speeches of the Reichskanzler [Hitler], that these were likely to appeal only to lunatics and the mentally insane. He has however made similar remarks in the presence of Sister Martha, with whom I have spoken in the last few days about this. He also commented that the speeches were directed at 'provincials', in other words the ill educated and lunatics.

This statement was made in the presence of Frau Stohwasser, a female patient who is perfectly sane and a National Socialist.

After the national government came to power Professor Forster remarked to other doctors, in the hearing of patients and in the presence of Sister Martha, that the present Minister for Education and Cultural Affairs . . . Rust, was an unsuitable choice since to avoid military service he had deliberately shot himself.

Braun then discussed another of Oklitz's charges: the support and encouragement that Forster had given to doctors from outside Germany.

Professor Forster favoured Jewish junior doctors and did not hold Christian doctors in the same esteem. Until recently the Hungarian Jew Zádor was the head junior doctor at the clinic. This spring he was sent on leave in compliance with the law on the purification of the professional civil servants and resigned from his job around 1 July [sic: he had been sacked in January].

Braun dealt next with Forster's alleged dishonesty and mistreatment of patients.

In the spring the purchase of another expensive tilting table was negotiated by Dr Zádor, for which he received a licence fee of 500 RM . . . While Dr Zádor was on leave [sic] a great many experiments were carried out using this table. Mentally ill people, as well as former patients, were being tilted around on this table, that is moving about while either lying down or standing up, and their responses were filmed. In my opinion those conducting the experiments, especially Dr Zádor, failed to treat these mentally ill patients with sufficient care and I often regarded what was being done as a form of torture. However, whenever I voiced my objections, I was told that there was no place in such research for sentiment.

Many thousand metres of film were used. It is possible that Zádor took some of them with him to Paris. I witnessed one female patient being jolted around on this tilting table for such a long time that she became utterly exhausted and had to be given an injection of camphor. This costly table is now standing idle. In June Dr Forster and Dr Zádor went to Budapest with these films. As far as I know this journey was paid for out of clinic funds (500 RM).

Finally, and it seems with considerable relish, Braun turned her attention to what she considered Forster's lewd conduct and his encouragement of similar immoral behaviour in others.

Standards of morality and decency within the clinic left much to be desired. Dances and dinners were held in the doctors' refectory at which female laboratory workers were present. I have witnessed how, early in the evening, Laboratory Assistant Frau Rietzkow from Greifswald and Fräulein Wilder came to the refectory in ball gowns and partied there with the junior doctors Zádor, Weiss and Zucker. Later the same night everyone, including Professor Forster, would drive off in a small car obviously in high spirits, with a great deal of screaming despite the late hour. They would then return in the early hours and all sleep in to about eleven or twelve o'clock, so that the work of the clinic suffered tremendously as a result.

Dr Goralewski, who left recently, and Dr Wayda, together with some student doctors . . . held a farewell party in Dr Goralewski's room with a great many female nurses from what is called the 'disturbed' ward. Naturally this placed patients in considerable danger. Also the celebrations went on until about six o'clock in the morning.

A few years ago Professor Forster had an affair with Fräulein Rietzkow. At the same time Dr Zucker, who was employed at the clinic, also started an affair with Fräulein Rietzkow . . . When Professor Forster found out that Fräulein Rietzkow had started an affair with Dr Zucker, there was an argument, the upshot being that both left the clinic. Laboratory Assistant Fräulein Wilder said that after parties they would drive to the beach and bathe in the nude.

As Professor Forster attended all these parties I assume he also took part in the nude bathing. Fräulein Wilder . . . once showed me and Sister Elfriede, who is still in the clinic, a photo depicting Professor Forster and Junior Doctor Marienfeld with my predecessor Lotte Kaiser sitting on Professor Forster's lap while Dr Marienfeld had Frau Professor Forster seated on his lap . . . Frau Professor Forster used to be the private secretary of Erzberger. Her reputation where decency and morality are concerned is very bad. She is said to fool around with every student . . . Nurse Thürk can provide you with information about orgies that have taken place in Professor Forster's house.

Dr Zádor had a very close relationship with a student doctor called Wayda who is still at the clinic. During the last fortnight he has started to call himself von Wayda and recently also obtained the flag of the Hungarian National Socialist Party.

While guests were drinking coffee at one of the numerous farewell parties at which Dr Zádor and Frau Professor Forster were present, Dr Wayda indecently assaulted a nurse called Schulz.

I have heard that Professor Forster then made an indecent proposal to Fräulein Oklitz, a laboratory assistant. It is not surprising that under these circumstances Professor Forster lacked the respect of his staff.

One afternoon, with my own eyes, I saw Frau Forster, the wife of Embassy Councillor Forster, leaving Dr Zádor's room at the clinic. I did not tell any of the other doctors about this, but the former junior doctors Weiss, Goralewski and Dr Facilides all told me, independently, that Dr Zádor had had an affair with Embassy Councillor Forster's wife. Whenever the wife of Embassy Councillor Forster was in Greifswald staying with her brother-in-law Professor Forster, Dr Zádor would hardly be seen around the clinic since he spent all the time in their home.[14]

Far from dismissing her wild and unsupported allegations as the farrago of innuendo and tittle-tattle they undoubtedly were, both the university and the Education Ministry took Edith Braun's accusations extremely seriously, with Curator Sommer stressing what an honest and truthful individual she was.

But the internal investigation, which, from the Education Ministry's point of view, had started so favourably, then rapidly began to unravel. Edith Braun was obliged to withdraw several of her accusations when Max Thürk, whom she said would substantiate her claims, refused to do so. From then on, none of the witnesses called was prepared to offer much support for Oklitz's allegations. A Professor Krisch, while conceding that Forster had described a speech by the Führer as 'lacking in any distinction whatever', also insisted his remarks were not prompted by antagonism towards the Nazis.

Professor Forster, as far as I can see, has no comprehension and no understanding of the National Socialist movement and its ideals . . . I never heard anything which could be considered as ridiculing or blackening the name of the Führer, of his leading officials or the National Socialist movement. For example I never heard Professor Forster talk about a 'fourth Reich' and I would never class him as a particularly vehement anti-National Socialist. He really isn't enough of a politician for that to apply. I am also certain that Professor Forster has no Jewish blood in his veins.

Alone and accompanied by my wife I was a frequent visitor in the Forster household, where the atmosphere was never formal but always very casual and relaxed. Neither in my own nor my wife's presence did anything happen that would have infringed on normal manners and decencies.

It is absolutely impossible that in my presence Forster ever disappeared upstairs with a lady and returned in his pyjamas, totally impossible. Yesterday, for the first time, I heard from the Curator and saw in the files the allegation that Professor Forster was supposed to have had sexual intercourse with female clinic employees. I only know that the laboratory assistant Fräulein Rietzkow is alleged to have had a relationship with Dr Zucker and that during this affair Dr Zucker was supposedly visiting this woman in one of the rooms at the clinic.

I also attended, with my wife, social events held in the clinic's refectory where the atmosphere was always very relaxed and friendly. There was dancing. In my presence there were never any occasions when there was indecent behaviour or anything bordering on the indecent. I am extremely surprised to hear what Matron Braun says about Professor Forster's relationship with Fräulein Rietzkow. I have never heard about or seen any photographs depicting Professor Forster in the nude with one or two others. Nor have I seen the picture in which Sister Kaiser is allegedly sitting on the Professor's lap and Frau Forster was supposed to be sitting on the lap of a junior doctor.

I am not sure whether Dr Zádor derived any personal financial advantage from the neurological department acquiring the so-called tilting table. This table Dr Zádor used for quite a number of scientific research experiments and was hoping that if his tilting-table examination methods were adopted as standard clinical practice he would receive some patent fees for distributing this table. I also consider the tilting-table experiments conducted by Dr Zádor to be both important and scientifically valid . . . I never had any reservations about these experiments.

I heard for the first time today that Professor Forster is alleged to have taken the former laboratory assistant Fräulein

Rietzkow with him in his car and is alleged to have allowed himself be photographed in the nude with Fräulein Rietzkow. I know Professor Forster brought back presents for Fräulein Rietzkow and his secretary from Paris . . . I never saw anything wrong with these gifts, because I knew how much time outside normal working hours both his secretary and the laboratory assistant had spent on preparing Professor Forster's speeches for the congresses.[15]

Other witnesses, even those professing themselves to be Nazis, also contradicted the matron's allegations that Forster had attacked Hitler or the Nazis. Junior Doctor Kroll told the investigation:

'Without being a member of the party, I have been a National Socialist for a considerable period of time and . . . in my presence Professor Forster never made a political remark slandering the Führer Adolf Hitler or ridiculing him or his officials or indeed the whole National Socialist movement and its activities . . . I do not at all regard Professor Forster as someone who actively is against National Socialism or acts as a serious opponent of it.[16]

On Tuesday 29 August, with the interrogations continuing, Herr Rinke, a university administrator working in the Curator's office, forwarded the three witness statements so far obtained to Greifswald's Oberbürgermeister (senior mayor), a Nazi Party member who was also head of the local police authority, marked 'for your attention and possible action'. He requested that the documents receive urgent attention and be returned promptly to the Curator.[17]

This request was complied with the following afternoon, the returned files being accompanied by a note which read, in part:

I have taken copies of the protocols and intend to send them on to the State Police in Stettin for review and possibly forwarding to the Secret State Police [Gestapo] in Berlin, taking into account the fact that the Ministry for Science, Culture and Public Education already possesses further evidence. Reasons of state security mean that, at present, I shall be taking no further action.[18]

The following day, Thursday, an Education Ministry official named Achelis wrote to Sommer, ordering Forster's suspension from duty:

Based on the law of the re-establishment of professional civil servants of 7 April 1933 (RGB1.S.175ff) I deem it necessary to remove the Professor at the Medical Faculty of the university Dr Edmund Forster from office until a final decision has been made, this is with immediate effect. This suspension also applies to those activities which Dr Forster carries out in connection with his position at the university . . . I request that Professor Dr Forster is informed of this immediately.[19]

Sommer telephoned Forster at home, only to be told by Mila that he had just left to drive to Berlin to seek an urgent meeting with senior officials at the Education Ministry. The Curator then told Mila that her husband was forbidden from entering the clinic or any other department of the university, and must, until further notice, remain confined to his home.

Not long after, Sommer received a call from Schnoering, ordering him to impound the clinic's account books and the 16mm films of Zádor's 'tilting-table' experiments. With insufficient evidence having been produced to provide grounds for Forster's dismissal under new civil service rules regarding defamation of Adolf Hitler or the Nazi Party, the bureaucrats now intended to go through the clinic's accounts entry by entry in the hope of discovering irregularities sufficiently serious to merit Forster's dismissal. However, this scheme also came to nothing, with the accountant reporting no evidence of any fraud as suggested in the Oklitz letter. The equipment for the new X-ray building, the auditor noted, had been purchased from a highly reputable supplier, Reiniger, Gebbert & Jeifa, and it was, in his view, impossible that any monies were paid to either Professor Forster or anyone else in return for the contract. The auditor also confirmed that 'only the normal payments had been made to the doctors involved, as well as to a technical assistant for the X-ray apparatus, films, etc. that had already been there and purchases were only made once the quotations had been carefully scrutinised'.[20] The only grounds for concern, he concluded, regarded the payment of approximately six hundred Marks to purchase artworks from Konrad Lattner.

Even before they received this unhelpful auditor's report (which was not presented to them until 8 September), faced with the collapse of their scheme to have Forster disgraced and dismissed, Education Ministry officials instructed the ever compliant Curator to try a new tactic. He was to win support from the other Medical Faculty professors to have their colleague dismissed by casting doubt on his sanity while, at the same time, offering Forster a substantial financial inducement not to contest his dismissal and to leave quietly.

Sommer obediently arranged a faculty meeting for the morning of Tuesday 5 September, later informing Schnoering:

Today I discussed the suspension of Professor Forster with all five of his colleagues who unanimously agreed he could no longer remain at Greifswald. They requested that I approach Professor Forster and ask him to resign voluntarily on the understanding that I would secure him a pension amounting to three-quarters of his present salary. The professors believed that this would be the best solution both for the university, to avoid a scandal, and for Professor Forster himself. He is said to be a psychopath, sometimes highly emotional while at others very prone to depression [*ein Psychopath und zu Zeiten leicht erregbar, zu anderen Zeiten wieder sehr zu Depression geneigt].* None of his colleagues with whom I discussed Forster's personality in detail was in favour of allowing him to retain his job at Greifswald.[21]

That same afternoon he asked Forster to call at his office, noting afterwards:

> Dr Kroll had previously told me that he [Forster] was suffering from severe depression and asked me to treat him gently. I therefore carefully explained all the accusations made against him. He considered the comments of the matron . . . to be utterly fantastic . . . He denies ever having made any derogatory remarks about Minister Rust but does admit to the possibility that he might have made remarks about the Reichstag fire, although not quite in the way that has been alleged. He also denies ever having made any statements or offered any opinions about the speeches of the Reich Chancellor Adolf Hitler. He believes that his political activities in no way give cause for the Ministry to dismiss him from service. He frankly admitted that where the accusations of immorality were concerned his position at Greifswald was compromised, unless one also took into account the fact that the relationship had occurred several years ago, and that he himself had brought it to an end.
>
> After receiving your telephone instructions I once again made it clear to him that in order to grant him a pension the Ministry would have no option but to dismiss him from service on the grounds of his political activities.
>
> He replied that he understood this, requesting only that if at all possible, news of his dismissal from the service on the basis of Paragraph 4 of the Professional Civil Service Law would not be made public. He said that if he could receive a pension to the value of about three-quarters [of his old salary] he would regard this as acceptable. He also asked me to talk to his brother who happened to be in Greifswald at the time.

I happily agreed to this, since it enabled me to shift responsibility for advising Professor Forster who was very unwell. Forster then said goodbye to me in a calm and completely composed manner. I talked to Ministerial Councillor Schnoering by telephone about the possibility of setting aside the accusations of immorality and indecency against Forster, which was what five of the university's clinical directors and the university council had proposed. Forster would then resign voluntarily, so avoiding disciplinary proceedings and the consequent damage to his own and the faculty's reputation this would involve. Ministry Councillor Schnoering said he was in favour of my suggestions and asked me to put them in writing.[22]

Half an hour later Dirk called to see Sommer, who noted in his diary:

I read out to him the complete contents of the file and together we drew up a letter of resignation for Professor Forster and an accompanying letter, which was intended to secure the three-quarter pension. Embassy Councillor Forster took both of these with him, and said that he wanted to think the matter over further before advising his brother whether to accept. He too considered the offer of a three-quarter pension would be the best outcome.

Embassy Councillor Forster also asked for the accusations regarding his own wife to be clarified and for him to be informed of this immediately.[23]

A short while later Sommer wrote:

Schnoering has just telephoned to say that he and Achelis have agreed in principle to my proposal, although this should not be regarded as a formal decision by the Ministry. I knew, however, that if he and Achelis were in agreement, I could accede to Forster's pension request. At my request Schnoering assured me that it would be in order to inform Forster of their consent and this I immediately did.[24]

Forster then sent the Curator his brief note of resignation, addressed to the Education Minister: 'I would ask to be released or dismissed from the Prussian State Service.' With it he appended a note addressed to the Curator outlining the circumstances under which he would be willing to request voluntary retirement.

> After you informed me today that, following your telephone conversation with Ministerial Councillor Schnoering, the Ministry is prepared to award me a pension amounting to three-quarters of the legal pension and to grant me this as soon as I have handed in my request for dismissal, I enclose this request. I ask that you only forward my request to the Ministry once their offer of the three-quarter pension has definitely been secured for me.[25]

Despite Forster's agreement to retire quietly, the authorities continued to interview his medical colleagues in the hope of unearthing any evidence that would justify having him dismissed under Paragraph 4 of the Professional Civil Service Law. In this they were unsuccessful, with many of the staff, from junior assistants to senior physicians, courageously rejecting the allegations and standing by their beleaguered Director.

In the absence of any substantial evidence in support of Eugen Oklitz's wild allegations, Mila Forster clearly believed that it would be only a matter of time before her husband was vindicated and reinstated. Her first move, following Edmund's suspension, was to approach Dr Hermann Brüske, the Greifswald Nazi and lecturer who had been the intended blackmail victim of the Oklitzes, and appeal for his assistance. His response was to contact the university's rector, Professor Wilhelm Meisner. The latter subsequently noted in his diary:

> Dr Brüske informed me today that Frau Professor Forster had asked him to intervene, alleging that the Curator had pressured her husband into agreeing to a voluntary resignation. I gave Dr Brüske all the files and suggested he advise Frau Forster after reviewing the documents. When Dr Brüske returned the files to me it was with the comment that even if three-quarters of the allegations were false and only one-quarter of them were true then Forster could no longer be tolerated at Greifswald.[26]

Given that the plot against Forster had been initiated from the top of the Nazi Party, his response was hardly surprising. One telephone call to Berlin was all it would have taken for him to have backed off immediately. But the fact that Mila had approached him in the first place, together with her vehement opposition to Edmund accepting Sommer's offer of voluntary retirement, makes it highly likely that she was unaware of the extent of her husband's dealings with the Paris émigrés and blissfully ignorant of the true reason behind the Nazis' determination first to ruin and then to eliminate him. We may presume that Edmund kept the truth to himself to avoid placing her in needless danger.

Mila, in her ignorance, appears to have clung desperately to the belief that her husband would somehow be allowed to keep his job. The favourable auditor's report which appeared on Friday 8 September must have strengthened her resolve still further. One by one Oklitz's wild charges were being shown up as baseless slurs. Certainly she seems to have applied considerable pressure on Edmund not to go quietly but to fight to clear his reputation and win back his job in the face of such ridiculous and unfounded accusations. Perhaps she even challenged him to demonstrate the same will-power he had so often exhorted his hysterical patients to display.

Whatever approach she adopted, it worked. On the Friday after-noon Forster first telegraphed the Education Ministry to withdraw his letter of resignation and then telephoned Sommer to tell him that, on the advice of his wife, he had decided to continue the fight. Clearly shaken by this unexpected and unwelcome refusal to give in gracefully, Sommer immediately phoned Schnoering to ask what he should do next, only to be informed that he was 'not in a position to offer any advice and that Professor Forster should think things over for perhaps a week or so before deciding and meanwhile he would leave the letter of resignation locked up in his desk'.[27]

Meanwhile, news that Edmund Forster was being uncooperative was undoubtedly passed up the chain of command, until the decision was taken that more extreme measures would have to be adopted. If the dangerous professor would not jump, then he would have to be pushed.

That the whole sorry saga, from Oklitz's letter of denunciation to the Greifswald witch hunt that followed, was deliberately contrived to discredit and dismiss a man the Nazis considered a threat to their Führer's reputation is virtually certain. But what, if any, truth was there in his allegations of indecency and immorality? Apart from a brief affair with Fräulein Rietzkow, which Forster himself had quickly brought to an end, the remaining charges against him seem to have been nothing more than salacious gossip stemming from a clash of lifestyles and social attitudes.

Edmund Forster was a man of liberal views who, perhaps in part because he had been educated in the Netherlands and travelled widely, had a far more cosmopolitan and internationalist outlook than most of his colleagues. Although a staunch patriot who, shortly before his death, told his eldest son Balduin that he would certainly fight for his country in the event of another war, he alone at Greifswald had encouraged the employment of foreign doctors, supported his Jewish colleagues and refused to participate in the faculty's anti-Semitic or xenophobic acts. Conduct that would have passed unremarked upon in the sophisticated liberalism of Berlin rapidly became the topic of prurient tittle-tattle in this bleak little town on the plains of Prussia.

September had always been a significant month for Edmund Forster. He had been born on the 3rd and had married Mila on the 12th. The investigations into his alleged misconduct had started hearing evidence from witnesses on his fifty-fifth birthday and exactly one week later, at eight o'clock in the morning, Mila found him lying dead in their bathroom. He had a close-range bullet wound to the head. The bullet had been fired from a pistol that no one had known he possessed.

At around the time he had revealed the truth about Hitler's blindness to the émigré writers in Paris, a Nazi show trial was taking place in Cologne, where seventeen communists faced charges of murdering two SA men and wounding a third during a gun battle. On 24 July in anticipation of death sentences being passed on the accused, the local Nazi newspaper, *Westdeutscher Beobachter*, proclaimed: 'The iron desire for order of the National Socialist movement lies heavily and powerfully upon our people. There are to be no more halfway measures of sentimentality. Every act of opposition will be nipped in the bud.'[28]

Six of the accused were, as predicted, sentenced to death and a short time later executed in Klingelpütz Prison. They were beheaded not, as was normal practice, by guillotine, but, on Göring's specific orders, using an axe. It was a gruesome and bloody business that more than fulfilled the *Westdeutscher Beobachter* prediction that their end would offer a 'frightful warning to the entire German people'.[29]

Was Edmund's death suicide brought on by depression, as the university authorities insisted at the time? Or was it, like the fate of those Cologne communists, a 'frightful warning' to any other academics who might also be tempted to speak their minds?

Chapter Fifteen
THE STRANGE SUICIDE OF EDMUND FORSTER

Red of the morning, red of the morning, Thou lightest us to early death. Yesterday mounted on a proud steed, Today a bullet through the breast.
        Diary of Viktor Lutze, SA Commander, Hanover.[1]

After brooding over his fate all weekend, Edmund Forster woke early on the morning of Monday 11 September 1933 having decided, at some time during the long and sleepless night, to take his own life. Over the days of the disciplinary hearing he had become increasingly depressed and unbalanced. Dismissed from his job and with any future academic employment depending on Bernhard Rust, his professional life was effectively at an end. Furthermore, he lived in dread of the knock on the door that would announce a visit from the Gestapo. Between Thursday 31 August and Monday 4 September, he had, according to Mila, already twice attempted to take his own life, the first time by hanging and the second by swallowing pure nicotine, which is deadly when concentrated. On each occasion only her speedy intervention had prevented him from succeeding.

After dressing in his bedroom on the second floor of the Director's house, he went down to the basement kitchen, where his sons, thirteen-year-old Balduin and twelve-year-old Ruprecht, were finishing breakfast before leaving for the *Gymnasium* soon after seven o'clock. Lessons started promptly at 7.45 a.m. and the walk from their home on Ellernholzstrasse to the Friedrich-Ludwig-Jahn *Gymnasium* in Thälmannplatz took around fifteen minutes. Having bid them farewell, Edmund left Mila to clear the dishes and retired to his study, where he spent the next forty minutes morosely contemplating his fate. Ahead of him, he could see not only professional and personal disgrace but arrest and possibly imprisonment in the recently opened concentration camp at Dachau outside Munich. He was well aware of the fate that had befallen a fellow academic, sixty-year-old Professor Karl Wilmanns of Heidelberg University, who, only a few months earlier, had been accused of defaming Hitler. He was alleged to have likened the Führer to the founder of a crazy religious sect and prophesied he would end up in a lunatic asylum. According to Wilmanns's daughter, Ruth Lidz, then a twenty-three-year-old medical student and later a professor of psychiatry at Yale, her father had also claimed Hitler suffered from hysterical blindness at the end of the First World War and described Hermann Göring as a morphine addict. Wilmanns had immediately been arrested and imprisoned.[2] Forster realised his own case would be treated far more seriously because he had not merely betrayed confidential medical knowledge about his treatment of Hitler but handed over details from his former patient's medical file to enemies of the state abroad. Later Mila would confide to Balduin that his father believed, no matter where he went, the Gestapo would still be able to track him down and silence him.[3]

In an academic paper published earlier that same year he had stated that suicide need not always be considered pathological if it was the only rational answer to an impossible situation.[4] Now he saw that this was his only honourable way out. If, having rejected the offer of voluntary retirement, he was now sacked in disgrace from his directorship of the Nerve Clinic, no pension was likely to be paid and, banned from ever again working in Germany, he and his family would have to survive on his modest military pension. If, as he fully expected, he was then arrested and imprisoned, not only would his family's financial situation become even more precarious, but Mila's freedom too might be in jeopardy. Furthermore, as the children of a man branded an enemy of the Reich, Balduin and Ruprecht's prospects might also be blighted.

By taking the 'honourable' way out and shooting himself, he would ensure that his wife and sons would be left in peace by the Nazis and, with his university pension and the proceeds of a life insurance policy[5] to support them, they would be financially secure. Taking a 9mm service pistol from his desk drawer, he went up to the bathroom, sat down on the edge of the bath and shot himself through the head.[6]

Mila, working in the kitchen two floors below, heard the shot. Having run upstairs, she discovered her husband's body. Doctor Kroll, whom she fetched from the clinic, pronounced Edmund dead and had his body taken immediately to the hospital mortuary. The Greifswald police department was informed but no investigation took place, no post-mortem was conducted and no inquest was held. Three days later he was buried.

The day after Edmund's death Curator Sommer had sent Mila a handwritten letter that combined hypocrisy and humbug in equal measure:

Dear Lady,

Please allow me to express my sincerest sympathy following the death of your husband. I worked with your husband for five and a half years. By working together the two of us were able to come up with satisfactory solutions to many difficult problems. It was with great regret that I recently learned of the serious difficulties that your husband was faced with and, on the 4th of this month, from Dr Kroll about his severe depression and the overwrought emotional state. I was very grateful to Dr Kroll for letting me know because, one hour later, your husband visited me for the last time in his life and I was able, by a show of great friendliness and tact, to make our very difficult conversation less embarrassing for him. When he left me I was very happy to see that, as a result, he had calmed down completely. When shortly afterwards, on the advice of his brother, he presented me with his request for voluntary resignation, I hoped that the matter had been resolved in his own and his family's best interests. I am, therefore, especially deeply saddened that yesterday your husband came to a different conclusion and decided on a different course of action. By this final act all criticisms against him have been expunged. As a memorial he leaves many positive achievements as a doctor, as a scientist, and as a civil servant.

When I, as a Curator of the University, laid a wreath on his coffin, dear lady, it was with cordial sympathy towards you and your children, who have suffered such a tragic fate.'[7]

This was the official version of Forster's death and the official verdict, then as now, was that Forster cracked under the stress of the investigation and killed himself in a bout of depression. Such an outcome was only to be expected, so the argument runs, because even at the best of times Forster was always a little unbalanced. When, in 1973, Rudolph Binion carried out his researches at what was by then Greifswald's Ernst-Moritz-Arndt University, he met two archivists who chuckled at the mention of Forster's name: 'He was crazy,' one said while the other nodded in agreement.[8]

But what evidence is there to support the judgement that Forster killed himself, while the 'balance of his mind was disturbed'? And how much credence should be given to such a claim in the light of his resigned comment to the German émigrés in Paris: 'If in a short time you hear I have committed suicide . . . don't believe it'?

Let's start with the suggestion that, in the words of Curator Sommer, he was a 'psychopath' who displayed the extraordinary emotional highs and profound lows, characteristic of bipolar affective disorder also known as manic depression. While his medical colleagues regarded Forster as volatile, impatient and quick to anger, they never reported any signs of clinical depression, generally describing him as energetic, positive and optimistic. Not terms one can easily apply to someone experiencing regular bouts of depression.

When interviewed by Rudolph Binion, in 1973, Balduin insisted that his father was 'never depressed, did not possess an uncontrollable temper and was always thoughtful'.[9] Accepting that someone's persona can be very different in his personal and in his professional life, it would have been virtually impossible for anybody manifesting the violent mood swings alleged by the Curator to have concealed this fact from his family. Nor is there anything in the descriptions of his behaviour or mood during those final days to suggest he was becoming deeply depressed. Although Forster was, unsurprisingly, outraged by Oklitz's absurd allegations, distressed that they were taken seriously by the University and, probably, hurt that his Faculty colleagues refused to support him, his actions were never those of a man declining into suicidal depression.

His teenage son Balduin, who later became a specialist in forensic medicine, refuted the suggestion his father had ever appeared suicidal and Professor Nissen, a friend and colleague Forster met only a few weeks before the Oklitz letter was sent, described him as being his usual self: 'very sociable and talkative'.[10] There is also evidence from his surviving relatives that even during this period of crisis he continued to carry out mundane chores such as paying his domestic bills.

On learning about Oklitz's accusations, he drove immediately to Berlin to hold discussions with colleagues at the Charité and senior officials at the Education Ministry. He also telephoned his lawyer brother Dirk at the German Embassy in Paris asking him to come to Greifswald at once to give him legal advice.

During his last meeting with Curator Sommer Forster had argued his case cogently and had successfully negotiated an outcome designed to ensure his family's financial security. All of which suggest that far from being deeply depressed, he was dealing rationally, energetically and courageously with events.

Later, when stories of his involvement with Hitler at Pasewalk became known, it was also suggested that he had been driven to take his own life by terror over Nazi retribution and the belief that there was nowhere in the world where he could escape their vengeance. This is the explanation which Mila gave Balduin on the one and only occasion she ever made reference to the reasons for his father's death. Rudolph Binion recalls how, during his interview, he had asked Balduin why Edmund hadn't fled abroad: 'He replied, after a characteristically long pause, that Papi had told Mutti it was pointless, the Gestapo would pursue him abroad just the same.' Binion never doubted Balduin's total veracity. 'He spoke with deep earnestness and with a scrupulous sense of the importance of each and every word he uttered, as if he were before a high tribunal in permanent session.'[11]

Balduin accepted this explanation because that was what his mother told him. But since, as I shall show in a moment, there are reasons for suspecting Mila's role in her husband's death this explanation cannot be taken at face value.

If he was so fearful of arrest then why did he not did simply flee the country? He was not under house arrest or even surveillance. Nor, apart from the ban on his entering the clinic, were any restrictions placed on his movements. It is hard to believe that a man with the foresight to leave a copy of Hitler's damning Pasewalk medical notes in a Swiss bank vault before meeting the émigrés in Paris would not have given some thought to ways of escaping if the situation became desperate. He had, after all, expected Schwarzschild to publish the medical dossier, an action which must inevitably lead the authorities directly back to him. Perhaps, as Oklitz claimed in his letter, he did have his suitcases packed in readiness for immediate flight. In Opel-Popel he could have been in Poland within a few hours or France within a day or so. Had he decided to travel further afield, Greifswald was a harbour town and the Baltic was only twenty miles away. Although, as events transpired, he would have faced increasing dangers had he moved anywhere in Europe as the years passed, in 1933 he had no reason to know that.

As to worries over their financial situation, Forster had, as we have seen, succeeded in negotiating a settlement of three-quarters pension from the Ministry of Education. This meant that even though he would be prevented from working in Germany while the Nazis remained in power, he could enjoy a comfortable retirement. Furthermore, even though unable to work in Germany, Forster's fluency in Dutch, English and French together with his qualifications, experience and international reputation would have enabled him to find a job almost anywhere in Europe or even in the United States. By moving abroad, he could not only have found well-paid employment but also safeguarded himself and his family against Nazi reprisals.

But while Edmund might have almost welcomed the opportunity this would have given him to work abroad, unlike her cosmopolitan husband, Mila was a small-town girl whose knowledge of other countries seems to have been limited to occasional trips to France. Although speaking a little French, she does not appear to have been proficient in it or any other language. Living among strangers in a strange land cannot have held much appeal. 'It took courage even to flee,' says Otto Friedrich, 'courage and a certain amount of money, or friends abroad, or at least a sense that one did have the ability to make a new life for oneself and one's children. Flight also required a quality of despair, a conviction . . . that things would never get better, and that the only alternative was death.'[12]

But Mila was far from despairing. Indeed, as the days passed with most of her husband's colleagues failing to support Oklitz's more outrageous allegations, she became even more certain he would be vindicated and reinstated. When on 8 September the auditor's report cleared Forster of any financial malfeasance, Mila must have concluded that victory was within their grasp. That, once this disagreeable episode had been forgotten, their lives would return to normal and she could continue to enjoy the social status and financial security that came from being the wife of Herr Professor Doktor Forster. It was almost certainly for this reason that she persuaded Edmund to change his mind about Sommer's offer of a generous pension in exchange for his agreement to dismissal.

Her confidence in the outcome can have been due only to her ignorance about the true reason for her husband's persecution. An ignorance revealed by Mila's naive appeal for help to Dr Brüske who, for almost a decade, had been a dedicated member of Greifswald's long-established Nazi Party.

At first sight it may appear that her assertion, following his death, that Edmund had made two previous attempts to kill himself, once by hanging and the second time by taking nicotine, and been saved only by her prompt intervention, strongly supports the case for an ultimately successful suicide. In fact, it points in a far more sinister direction.

Everything we know of Edmund's character and his sense of honour as a German officer suggests that both hanging, the fate of the felon, and taking poison, the choice of the coward, were the least likely methods he would have chosen to end his life, especially if he already possessed a loaded pistol. But then, even his putative ownership of such a weapon, which was illegal under Prussian law, raises a further question over Mila's version of events. If Edmund had a gun, why would he have wasted time attempting death by hanging or poisoning?

No one seems to have known of the existence of this weapon before Mila found it lying beside his body. And if Edmund was not the owner of the gun, then, clearly, murder becomes far more likely than suicide. Mila's other claim that Edmund had attempted to poison himself by taking nicotine is equally curious and implausible, given that this colourless alkaloid is three times as toxic as arsenic and one and a half times as poisonous as strychnine. For a man of Forster's weight, a fatal dose would have been around 200mg of arsenic or 75mg of strychnine a fact of which someone with Forster's extensive pharmacological knowledge could scarcely have been unaware. If he had ingested this amount of the drug, either by swallowing or more likely, given the intense burning sensation it produces in the mouth, via an injection, only prompt and specialist medical attention could have prevented convulsions, followed by death from heart failure. Forster would have needed to have his stomach washed out and, probably, a drug such as atropine rapidly administered. Since she lacked both the training and the resources to accomplish this, Mila would have had to summon help from medical staff at the Nerve Clinic which would have made his attempted suicide public knowledge. Yet, according to Curator Sommer, the first he heard about this supposed earlier attempt was when he was informed of it by Dr Kroll.

If Mila lied about Edmund's two previous suicide attempts, she can only have done so in order to add greater credence to the notion that his death by gunshot was self-inflicted, which obviously points to her involvement in his murder. But what might this role have been and what would have persuaded her to collude with the Nazis in her husband's murder?

Although, in the absence of any surviving documentation, the following account is, inevitably, speculative, it matches the known facts and helps explain a number of otherwise inexplicable features of the case. Confronted with Edmund's refusal to accept voluntary dismissal the Nazis decided to have him killed and to pass off his murder as suicide. In this event it was important to ensure Mila did not raise any awkward questions about the manner of her husband's death and that she was away from home when the killing occurred. Had she been present to witness the arrival of the state authorised executioner then, of course, she too would have had to be killed to keep the matter secret, adding an unnecessary complication to the plan. Sometime over the weekend preceding his murder she was invited to the Curator's office on the pretext of discussing her objections to Sommer's proposed plan for her husband's dismissal. It is doubtful that Sommer himself would have dealt with her and more likely she met someone who presented himself as an official from the Ministry of Education. After swearing Mila to absolute secrecy he told her that Forster was going to be dismissed for betraying both his professional oath and the Reich by revealing highly confidential medical secrets concerning the Führer to enemies of the State. Acts of treason for which he could quite properly be arrested and imprisoned.

The extent of the details about the nature of Hitler's illness and the type of treatment Forster had employed cannot be known. What we do know, however, is that Mila was at some point made aware that Hitler had suffered from hysterical blindness since, many years later, she confided this fact to Balduin. If, as suggested in the previous chapter, Edmund sought to protect her by remaining silent about this fact as well as his meetings with the German émigrés then she can only have learned of the matter from the Nazis themselves. Having made this terrifying disclosure, the official then presented Mila with a simple choice. She must either drop her objections to her husband's dismissal or face extremely grave consequences, including Edmund's sacking and the removal of all his pension rights followed by his arrest and imprisonment. She and her sons would then have to survive as best they could under the stigma of having a husband and father imprisoned for treason. Not only would Balduin and Ruprecht grow up in poverty but their educational and employment opportunities would be severely jeopardised. Such a prospect would have clearly terrified Mila who, having experienced great poverty during childhood, would have been determined to spare her sons the same fate.

The extent of her concern about ensuring their financial security can be judged from a comment which Lilly made in a letter to Dirk following Edmund's funeral: 'Mila does not say a word about his death,' she told her husband. 'All she talks about is money!'[13]

Having painted the bleakest picture of what would happen if Edmund refused to go quietly, the official now sought to reassure the despairing Mila that there still remained one final opportunity for her to safeguard her family's future.

Early on Monday morning an official from the Ministry of Education would visit her husband at home and make one final attempt to persuade him to accept voluntary dismissal on the terms already agreed. If he consented then, despite the seriousness of his conduct, no further action would be taken. He next suggested that, since her husband would find it easier to discuss matters frankly were the two of them alone in the house, Frau Forster must ensure she was absent from home between seven thirty and eight o'clock on Monday morning. The official then concluded with a grim warning that if she mentioned their conversation to anyone, her sons included, she would face immediate arrest and lengthy imprisonment. Whether Mila understood the true implication of his order that she stay away from the house on Monday morning is unlikely ever to be known. Perhaps she took the official at his word and believed something good might still be salvaged from the mess that Edmund's indiscretions had created. In the event she simply obeyed his instruction. With breakfast over Mila told her sons that, since it was a fine morning, she intended walking with them to the gymnasium.

No sooner had they left the house than a waiting Nazi killer climbed the stone steps to the front door and rang the bell. Unsuspectingly, Edmund, whom Mila would have told to expect a visitor from the Ministry of Education, let the man inside. The moment the door closed behind them, the Nazi drew out a 9mm pistol, ordered Edmund into the bathroom on the first floor and shot him once through the head at point blank range. Then, dropping the gun beside the lifeless body, he casually left the house and returned to Berlin where he reported his mission accomplished. A fact confirmed the following day in a letter from Dr K. Deibner, the University's Director, to Bernhard Rust: 'This is to most obediently inform you that Professor Doctor Forster at present on leave took his own life on the 11th of this month.'[14]

That the Nazis were sufficiently ruthless to have carried out such an assassination is not open to doubt. Between Hitler's accession to power and Forster's death, more than five hundred individuals met violent deaths at the hands of the Nazis. Some were simply gunned down, kicked or beaten to death, others were said to have been 'shot while trying to escape from custody'. But a significant number of senior academics and political leaders were, like Forster, alleged to have 'committed suicide'. For example, Dr Hermann Neumann, honorary member of the senate of Giessen University, who it was claimed had killed himself after being informed of his forcible retirement.

Less than a year after Forster's death, on Saturday, 30 June 1934 – the infamous 'Night of the Long Knives' – hundreds were slaughtered, frequently in the most brutal manner and often for the most banal of reasons. Among the victims was Gustav von Kahr, the official who eleven years before had failed to support Hitler's *Putsch*. Now aged seventy-three and living in quiet retirement Kahr was dragged from home and his grossly disfigured body later discovered in a swamp close to Dachau concentration camp. He had been hacked to death with pick-axes. Even complete innocence offered no protection. Willy Schmidt, a music critic, was the victim of mistaken identity when his SS killers confused him with another man of the same name. When his fiancée contacted the police to ask them to find out what had happened, she was told contemptuously: 'Do you really think he is still alive?'[15] A few days later his remains were returned to his relatives in a coffin marked with a warning that it was not to be opened.

Finding a willing assassin from within the ranks of the Gestapo or SA would have caused no difficulties, since there were scores of men only too happy to commit murder without ever wondering, let alone asking, why. As Heinz Höhne points out: 'They did not think; they simply obeyed. They did not grumble; they simply acted. Without a word they carried out the duty assigned to them . . . All they wanted to know were the names of their victims.'[16]

Many of these killings were faked to look like suicide. After SS Hauptsturmführer Kurt Gildisch shot Erich Klausener, former head of the Police Section of the Prussian Ministry of the Interior, on the orders of Reinhard Heydrich, he telephoned his boss from the victim's office to ask for further instructions. 'The unnaturally high-pitched voice from the Prinz-Albrecht Strasse ordered him to fake a suicide,' reports Heinz Höhne, 'so he placed the Mauser near Klausener's limp right hand and put a double guard on the door. As far as the Third Reich was concerned, the Klausener Case was settled.'[17]

Did Mila know that Edmund had been murdered or did she convince herself that he had, indeed, taken his own life in a state of deep depression? Certainly Dirk and Lilly Forster seem to have believed she colluded, if only by keeping silent, in Edmund's violent end. But even if they had their suspicions, given the circumstances of the time, there was absolutely nothing they could have done about it. Dirk would never have dared to challenge the authority of the state, especially as to do so would have placed Lilly, with her Jewish background, in grave danger. Dirk's feelings towards his brother's death may, however, be judged from his refusal to attend the funeral, sending Lilly in his place. As for her, she refused ever to speak to Mila again, although she remained on good terms with Balduin and Ruprecht. Within the family she scathingly referred to Mila as 'that old Nazi in a fur coat'.[18] Even today, Dirk's daughter-in-law Pam and his granddaughter Marie Rose believe that Edmund was murdered and that Mila may well have colluded in his death.

Reactions to Forster's death and explanations for it differed widely. At the Charité Hospital his former boss Karl Bonhöffer attributed it to a 'depressive crisis'[19] while Wilhelm Meisner, the Rector at Greifswald, commented, somewhat curiously, that 'If Forster had had a different wife and a different consultant he would not have come to such a sad end but would have been able to cope with events.'[20]

An announcement of Forster's death appeared in the local newspaper and subsequently brief obituaries appeared in a number of foreign newspapers. On 12 September the *New York Times* published a short report by their Berlin correspondent:

> Professor Edmund Forster, head of the university clinic for nervous diseases, shot himself dead at his home here today. He had been put 'on leave' by the Nazi Minister of Education pending an investigation into 'offences' against him.

No hint was ever published by the authorities as to what these alleged offences might be. The following day *Le Temps* noted that 'The Jewish [*sic*] Professor Forster, a specialist in nervous disorders, suspended from his position at the University of Greifswald, has committed suicide.' Three days later the London *Times*' 'own correspondent' noted simply that 'Professor Edmund Forster, who was recently retired from his post as director of the clinic for nervous disorders at Greifswald University, has committed suicide.'

Edmund's funeral took place at half-past three in the afternoon on Thursday 14 September in the chapel of the Nerve Clinic.[21] A Protestant priest, Pastor Schwedendick, from nearby St Jacob's, presided over the proceedings. Senior members of the faculty, who only days earlier had been determined to disgrace Forster, turned out in force. Several read eulogies. Professor Bonhöffer and several former colleagues from the Charité made the journey from Berlin. Lilly Forster was unimpressed by the service, writing to Dirk that same evening:

> I do not know whether you will get my letter before you leave for Paris, but I promised to write to you. You asked about the funeral. It is hard to describe, and I shall have to tell you about it when we meet. A great many people were present. The priest was very bad and mother told him so afterwards in no uncertain terms.
>
> Bonhöffer's speech was half-hearted, but went down well,

mainly because he had merely bothered to attend. The Rector was very moving. A great many flowers and sincere expressions of grief from the [clinic] staff. Salutes fired by the Marine Association. You should have been here to say something nice. That was what was missing the most.[22]

Edmund Forster's body was interred in Greifswald's Neuer Friedhof cemetery. Today the simple granite headstone, bearing only his name, dates and title, marks the final resting-place of a man described by his friend and colleague Ludwig Zürn as: 'an excellent scholar, an outstanding teacher, and the saviour of the sick'.[23]

His grave in the quiet cemetery, hardly visible behind a tangled screen of undergrowth, appears as neglected and forgotten as the strange story of Edmund Forster himself.

Chapter Sixteen
AFTER THE FUNERAL

The tumult and the shouting die, the Captains and the Kings depart.

Rudyard Kipling, 'Recessional', 1897[1]

On Tuesday, 3 October 1933 Mila and her sons left Greifswald for ever. They went first to Munich and then, in 1934, to Berlin, moving into a well-appointed apartment at 30 Stübbenstrasse in the fashionable Bayrisches Viertel district. Over the next ten years she devoted herself to raising Balduin and Ruprecht, who had inherited both their father's brain and his interest in medicine. She is officially listed throughout this decade as a widow and never appears to have gone out to work. Early in the spring of 1944 she moved to Göttingen, and a week later her former apartment block at 30 Stübbenstrasse was totally destroyed by an Allied bombing raid.

Relationships with the rest of the family remained strained. When Mila and Dirk did correspond it was mostly to argue over money. In December 1940 he wrote to Mila's brother Paul Bretschneider:

> There is nothing good to be said about Mila. The row over her inheritance [following the sale of her house in Deisenhofen] is drawing to an end but what she finally gets her hands on will be only a small part of what she expected to get her hands on. As you know, I was opposed to this settlement, since I am convinced that she will immediately spend all the money.

But she placed me under so much pressure that in the end I agreed just to put an end to the matter . . . Mila is extremely difficult to deal with. So far as the inheritance is concerned it was I who bore the brunt of her strange behaviour.[2]

In March 1941 Dirk again wrote to Paul, thanking him for a letter and adding: 'I have given up worrying about Mila, although I feel sorry for the boys. But I will only make contact with her again if she adopts a different and less hostile manner towards me.'[3]

Balduin and Ruprecht followed in their late father's footsteps and pursued careers in medicine. Balduin, who studied in Graz and Göttingen, gained his doctorate with a thesis on alcoholism and later became a professor at the Institute for Forensic Medicine in Göttingen. He died on 28 December 1999 aged seventy-nine and was buried in Bad Krozingen.

After the Anschluss, in March 1938, Ruprecht went to Switzerland to study, and later joined the anaesthesia department at Basle University Clinic, where he worked until his untimely death from cancer in August 1955 at the age of thirty-four.

Lilly, Dirk and their family were never reconciled with Mila, and when she died on 27 January 1970 none of the family, apart from Balduin, attended the funeral.

Dirk, because of his marriage to Lilly, had any prospects of advancement in the diplomatic service blocked after 1933, although he remained in his Paris job until 1936 when, his family claim, he was suspended following an argument with Hitler over the latter's renunciation of the Locarno Pact, a non-aggression treaty signed in 1925 by Germany, Italy, Great Britain, France and Belgium. During a meeting in the Chancellery, he said the Führer warned him: 'If you talk about this meeting to anyone you and your family will be killed.'[4]

If such an encounter occurred, then Dirk was certainly being uncharacteristically confrontational, since his normal response to conflict was to search for a compromise while keeping his head well below the parapet. When he discovered that one of his colleagues in the German Embassy in Paris was arranging passports for Jews to help them escape persecution, for example, he warned the man that he would get into serious trouble. But he neither reported nor assisted him. However, although suspended, he was not dismissed for another four years. In 1940, when he finally left the diplomatic service, Dirk moved with Lilly to Berlin, where they lived until 1943, when their apartment was destroyed in a raid. After the war he worked with the Allies and made occasional radio broadcasts. He died on 27 February 1975, and Lilly followed on 15 September of the same year.

After the First World War, Karl Kroner, the doctor whose account of Hitler's treatment at Pasewalk first identified Edmund Forster as the neuropsychiatrist concerned, practised as a neurologist at four different Berlin hospitals, as well as establishing a successful private practice. He published widely in his field and was the first physician to point out the value of the Wassermann test for syphilis in cases of drug and nervous disorders. On 11 November 1936, the day after the Nazis' anti-Jewish 'Crystal Night' pogrom, he was arrested and sent to the Sachsenhausen concentration camp. There he might well have perished but for a piece of extraordinary good fortune.

In 1920 he had married Dr Irmgard Liebich, a colleague he had met in one of the Berlin hospitals where he was a consultant. 'After a few years, they thought there were too many doctors in the family,' recalled their son Klaus Kroner, who was for thirty years Professor of Industrial Engineering at the University of Massachusetts, 'so she returned to university to study linguistics, especially Scandinavian languages.'[5] This led to friendships with university students from all over Scandinavia, especially those from Iceland. Soon the Kroners' Berlin home was playing host to Icelandic celebrations at which dozens would turn up to listen to folk music, talk and eat. On returning to Iceland, many of these students gained prominent positions in politics, medicine, the press and other professions.

Following her husband's arrest, Irmgard turned to Helgi Briem, Iceland's representative at the Danish Embassy,[6] for help. Briem immediately set to work to secure Kroner's freedom by applying subtle psychological pressure to von Jagow, the chief of the Berlin Storm Troopers, using his boasts about the amount of influence he possessed to challenge him to do something. After twelve days of imprisonment, Karl Kroner, his head shaven and his face gaunt from starvation, was brought to von Jagow's office, where a deal was arranged: he would be given his freedom as long as he left the country by midnight. It was a race against time, since the only flight out of Berlin that would meet von Jagow's deadline was leaving at six that evening. A call to the airline's office showed that all the seats had been taken, but once again Briem came to the rescue, using his influence to have a passenger bumped off the flight. He then accompanied Kroner to the airport, where Gestapo officers made a final attempt to rearrest Kroner. Using his diplomatic papers, Briem insisted on escorting Kroner on to the aircraft and then waited until it had taken off.

Kroner's wife and twelve-year-old son, Klaus, followed a few days later by train. They were permitted to take only ten Marks and whatever luggage they could carry; their home and all their other possessions were confiscated.

Once in Iceland, the family found that their friends had rented an apartment, stocked it with food and made interest-free loans to tide them over. Unable to obtain a licence to practise medicine, Karl remained unemployed, except for occasional labouring jobs for the British occupation force. Irmgard managed to find some work teaching languages at the university. Both had applied for visas to travel to the United States, and it may have been in the hope of expediting these documents that in 1943 Karl made a statement to an agent from US Naval Intelligence about his dealings with Hitler in 1918.

However, it was not until after the war had ended that their visas finally arrived and the family departed to make a new life in the

United States. There Karl worked as a specialist consultant at a number of hospitals, including the Professional Hospital in Yonkers. He died peacefully in August 1954; Irmgard died in 1973. Both had asked for their ashes to be returned to Iceland and today they are interred in Fossvog cemetery.[7]

Dr Julius Zádor, whose research with the tilting table caused Edmund Forster so much trouble, was less fortunate. When last heard of, in 1938, he was working as a doctor in a concentration camp hospital, and he is believed to have perished in Auschwitz.

Nothing further can be confirmed about Eugen and Louise Oklitz, whose names do not appear on any of the National Socialist Party records. One unsubstantiated story claims that Eugen was killed fighting on the Eastern Front.

In the year of Forster's death, Greifswald University changed its name to Ernst-Moritz-Arndt, after the eighteenth-century German writer and patriot who was educated there and at the University of Jena. Following Napoleon's invasion of Prussia in 1806, Arndt wrote a number of stirring polemics under the general title of *The Spirit of the Times* (*Der Geist der Zeit*), as well as several German patriotic songs.

In 1919 the Pasewalk *Lazarett* was returned to its civilian owner and converted back into a hostelry run by Paul Meyer. Thereafter it passed rapidly through a number of different hands, becoming increasingly run down and derelict until, in 1934, it was purchased by the Nazi Party. By this time it was in such a poor state of repair that much of it had to be demolished, with only the central portion remaining. Converted into a *Weihestätte* (shrine) by the party, with a bronze bust of Hitler in the alcove where his iron-framed bed had once stood, it became a place of pilgrimage for high-ranking Nazis, being a special favourite of the Pomeranian SA and SS. Hitler, however, never returned to the scene of his 'vision'.

The extent of the myth-information generated around Pasewalk can be judged from an introduction to a book of Hitler's early speeches, published in 1923 by Adolf-Viktor von Körber. In a biographical introduction to *Adolf Hitler – His Life and His Speeches*, Kürber, an ardent Nazi Party supporter, described his version of what had taken place there:

> In the infirmary of the Pomeranian village Pasewalk a solitary bed stands in a darkened room. A nurse lays cooling bandages on the patient's dead eyes. He starts in fright . . . The nurse's arms support the tortured one, who sits upright. She wants to push him back down on to the pillows, this uncanny patient brought there blind and mute, this – how does his personal form read? – 'lance corporal, collapsed in enemy gas attack. "Yellow-Cross gas" poisoning', she knows no more about him.
>
> Yet she sees the ineffable suffering of this semi-corpse whose facial expressions and whose gestures pointing into the distance indicate more and more definitely from day to day that he knows that something frightful has broken in upon Germany! The nurse holds the twitching, feverish soldier of the betrayed army in her arms. And a higher constraint brings good words to her lips, words of faith in Germany's resurrection. And a miracle comes to pass. He who was consecrated unto eternal night, who had suffered through his Golgotha in this hour, spiritual and bodily crucifixion, pitiless death as on the cross, with senses alert, one of the lowliest out of the mighty host of broken heroes – he acquires *sight*! The spasms of his features subside. And in a trance peculiar to the dying seer alone, new light fills his dead eyes, new radiance, new life![8]

In 1945 the town of Pasewalk became part of the Ocker Line, a desperate last-ditch stand against rapidly advancing Soviet forces. Allied bombing raids destroyed 80 per cent of the ancient buildings and most of the civilian population fled. Although the *Weihestätte* survived the war more or less intact, it was pulled down soon after by the Soviets, eager to obliterate all remnants of fascism. Later a small sports pavilion was constructed on the site and Herr Brose, curator of the town's museum, remembers that, as a child in the 1950s, he played in its cellar, little realising this was the only part of the former Schützenhaus to have survived. Today even that has gone and the disused sports pavilion is shuttered and decaying. There are plans to build houses on the site but, for the moment, only tall grass grows on the spot where Forster practised his draconian therapies, a blind lance-corporal's sight was 'miraculously' restored and Hitler became convinced of his divinely inspired destiny to lead Germany to victory.

On a moonless winter's night an icy wind blows across the Prussian plains and shakes the bare branches of poplars flanking the field where the *Lazarett* once stood. The rest is silence.

NOTES

Chapter One: 'Hitler Lacked the Personality Ever to Become a Leader!'

1 Viktor Lutze, SA leader. From a speech delivered on Reich Labour Day, September 1934.
2 Meteorological records for Nürnberg, 7 September 1948, show a high of 19°C with seven-eighths cloud cover.
3 Kempner is today best remembered as the man whose researches brought to light the notorious Wannsee Protocol, a verbatim record of the 1942 meeting at which the 'Final Solution' of the 'Jewish problem' was openly discussed.
4 The Trial of German Major War Criminals, Proceedings of the International Military Tribunal Sitting at Nürnberg, Germany, Part 1, page 50.
5 F. Wiedemann, *Der Mann der Feldherr Werden Wollte*, pages 23–4.
6 From an interview by journalist Julia Shearer, Regional Oral History Office, University of California.
7 Otto Friedrich, *Before the Deluge*, page 309.
8 Cross-examination taken verbatim from R. Kempner, *Das Dritte Reich im Kreuzverhör*, pages 73–4.
9 Wiedemann, *op. cit.*, page 26.
10 Rudolph Binion, 'Foreword' to E. Weiss, *The Eyewitness*, page i.
11 Lloyd George, who had recently met Hitler at Berchtesgaden, described him in these glowing terms in a *Daily Express* article

written at the request of Lord Beaverbrook. Cited in 'Hitler's Olympians', *Observer Magazine*, 29 September 1968.

12 Alan Wykes, quoted in David Calvert Smith, *Triumph of the Will – Original Screenplay*, page 4.

13 William Shirer, *Berlin Diary*, page 23.

14 Barrie Pitt, 'Pageantry of Power', in Alan Wykes, *The Nuremberg Rallies*, page 6.

15 Ernst von Weizsäcker, cited in Piers Brendon, *The Dark Valley*, page 95. Weizsäcker was the father of President Richard von Weizsäcker, and served as Ribbentrop's State Secretary between 1938 and 1943.

16 P. Merkl, *Political Violence under the Swastika*, page 539.

17 Martin Middlemarch, *The Nuremberg Raid*, page 87.

18 *Ibid.*, page 92.

19 Albrecht Dürer, born Nürnberg 21 May 1471, died there 6 April 1528. Painter and printmaker recognised as the greatest of the German Renaissance artists, with work including altarpieces, religious paintings, numerous portraits, self-portraits and copper engravings.

20 Hans Sachs, born Nürnberg 5 November 1494, died there 19 January 1576. Popular *Meistersinger* and poet whose work had a strong religious influence.

21 Neal Ascherson quoted in *Observer Magazine*, 22 September 1968.

22 The film's title, as with two others she made of the Reich Party Rallies, was taken from the title of the rally itself.

23 Brendon, *op. cit.*, page 95.

24 From a broadcast by Joseph Goebbels, 19 April 1945, to mark Hitler's birthday on the 20th. Quoted in *The Times* of London, 20 April 1945.

25 Brendon, *op. cit.*, page 95.

26 Joachim C. Fest, *Hitler*, page 266.

27 Otto von Wegener, *Hitler – Memoirs of a Confidant*, page 111.

28 Joachim von Ribbentrop, *The Ribbentrop Memoirs*, page 32.

29 *Frankfurter Zeitung*, 27 January 1923, repeating the story from a weekly 'political letter mailed confidentially by the Ring-Verlag'.

30 Karl II von Wiegand in *Cosmopolitan*, April 1939, page 152. He was quoting Hitler from 1921 or 1922.

Chapter Two: Thirty Days at the Shooting House

1 Quoted from 'Experimental Analysis of Hysterical Blindness: A Follow-up Report and New Experimental Data'. Archives of General Psychiatry, page 257.

2 In 1937 Lord Halifax, mistaking Hitler for a footman, was on the point of handing him his hat when von Neurath, the Nazi Foreign Minister, stopped him in the nick of time by frantically whispering, *'Der Führer! Der Führer!'*

3 The weather report for Pasewalk on 21 October shows a clear sky and almost seven hours of sunshine, with a maximum temperature of 16°C.

4 Although many biographers and historians follow Hitler's account in *Mein Kampf* by stating that the attack and his blindness occurred on the night of 13/14 October, original documents show that it was not until the 15th that this took place. See, for example: Namentliche Verlustliste: Ort und Tag des Verlustes La Montagne 15.10.18 Fünftägige Meldungen der Lazarette: Oudenaarde Zugang am 15.10.18, Abzug am 16.10.18; Res.Laz.Pasewalk Zugang am 21.10.18; Verlustliste des Res.Inf.Regiments 16: Am 15.10.18 bei La Montagne gaskrank ins Lazarett; Kriegsstammrolle: 15.10.18 bei Montagne gaskrank.

5 Adolf Hitler, *Mein Kampf* (Manheim translation), page 183; Hans Raub account in NSDAP archive.

6 Hans Raab letter, 5 August 1939. Copy in Bundesarchiv.

7 Kriegsministerium, 'Grundsätze für die Behandlung und Beurteilung der sogen. Kriegsneurotiker,' Berlin 29.1.1917; UA Tübingen, 308/89, cited by P. Lerner, *Hysterical Men*, page 333.

8 *Ibid.*, page 281.

9 Since no account of Hitler's journey from Ghent to Pasewalk exists, this description has been based on a number of contemporary reports and photographs.

10 The description of Pasewalk railway station is taken from a contemporary photograph.

11 The little town's only claim to fame was that it was the birthplace,

in the nineteenth century, of Oskar Picht, who invented the first typewriter for the blind.

12 Pasewalk museum archive.

13 *Ibid.*

14 *Ibid.*

15 Information about Dr Karl Kroner was kindly provided to me by his son, Professor Klaus Kroner.

16 Hitler's general attitude and conversations with other patients are all drawn from Ernst Weiss's novel, *Der Augenzeuge* (*The Eyewitness*). Although written as fiction, there are, as I shall explain in Chapter 13, excellent grounds for believing that this account is based on facts provided to Weiss in 1933 by Edmund Forster, shortly before the psychiatrist's death.

17 Account of Forster's attitude towards Hitler and quote regarding the doctor's therapy from *The Eyewitness*, page 103.

Chapter Three: The Hitlers of Braunau-am-Inn

1 August Kubizek, *Young Hitler*, page 23.

2 This description of Hitler's birth is based on J. Constantinesco, *Hitler Secret*. Constantinesco was a journalist who, shortly after Hitler's rise to power, visited all the places associated with him and interviewed many who had known him.

3 Albert Speer, *Erinnerungen*, page 313.

4 Description of Braunau-am-Inn from a booklet by Hermann Sprecht, *Ein Geschichts – Stadt und Landschaftsbild* (1900).

5 Konrad Heiden, *Der Führer*, page 40.

6 W. Maser, *Hitler*, page 10.

7 *Daily Mirror*, 14 October 1933.

8 Hans Frank, *Im Angesicht des Galgens*, page 330.

9 *Ibid.*

10 *Paris Soir*, 6 August 1939.

11 Frank, *op. cit.*, page 94.

12 Rudolph Binion, 'Hitler's Concept of Lebensraum', page 207.

13 B.F. Smith, *Adolf Hitler*, page 25.

14 Hugh Trevor-Roper, *Hitler's Secret Conversations*, page 520. Hitler made the comment on 20 August.

15 Cited in 'Hitler as his Mother's Delegate', an article by Helm Stierlin,

in *History of Childhood Quarterly*, Vol. 3, No. 4, 1976, page 492. Hitler uses the word '*Prügeln*', which can mean a thrashing, birching or beating.

16 Heiden, *op. cit.*, page 44.
17 Maser, *op. cit.*, page 33.
18 August Kubizek, *Young Hitler*, facing page 102.
19 Heiden, *op. cit.*, page 47.

Chapter Four: The Forsters of Amsterdam

1 Salman Rushdie, *Step Across the Line*.
2 G.H. Macdermott was a music-hall singer who achieved tremendous popular success with this song during the diplomatic crisis of 1878. Both the writer of the song, G.W. Hunt, and the singer saw themselves as serious commentators on foreign affairs. Ultimately Russia retreated from Bulgaria, restoring both it and Macedonia to Ottoman Turkish rule. Although hailed as a diplomatic coup for British Prime Minister Benjamin Disraeli, this meant that the Balkan Slavs suffered misrule under the Ottoman Empire for another generation. Macdermott died in 1901 and is buried in West Norwood Cemetery, south-east London.
3 The chorus continues: 'We've fought the Bear before . . . and while we're Britons true / The Russians shall not have Constantinople.'
4 The term comes from Gottlieb Biedermeier (*Bieder* meaning 'plain' and Meier being a common German surname), a fictitious character who featured in satirical publications during the nineteenth century, who was claimed to personify solid but unimaginative middle-class virtues. It describes a design style popular in Germany, Austria and northern Europe between 1815 and 1860. Although applied mainly to furniture, the term was also used to describe painting, sculpture, porcelain, glass and even music.
5 Deutsche Revolution (German Revolution) or Märzrevolution (March Revolution) is the term applied to events between March 1848 and 1849. Supporters and participants in the revolution are known as the Achtundvierziger (Forty-Eighters).
6 Karl Marx, born 1818 in Trier on the Mosel, studied law and political sciences before becoming editor of a liberal Cologne newspaper. This was shut down by the authorities in 1843 after

Marx had exposed the sufferings of agricultural workers and criticised censorship. He moved first to Paris and then to Brussels, where in February 1848, with his friend Friedrich Engels, he wrote *The Communist Manifesto*. His return to Cologne after the March Revolution was short-lived and his influence on it negligible.

7 During the Civil War Schurz commanded the 3rd Division of the Army of Virginia and later the 3rd Division of the Army of the Potomac, taking part in the Battles of Bull Run (July 1862), Fredericksburg (December 1862), Chancellorsville (May 1863) and Gettysburg (July 1863). His books included *The Life of Henry Clay* (1887) and *Abraham Lincoln* (1891). He died on 14 May 1906.

8 From his address to the Anti-Imperialistic Conference, Chicago, 17 October 1899.

9 Otto Dietrich, *Before the Deluge*, page 221.

10 *Ibid.*

11 Pam Forster, personal communication.

Chapter Five: Down and Out in Vienna

1 Konrad Heiden, *Der Führer*, page 61.

2 August Kubizek, *Young Hitler*, page 6.

3 *Ibid.*, page 10.

4 *Ibid.*, page 13.

5 *Ibid.*, page 11.

6 *Ibid.*, pages 11–12.

7 Rudolph Binion, personal communication.

8 Kubizek, *op. cit.*, page 41.

9 *Ibid.*, page 81.

10 Dr Eduard Bloch, 'My Patient Hitler', *Collier's Magazine*, 15 March 1941.

11 Binion, personal communication.

12 *Black's Medical Dictionary*, 1910, page 414.

13 Kubizek, *op. cit.*, page 82.

14 Binion, personal communication.

15 Kubizek, *op. cit.*, page 85.

16 NSDAP Central Archives NS26/65/38. Account by Bloch in his own handwriting dated 7 November 1938. Bloch handed a copy to the Gestapo in 1938 and took a second one with him to America

when he fled there as a refugee in 1940. Quoted by W. Maser, *Hitler*, page 41.

17 Kubizek, *op. cit.*, page 86.

18 Bloch, *op. cit.*

19 Binion, personal communication.

20 Kubizek, *op. cit.*, page 143.

21 In this, as in his other 'creative' endeavours, Hitler was hardly being original. In an article 'The Art Work of the Future', written in 1849, his musical hero Richard Wagner included a poetic version of the Nordic legend of Wieland the Smith that he intended to turn into an opera, an ambition that was never realised.

22 Nerin Gun, *Eva Braun*, page 48.

23 The problem was simply too big for the resources available. In 1901 some 103,000 impoverished people were in need of food and a night's lodgings. In 1911 the asylums of just one charitable foundation, run by the Epstein family, were caring for 226,000 men, 50,000 boys, 61,000 women and 46,000 children up to the age of fourteen.

24 E. Kläger, *Durch die Wiener Quartiere*, page 31.

25 Adolf Hitler, *Mein Kampf* (Manheim translation), page 20.

26 J. Greiner, *Das Ende des Hitler-Mythos*, pages 13–14.

27 Jean Constantinesco, *Hitler Secret*, pages 2–5.

28 Hitler, *op. cit.*, page 19.

Chapter Six: Journey into Mind

1 Garth Wood, *The Myth of Neurosis*, page 40.

2 Marie Rose von Wesendonk Family Archive, Tuscany.

3 *Ibid.*

4 'Versuche über das Verhalten des Muskels wenn Muskel und Nerv zugleich elektrisch durchströmt werden', dissertation, Kaiser-Wilhelms University, Strasbourg, 1901.

5 Wood, *op. cit.*, page 40.

6 Von Wesendonk, *op. cit.*

7 *Ibid.*

8 'Rapport sur deux cas d'adéno-papillomes multiples du gros intestine avec carcinoma cylindrique concomitant', Rev.méd. Suisse rom., Vol. 23, 1903, pages 562–70.

9 Von Wesendonk, *op. cit.*

10 Oliver Sacks, 'The Great Awakening', *Listener*, Vol. 88, pages 521–4.

11 Laplace, who was briefly Minister of the Interior under Napoleon Bonaparte, is said to have made this reply when on receiving a copy of Laplace's *Méchanique Céleste*, the Emperor commented: 'You have written this huge book on the system of the world without once mentioning the author of the universe.' Cited in Eric Temple-Bell, *Men of Mathematics*, page 63.

12 Editorial, *Medical Record*, Vol. 23, 1883, page 710.

13 Ernest Jones cited in Ben Shephard, *A War of Nerves*, page 6.

14 Cited in S. Wessely and T. Lutz, 'Neurasthenia', in G. Berrios and R. Porter, *A History of Clinical Psychiatry*, pages 509–44.

15 David Healy, *The Creation of Psychopharmacology*.

16 Cited in F.C. Rose and W.F. Bynum, *Historical Aspects of the Neurosciences*, page 8.

17 Von Wesendonk, *op. cit.*

18 Stefan George was a mystical poet, born in Rüdesheim in the Rhineland on 12 November 1868. His fame and influence as a poet, especially within a group of friends and followers known as the Stefan George Circle, were based largely on his idealised visions of ancient Greece and medieval Europe, together with a fanciful 'Oriental' culture. Among its members was Claus von Stauffenberg, the army officer who attempted to assassinate Adolf Hitler in 1944. George's book of poems, *Das Neue Reich* (*The New State*), published in 1928, describes a vision of a German Utopia that Goebbels and other leading Nazis viewed as an endorsement of their ideology. George, however, refused to collaborate with them and died in exile in Switzerland on 4 December 1933.

19 Von Wesendonk, *op. cit.*

20 'Die Klinische Stellung der Angstpsychose'.

21 Jan Armbruster, *Edmund Robert Forster (1878–1933)*, page 17.

22 *Ibid.*

23 Von Wesendonk, *op. cit.*

24 Luigi Barbasetti, cited in K. McAleer, *Duelling*, page 43.

25 *Stenographische Protokolle des Herrenhauses*, 10th Session, 8 May 1907.

26 McAleer, *op. cit.* page 43.

27 *Ibid.*, page 47.

28 Isabel V. Hull, *The Entourage of Kaiser Wilhelm*, page 196.

29 This building survived the war and has been converted into a rheumatics' clinic.

30 Robert Gaupp, 'Über den Begriff der Hysterie', *Zeitschrift für die Gesamte Neurologie und Psychiatrie*, Vol. 5, 1911, page 464.

Chapter Seven: Hitler goes to War

1 *Diary of Robert Wilson, January–March 1918*, Imperial War Museum.

2 Hans Freimark, *Die Revolution als Massenerscheinung*, pages 27–8. Some of the more important sources on enthusiasm for the war in the UK and Germany include: M. Eksteins, *Rites of Spring*, R.N. Stromberg, *Redemption by War*; and R. Rürup, *Der Geist von 1914 in Deutschland*.

3 Nigel Jones, *Rupert Brooke*, page 391.

4 Rupert Brooke, 'Peace', in Brian Gardner (ed.), *Up the Line to Death*. Nigel Jones, *op. cit.*, makes the point that, with his reference to 'sick hearts that honour could not move', Brooke specifically had in mind the brothers James and Lytton Strachey and other intellectuals and artists in the Bloomsbury Group who had failed to join up with him. Nevertheless, the enormous popularity of this poem shows the extent to which these sentiments resonated in the hearts and minds of the public as a whole.

5 Letter cited in Jones, *op. cit.*, page 390.

6 Words for this popular 1914 song were written by Paul Rubens (1875–1917), best known as the lyricist for *Floradora*, written in 1899.

7 Newman Flower (ed.), *The History of the Great War*, Vol. 1, pages 39–40.

8 K. Schwalbe, *Wissenschaft und Kriegsmoral*, page 21. Written for a rally of students and faculty on 8 August 1918.

9 B.W. Tuchman, *August 1914*, page 131.

10 Friedrich Meinecke quoted in Otto Dietrich, *Before the Deluge*, page 15.

11 Charles Péguy, born 7 January 1873 in Orléans; died, 5 September 1914. A French poet and philosopher, he fought to establish Alfred Dreyfus's innocence. Publisher of the influential journal *Cahiers de la Quinzaine* (*Fortnightly Notebooks*), which exercised a profound influence on French intellectual life for some fifteen years.

12 Auguste Marie Joseph Jean Jaurès, born 3 September 1859; died (assassinated), 31 July 1914. Co-founder of *L'Humanité* and member of the French Chamber of Deputies, he helped unify different factions into a single socialist party, Française de l'Internationale Ouvrière.

13 Tuchman, *op. cit.*, page 123.

14 *Ibid.*

15 Adolf Hitler, *Mein Kampf* (Manheim translation), page 150.

16 Heinz A. Heinz, *Germany's Hitler*, page 51.

17 Minute no. 248, 23 January 1914, Imperial Austro-Hungarian Consulate. Cited in W. Maser, *Hitler*, page 75.

18 W. Maser, *Die Frühgeschichte der NSDAP*, page 62.

19 Official confirmation dated 23 February 1932, Federal Archives, Coblenz, NS 26/17a. Cited in Maser, *Hitler, op. cit.*, page 76.

20 Hitler, *op. cit.*, page 148.

21 *Ibid.*, page 149.

22 *Ibid.*, page 150.

23 Heinz, *op. cit.*, page 63.

24 A copy of Hepp's letter can be found in the files of the Institute of Contemporary History, London.

25 Federal Archives, Coblenz, NS 26/4.

26 Heinz, *op. cit.*, page 67.

27 *Ibid.*, page 72.

28 *Ibid.*, page 84.

29 Federal Archives, Coblenz, NS 26/17a.

30 *Ibid.*

31 *Ibid.*

32 *Ibid.*

33 *Ibid.*

34 Hitler had acquired this picture as early as 1937 from Tandey's old regimental commander, Colonel Earle. Earle later explained how he had heard from Dr Schwend that Hitler had expressed a wish to have a large photograph of the Matania painting. Subsequently Fritz Wiedemann, Hitler's adjutant, wrote to Earle: 'I beg to acknowledge your friendly gift which has been sent to Berlin through the good offices of Dr Schwend. The Führer is naturally very interested in things connected with his own war experiences, and he was obviously moved when I showed him the picture and explained the thought which you had in causing it to be sent to him. He has directed me to send you his best thanks for your friendly gift

which is so rich in memories.' (Colonel Earle, *The Green Howards' Gazette*, UK. June 1937.)

35 Godin, cited in Maser, *Hitler*, *op. cit.*, page 88.

36 Full details of this story can be found on the Great War Society's website www.worldwar1.com, and the author can be contacted at archive@collector.org. It should be pointed out for balance that several historians dispute the veracity of the Tandey incident.

Chapter Eight: Forster goes to War

1 I. Beckett and K. Simpson (eds), *A Nation in Arms*, page 68.

2 B.W. Tuchman, *August 1914*, page 131.

3 Karl Liebknecht, born, 13 August 1871 in Leipzig; died (murdered), 15 January 1919 in Berlin. Imprisoned during the war for his pacifism, he later founded, with Rosa Luxemburg and other radicals, the Spartacus League, a Berlin underground group that later became the German Communist Party. He and Luxemburg were shot in 1919 on the pretext that they had attempted to escape from arrest.

4 Paul Lerner, 'Hysterical Men', page 34.

5 Bernd Ulrich, 'Krieg als Nervensache', *Die Zeit*, 22 November 1991.

6 Cited in Wolfgang Mommsen, 'The Topos of Inevitable War in Germany in the Decade before 1914', page 26.

7 O. Binswanger, *Die Seelischen Wirkungen des Kriegs*, page 10. Binswanger was a psychiatrist at Jena University.

8 Lerner, *op. cit.*, page 47.

9 K. Singer, 'Wesen und Bedeutung der Kriegspsychosen', page 177.

10 Quoted in B. Ulrich and B. Ziemann, 'Nerven und Krieg', page 164.

11 Dr Nippold in a review of the book *Medizin und Krieg* by A.A. Friedlander; Geh StA Berlin-Dahlem, Rep 76, Akte 4399, 'Medizinische unter Ärztliche Schriften'.

12 A. Sänger 'Über die durch den Krieg', page 567.

13 Lerner, *op. cit.*, page 36. Some 6,000 dentists, 1,800 pharmacists and a great many medical students also joined up. See, for example, Otto von Schjerning, *Die Tätigkeit und die Erfolge der deutschen Ärzte im Weltkriege*.

14 Karl Birnbaum, 'Ergebrisse der Neurologie und Psychiatrie' page 325.
15 Kurt Mendel, 'Psychiatrisches und Neurologisches aus dem Felde', *Neurologisches Centralblatt*, Vol. 34, 1915, page 3.
16 R. Gaupp, 'Hysterie und Kriegsdienst', *Münchner Medizinische Wochenschrift*, Vol. 62, 1915, page 361.
17 Cited in Lerner, *op. cit.*, page 60.
18 Cited in B. Ulrich and B. Ziemann (eds), *Frontalltag*, page 102.
19 Lerner, *op. cit.* page 3.
20 Robert Weldon Whalen, *Bitter Wounds*, page 89.
21 Harold Wiltshire, *Lancet*, i, 17 June 1916, pages 1207–12.
22 Quoted in B. Shephard, *A War of Nerves*, page 30.
23 C.S. Myers, *Shell-Shock in France*, pages 25–9.
24 S. Wessely and T. Lutz, 'Neurasthenia and Fatigue Syndrome', in G. Berrios and R. Porter (eds), *A History of Clinical Psychiatry*, pages 509–44.
25 G.M. Beard, *American Nervousness*, quoted by *Ibid*, page 534.
26 Wessely and Lutz, *op.cit.*, page 535.
27 J. Certhoux, 'De la neurasthénie aux neuroses: le traitement des neuroses dans le passe', *Annales Medico-Psychologiques*, Vol. 119, 1961, pages 913–30.
28 A. Clark, 'Some Observations Concerning What Is Called Neurasthenia', quoted by Wessely and Lutz, *op. cit.*, page 517.
29 Shephard, *op. cit.*, page 10.
30 Schindler, 'Psychiatrie im Wilhelminischen Deutschland', quoted by Lerner, *op. cit.* pages 40–1.
31 L.J. Rather, *Mind and Body in Eighteenth Century Medicine*, page 191.
32 Willy Hellpach, quoted by Esther Fischer-Homberger, *Die traumatische Neurose*, page 133.
33 Alfred Goldschieder, 'Über die Ursachen des günstigen Gesundheitszustandes', page 170.
34 Binswanger, *op. cit.*, page 18.
35 J. Brunner, 'Psychiatry, Psychoanalysis and Politics', page 353.
36 Cited in Lerner, *op. cit.*, page 222.
37 Charcot, quoted by G. Guillain, *J.M. Charcot*, page 216.
38 H.J. Grosz and J. Zimmerman, 'Experimental Analysis of Hysterical Blindness', page 257.
39 W. Hellpach, 'Lazarettdisziplin als Heilfaktor', page 1210.
40 Cited in Lerner, *op. cit.*, page 253.

41 Cited in F. Kennedy, *The Making of a Neurologist*, page 62.

42 Shephard, *op. cit.*, page 48.

43 J. Purdon Martin, 'Reminiscences of Queen Square', *British Medical Journal*, Vol. ii, 1981, pages 1640–42.

44 Dr Maring, 'Vorschläge zur Neurotikerfürsorge. Ergänzung des badischen Systems', Ulm, 15 March 1918; UV Tübingen, pages 308–9.

Chapter Nine: Battlefields of the Mind

1 Brecht, quoted by Otto Friedrich, *Before the Deluge*, page 16. There is some evidence that Brecht was exaggerating, or indulging in a morbid joke. One scholarly account insists that he spent the war years working in a clinic for venereal disease, but perhaps he was simply expressing, in another form, the truth of his own poetry.

2 Kriegsministerium, 'Nachprüfung beim Prüfungsgeschäft', Munich, 14 May 1917; BayHStA Munich, Stellv. Gen. Kom des I. A.K., page 156.

3 A. Mendelssohn-Bartholdy, *The War and German Society*, pages 202–3.

4 Babinski is today best remembered for the Babinski sign, an upward movement of the big toe when the sole of the foot is tickled.

5 B. Shephard, *A War of Nerves*, page 12.

6 E. Trillat, *Histoire de l'hysterie*, pages 199–212.

7 Shephard, *op. cit.*, page 12.

8 M. Nonne, *Anfang und Ziel Meines Lebens*, pages 177–8.

9 M. Nonne, 'Therapeutische Erfahrungen', page 109.

10 Shephard, *op. cit.*, page 99.

11 Otto Muck, 'Über Schnellheilungen', pages 165–6.

12 Kaufmann, cited in P.F. Lerner, *Hysterical Men*, page 187.

13 D. Kaufmann, quoted by Shepherd, *op. cit.*, page 100.

14 Lerner, *op. cit.*, page 188.

15 M. Raether, 'Neurosen-Heilungen der "Kaufmann-Methode"', pages 492–3.

16 Rafael Weichbrodt, 'Zur Behandlung Hysterischer Störungen', *Archiv für Psychiatrie*, Vol. 57, 1917, pages 519–25.

17 Oskar Maria Graf, *Prisoners All*, page 160. Lerner, *op. cit.*, page 212, makes the point that Graf was placed in the bath to calm

him down rather than to try to cure a hysterical condition, but notes that the experience would have been identical to that suffered by Weichbrodt's patients, who might lie like this for up to forty hours.

18 Stier, quoted by R. Weichbrodt, 'Einige Bemerkungen zur Behandlung von Kriegsneurotikern', page 266.
19 Lerner, *op. cit.*, page 6.
20 F. Kehrer, 'Zur Frage der Behandlung der Kriegsneurosen', page 13.
21 K. Goldstein, 'Über die Behandlung der Hysterie', pages 757–8.
22 M. Rothmann, 'Zur Beseitigung psychogener Bewegungsstörungen', pages 1277–8.
23 Robert Sommer, 'Beseitigung funktioneller Taubheit', page 68.
24 *Ibid.*
25 Edmund Forster, 'Hysterische Reaktion und Simulation', pages 298–324.
26 *Ibid.*

Chapter Ten: Gas Attack

1 *Surgeons' Journal*, 23 July 1917, page 166.
2 NSDAP publishing house, Munich, 1936.
3 Adolf Hitler, *Mein Kampf* (Manheim translation), page 183.
4 *Mein Kampf* was written in two volumes, the first entitled *Eine Abrechnung* (*A Reckoning*), published on 19 July 1925 in an impression of ten thousand copies by Max Amann, who had been a sergeant-major and regimental clerk in the 16th Regiment. The second volume, *Die Nationalsozialistische Bewegung* (*The Nazi Movement*), was published on 11 December 1926.
5 The most notable exception was historian Rudolph Binion, who first challenged many aspects of the account as long ago as 1976.
6 Sven Hedin, *With the German Armies in the West*, pages 357–8.
7 History of the 30th Division.
8 *Ibid.*
9 148th Brigade R.F.A., Sheet 28, 19 October 1918. Public Record Office, London.
10 History of the 30th Division. Thermite, in use since mid-1917, was a mixture of powdered aluminium and iron oxide, which, when

combined with an explosive called ophorite, doused enemy trenches in molten fragments.

11 Ignaz Westenkirchner, interviewed by Julius Hagemann; Harry Schultze-Wilde Collection, Ottobrunn bei München.

12 Heinz A. Heinz, *Germany's Hitler*, page 83.

13 *Official History of the War*, quoted by John Terraine, *The Great War*, page 137.

14 *Ibid.*

15 C.R.M. Cruttwell, *A History of the Great War*, page 139.

16 L.F. Haber, *The Poisonous Cloud*, page 223.

17 The classification 'gas' was not introduced until 1915 by the British, January 1916 by the Germans, and January 1918 by the French.

18 In January 1916 the British government bought four and a half square miles of land at Porton, near Salisbury, in the west of England. The site was chosen due to a similarity between the Hampshire Downs and the ridges east of Ypres. By the time the war ended it had expanded to around ten square miles.

19 C.H. Foulkes, *Gas!*, page 137.

20 W.G. MacPherson *et al*, *Official History of the Great War*, 'Medical Services: Diseases of the War', page 319.

21 *Ibid.*, pages 428–32.

22 *Ibid.*, page 256.

23 If the British troops were not being supplied with the gas by their own side, however, they were not averse to shelling the German troops with captured Yellow Cross canisters well before September 1918.

24 Foulkes, *op. cit.*, page 209.

25 Matthew Buck, personal communication.

26 Foulkes, *op. cit.*, page 162.

27 W.G. MacPherson, *et al*, page 463.

28 H.R. Trevor-Roper, *Hitler's Secret Conversations*, page 177, said on the night of 16/17 January 1942.

29 By 1938, Hitler's doctors *were* advising him against visiting the Eagle's Nest on the Kehlstein because of a shortage of breath, but, of course, by then Hitler was well into middle age.

30 During the whole of 1918 Germany suffered some 70,000 gas casualties, around 65 per cent of their estimated total casualties. Twelve thousand of these occurred between 1 October and 11 November.

31 D. Winter, *Death's Men*, page 64.

32 A.G. Butler, *Moral and Mental Disorders in the War*, page 113.

33 Winter, *op. cit.*, page 64.

34 *'Bei Montagne gaskrank'* (Bavarian Army HQ records); '21.10.1918 *Zugang vom LKZ [Leichtkrankenzug] Gent wegen Gasvergiftung ins Res. Laz. Pasewalk'*; Pasewalk Records; Hans Raab, 5 August 1939, to Hauptarchiv in Munich, 'Bis wir im Okt. 18 bei Werwic-Sued mit Gas ... beschossen wurden'; Hans Bauer, 15 May 1940, *'Gas'*; Heinrich Lugauer, 5 February 1940, *'gasvergiftet'*; Regimental notice, *'gaskrank'*; Mayor of Rothenburg in personal communication to Rudolph Binion, *'Gasvergiftung'*; Hermann Heer's niece in personal communication to Rudolph Binion, *'Gasangriff'*; Hermann Heer, *'Gasvergiftung'*; Wilhelm Hoegner both in his book *Gaskrankheit* and in a personal communication to Rudolph Binion.

Chapter Eleven: The Ways of the Wolf

1 Goebbels, quoted by Otto Friedrich, *Before the Deluge*, page 382.

2 In Heinz A. Heinz, *Germany's Hitler*, page 93.

3 *Ibid.*

4 Lorenz Frank report, 23 August 1919; HStA München Abt. II, Gruppen Kdo 4, Vol. 50/3.

5 Allan Bullock, *Hitler*, pages 58–9.

6 Konrad Heiden, *Der Führer*, page 43.

7 Hitler, quoted in *ibid.*, page 78.

8 *Ibid.*, pages 78–9.

9 Hjalmar Schacht, *Abrechnung mit Hitler*, page 206.

10 Konrad Heiden, *History of National Socialism*, page 31, quoting *Völkischer Beobachter*.

11 Quoted in Heinz, *op. cit.*, page 119.

12 This was Point 18 in the party's 25-point manifesto; cited by Robert Payne, *The Life and Death of Addf Hitler*, page 194.

13 Quoted by Heiden, *Der Führer*, *op. cit.*, page 79.

14 Adolf Hitler, *Mein Kampf* (Murphy translation), page 317.

15 Kurt Ludecke, *I Knew Hitler*, page 22.

16 Heiden, *Der Führer*, *op. cit.*, page 113.

17 Hitler in an unsigned article for *Völkischer Beobachter*, cited by Payne, *op. cit.*, page 200.

18 Heiden, *History of National Socialism*, *op. cit.*, pages 44–5.

19 Seymour Lipset, quoted in Otto Braun (ed.), *Von Weimar zu Hitler*, page 114.

20 Heiden, *Der Führer, op. cit.*, page 113.

21 Hans Peter Bleuel, *Sex and Society in Nazi Germany*, page 46.

22 Ernst Hanfstaengl in an interrogation conducted by the Office of Strategic Service; cited in Glenn Infield, *Eva and Adolf*, page 22.

23 Ernst Hanfstaengl, *Hitler: the Missing Years*, page 43.

24 H.R. Trevor-Roper, *Hitler's Secret Conversations*, page 202. Spoken on the night of 25/6 January 1924.

25 Houston Stewart Chamberlain, *Foundations of the Nineteenth Century*, page 623.

26 Heiden, *Der Führer, op. cit.*, page 198.

27 *Ibid.*, pages 129–30.

28 Quoted by William Shirer, *Rise and Fall of the Third Reich*, page 70.

29 Payne, *op. cit.*, page 242.

30 *Ibid.*, page 247.

31 Edouard Calic, *Ohne Maske*, page 46.

32 Geoffrey Pridham, *Hitler's Rise to Power*, page 41.

33 Letter from Fremdenverkehrsverein München und Bayerisches Hochland to the State Ministry of the Interior, 2 August 1924; cited in Pridham, *op. cit.*, page 35.

34 *Ibid.*, page 43.

35 *Mein Kampf* ultimately became a bestseller and made Hitler a fortune. By 1939 more than five million copies had been printed, a number which had doubled by 1943. It was translated into sixteen languages and even after 1945 was published outside of Germany. From 1936 a copy was handed out to newly married German couples along with their marriage certificate.

36 Quoted by Roger Manvell and Heinrich Frankel, *Doctor Goebbels*, page 65.

37 Pridham, *op. cit.*, pages 72–7.

38 NSDAP headquarters order dated 9 March 1927; Federal Archives.

Chapter Twelve: Before the Deluge

1 Mary Wollstonecraft Shelley, *Frankenstein*, New York, Dover Publications, page 34

2 Jan Armbruster, *Edmund Robert Forster*, inaugural dissertation, Ernst-Moritz-Arndt University, page 24.

3 Hanns Schwarz, cited in *ibid.*, page 25.

4 Erwin Gohrbandt, cited in *ibid.*, page 24.

5 Karl Bonhöffer, cited in *ibid.*

6 Otto Friedrich, *Before the Deluge*, pages 60–61.

7 *Ibid.*, page 76.

8 *Ibid.*, pages 76–7.

9 Ilya Ehrenburg, quoted in *ibid.*, page 82.

10 *Ibid.*, page 52.

11 Lovis Corinth, born, 1858; died, 1925. Although often described as a German Impressionist, he never regarded himself as one, nor as an Expressionist, citing as his major influences the works of Rembrandt and Rubens. He explored most printing techniques, with lithography being his favourite. A prolific artist, Corinth produced some nine hundred graphic works, including sixty self-portraits, over his lifetime. In 1925, while in Holland to look at Dutch masters, he caught pneumonia and died in Zanvoort. After Hitler came to power much of his later work was condemned as 'degenerate' and burned on Nazi bonfires.

12 Margot wrote these comments at the front of a photo album she gave to her father for his eightieth birthday; Marie Rose von Wesendonk Family Archive.

13 Paul Schröder, born, 1873; died, 1941. His main area of research was the histopathology of the brain. Publications included *Atlas des Gehirns* (*Atlas of the Brain*) and *Chronische Alkoholpsychosen* (*Chronic Alcohol Psychoses*).

14 In 1933 it was renamed the Ernst-Moritz-Arndt University of Greifswald.

15 Von Wesendonk, *op. cit.*

16 Armbruster, *op. cit.*, page 28.

17 Letter on Greifswald notepaper, dated 5 August 1927. The Curator was a civil servant with responsibility for administration, while the Rector was in charge of academic matters.

18 Mick Hamer, *New Scientist*, 22 June 2002, pages 39–41, on studies undertaken by Rosalia Lelchuk Staricoff at the Chelsea and Westminster Hospital, London.

19 K.A. Lattner, born, Anklam, Pomerania, 15 January 1896. Studied in Düsseldorf and Hamburg.

20 H.W. Cushing, born, 1869; died, 1939. Made his name with a

book entitled *The Pituitary Body and its Disorders* while still a young doctor. Also achieved a reputation as a medical historian and wrote a biography of Sir William Osler.

21 'Gleichgewichtsreaktionen bei Erkrankungen des Zentralnerven-systems (Filmdemonstration)', *Deutsche Zeitschrift für Nervenheilkunde*, Vol. 130, 1933, pages 25–43.

22 Von Wesendonk, *op. cit.*

23 This anecdote was recounted to Rudolph Binion by a Greifswald archivist who had been at the university during Forster's time; personal communication.

Chapter Thirteen: Vision at Pasewalk

1 *The Collected Poems of Wilfred Owen*, ed. C. Day Lewis.

2 Edmund Forster, 'Hysterische Reaktion und Simulation', pages 298–324.

3 The descriptions of Hitler's behaviour at Pasewalk are taken from E. Weiss, *Der Augenzeuge*, pages 114–26, and are my translations of Weiss's original German text.

4 *Ibid.*

5 *Ibid.*

6 R. Binion, *Hitler among the Germans*, pages 11–12.

7 UAG Kurator 449, Blatt 280 R.

8 P. Horn (1915) cited in J. Brunner, 'Psychiatry, Psychoanalysis and Politics', page 354.

9 Archiv der Gesellschaft für Rassenbiologie, Berlin, 18 August 1938.

10 Quoted in an article by Leopold Schwarzschild, *Das neue Tage-Buch*, 16 September 1933.

11 Postcard in Marie Rose von Wesendonk Family Archive, Tuscany.

12 UAG Kurator 449, Blatt 284.

13 Marie Rose von Wesendonk, personal communication.

14 Attempts to track down this document by Arne Forster, Edmund's grandson, myself and reporters from *Der Spiegel* have proved unsuccessful. The most likely explanation is that Edmund deposited the *Krankenblatt* under a false name, a reasonable precaution given the risks he was already running in openly discussing what was, by this time, an official state secret.

15 Walter Mehring claims that this meeting took place 'in the Café Royal'. However, there was no such café in Paris at that time. The Registry of Commerce for 1930 does show Le Royal located on the corner of 1 Place du Théâtre Français and 248 rue St Honoré. It is still there today, although the square in front of the café has been renamed Place André Malraux.

16 Born, 1896, Berlin; died, 1981, Zurich. Mehring was an Expressionist poet and author of novels such as *The Infernal Comedy* (*Die höllische Komödie*, 1932), *The Night of the Tyrant* (*Die Nacht des Tyrannen*, 1937) and *The Lost Library* (*Die verlorene Bibliothek*, 1951). However, his reputation was made as the writer of the anti-bourgeois *The Political Cabaret* (*Das politische Cabaret*, 1920) and *Noah's Ark SOS* (*Arche Noah SOS*, 1931).

17 The continuation in exile of a publication he had founded in Germany several years earlier, it was published in Paris from July 1933 to May 1940.

18 Medaille des olympischen Kunstwettbewerbs, 1928, and Adalbert-Stifter-Preis für Literatur des Landes Oberösterreich, 1930.

19 Walter Mehring quoted by Binion, *op. cit.*, page 8.

20 *Ibid.*, pages 8–9.

21 Edmund Forster, 'Das Nervensystem', in Hermann Lüdke and Carl Robert Schlayer (eds), *Lehrbuch der pathologischen Physiologie*, pages 269–334.

22 Klaus-Peter Hinze in a postscript to the 1977 American edition of *The Eyewitness*, page 202.

23 Weiss, *op. cit.*, page 5.

24 *Ibid.*, pages 152–69.

25 Mona Wollheim in a letter dated 29 November 1973 to Rudolph Binion.

26 Karl Kroner in Washington National Archives of the OSS, Navy Intelligence Report 31983, Reykjavik 21 III 43.

27 Jürg Zutt in a letter to Rudolph Binion, quoted by Binion, *op. cit.*, page 7.

28 Warren Bennis and Robert Thomas, *Geeks and Geezers*, pages 87–120.

29 Quoted by Hinze, *op. cit.*, page 201.

Chapter Fourteen: Decline and Fall

1 Remark made to Rudolf Diels, first chief of the Gestapo, in front of the blazing Reichstag on the night of 27/8 February 1933.

2 Translated from the original handwritten letter from Oklitz on file in the Geheimes Staatsarchiv 'Preussischer Kulturbesitz', Berlin.

3 Jan Armbruster, *Edmund Robert Forster*, pages 63–6.

4 *Ibid.*

5 W. Shirer, *Rise and Fall of the Third Reich*, page 248.

6 Professor Stephen Roberts, quoted in Stefan Lorant, 'Is He Hitler's Successor', *Picture Post*, Vol. 5, No. 11, 16 December 1939, pages 19–33.

7 Diels rose to the rank of SS-Standartenführer (colonel) and in 1943 married Ilse Göring, widow of Göring's younger brother Karl. He was eventually defeated by Himmler and Heydrich of the SS, ending up as a prisoner in the basement of his own former headquarters. He survived the experience, and the war, only thanks to the personal intervention of his former boss, Hermann Göring.

8 Lorant, *op. cit.*

9 *Ibid.*

10 *Ibid.*

11 *Ibid.*

12 This is, of course, speculation, but if we accept that the campaign to neutralise Forster's potentially highly politically damaging revelations by having him disgraced, dismissed and, probably, killed originated in the highest levels within the Nazi Party, then Göring is certainly the most likely candidate. He was intensely protective of Hitler's reputation and, as we have seen, utterly ruthless in pursuit of that goal. He was also sufficiently intelligent and subtle to recognise that, at that stage, it would be inappropriate merely to have Forster murdered.

13 Ernst-Moritz-Arndt Universität Archiv UAG.

14 UAG PA486 Blatt 75 ru.v. Aufzeichnungen des Universität Kurators Zum Gespräch mit Forster.

15 *Ibid.*

16 *Ibid.*
17 Ernst-Moritz-Arndt Universität Archiv UAG.
18 *Ibid.*
19 *Ibid.*
20 *Ibid.*
21 *Ibid.*
22 *Ibid.*
23 *Ibid.*
24 *Ibid.*
25 *Ibid.*
26 *Ibid.*
27 *Ibid.*
28 Quoted in Adolf Klein, *Köln im Dritten Reich*, page 136.
29 *Ibid.*

Chapter Fifteen: The Strange Suicide of Edmund Forster

1 Lutze, quoted by Heinz Höhne, *Order of the Death's Head*, page 113.
2 Jan Armbruster, *Edmund Robert Forster*, pages 91–2.
3 Balduin Forster, interviewed by Rudolph Binion, 1973; personal communication.
4 'Wann muß der praktische Arzt Suizidneigung vermuten und wie verhält er sich dann', *Münchener Medizinische Wochenschrift*, Vol. 80, 1933, pages 766–9.
5 Although it might seem strange that an insurance company would pay out in the event of a suicide, this was the case in Germany at the time.
6 Arne Forster, 2002, personal communication. This is the only source for where Edmund's body was found. No official documents relating to his death have survived.
7 Ernst-Moritz-Arndt-Universität Archiv UAG.
8 Rudolph Binion, personal communication.
9 Balduin Forster, interviewed by Rudolph Binion, 1973.
10 Letter to Rudolph Binion.
11 Rudolph Binion, personal communication.

12 Otto Friedrich, *Before the Deluge*, page 391.

13 Postcard from Lilly to Dirk Forster dated 15 September 1933; Marie Rose Von Wesendonk Family Archive, Tuscany.

14 Ernst-Moritz-Arndt-Universität Archiv UAG. summer 2002.

15 Konrad Heiden, *op. cit.*, page 600.

16 Höhne, *op. cit.*, page 121.

17 *Ibid.*, page 120.

18 Pam Forster, personal communication.

19 Armbruster, *op. cit.*, page 62.

20 Ernst-Moritz-Arndt-Universität Archiv UAG.

21 This building is still standing but was converted into a gymnasium under the East German regime.

22 Letter from Lilly to Dirk Forster dated 14 September 1933; von Wesendonk, *op. cit.*

23 Von Wesendonk, *op. cit.*

Chapter Sixteen: After the Funeral

1 Rudyard Kipling, 'Recessional'.

2 Marie Rose von Wesendonk Family Archive, Tuscany.

3 *Ibid.*

4 Pam Forster, personal communication. Hitler renounced the Locarno Pact on 7 March 1936 following his reoccupation of the Rhineland. Given that Dirk ranked only fifth in the diplomatic pecking order at Paris, it is rather surprising that Hitler bothered to discuss the matter with him at all. Furthermore, while he was certainly capable of making such a threat, Hitler was, perhaps, too conscious of maintaining his dignity before a subordinate to have done so.

5 Klaus Kroner, personal communication.

6 In 1938 Iceland was still in a 'personal union' with Denmark, in spite of achieving nominal independence in 1918. Iceland's affairs in Germany were dealt with by the Danish Ambassador in Berlin. However, since there was a German Consul-General, Herr Gerlach, in Reykjavik, there was also an Icelandic Consul-General in Berlin.

7 Klaus Kroner, personal communication.

8 Körber's introduction was circulated as a page proof shortly before the 1923 *Putsch*, but when published a year later the book was

immediately confiscated and pulped. When reissued several months later, Körber's flowery contribution had been removed. Although no reason was ever given, it may be that the Nazis were concerned at giving offence to the Church by such overt comparisons with Christ.

ARCHIVAL REFERENCES AND BIBLIOGRAPHY

Archives, Institutions, and Individuals Consulted

Rudolph Binion Archive, Boston.

Marie Rose von Wesendonk Family Archive, Tuscany.

Stadt Pasewalk, Museum (special thanks to Herr Brose).

Bundesarchiv Berlin (BArch).

Humboldt-Universität zu Berlin, Universitätsbibliothek, Universitätsarchiv.

Geheimes Staatsarchiv Preußischer Kulturbesitz Berlin (GStA PK).

Ernst-Moritz-Arndt-Universität Greifswald, Universitätsarchiv (UAG).

Bildarchiv Preußischer Kulturbesitz, Berlin.

Bilddatenbank Deutsches Historisches Museum.

Stadtarchiv Hansestadt Greifswald (special thanks to Frau Neitzel).

Haupt- und Kulturamt Anklam.

Bildarchiv am Institut für Geschichte der Medizin/ZFA (HU zu Berlin).

Archiv der Hapag Lloyd AG, Hamburg.

Freie Universität Berlin, Institut für Geschichte der Medizin (special thanks to Frau Kliesch).

Archiv der Siemens-AG.

Bundesarchiv Militärarchiv Freiburg.

Bundesbeauftragte des Staatssicherheitsdienstes der ehemaligen Deutschen Demokratischen Republik.

Leonaris Film.

Deutsche Gesellschaft für Psychiatrie, Psychotherapie und Nervenheilkunde.

Universitätsarchiv Heidelberg.

Bundesarchiv Filmarchiv.

Landesarchiv Berlin.

St Jakobi Gemeinde, Greifswald (special thanks to Pastor Hanke).

Bundesbank Bundesrepublik Deutschland.

Deutscher Wetterdienst, Regionales Gutachtenbüro, Potsdam.

Musikabteilung der Staatsbibliothek zu Berlin Stiftung Preußischer Kulturbesitz.

Ärztekammer Berlin.

KZ Gedenkstätte Oranienburg.

Lehrstuhl Prof. Dr Lück für Bürgerl. Recht, Europäische, Deutsche und Sächsische Rechtsgeschichte, Martin-Luther-Universität Halle-Wittenberg.

Bereichsbibliothek Rechtswissenschaft, Universitätsbibliothek Mannheim.

Akademie der Künste, Abteilung Bildende Kunst.

Gesamtverband der Deutschen Versicherungswirtschaft.

Standesamt Greifswald.

Ministry of Labour (RAM) Collection.

Ministry of the Interior (MdI) Collection.

Karl Bonhöffer Papers Charité Nervenklinik Collection.

Bayerisches Hauptstaatsarchiv, Abteilung IV Kriegsarchiv (BayHStA), Munich.

Bavarian Ministry of War, Medical Department.

Deputy General Command, Bavarian I. Army Corps. Sanitary Dept.

Militärarchiv Württemberg (MA), Stuttgart. Deputy General Command, XIII Army Corps.

Sächsisches Hauptstaatsarchiv (SHSA), Dresden.

Saxon Ministry of War, Medical Department.

Nonnenhorn Museum.

Schularchiv des Jahn-Gymnasiums, Greifswald.

La Bibliothèque Historique de la Ville de Paris.

Bibliothèque Nationale de France (special thanks to Madame Monique Moulène).

Les collections de la Documentation Française et les Collections Photographiques de la Documentation Française.

Documents Accessed

Bundesarchiv Berlin

BArch, NS 26/2214

BArch, NS 26/47

BArch, NS 26/17a

Geheimes Staatsarchiv Preußischer Kulturbesitz Berlin

GStA PK, I. HA Rep. 76 Va Sekt. 7 Tit. IV Nr. 21 Bd. 12: Acta betreffend die Anstellung und Besoldung der ordentlichen und außerordentlichen Professoren in der Medizinischen Fakultät der Universität zu Greifswald vom Juli 1922 bis Februar 1929;

GStA PK, HA I Rep. 76 Va Sekt. 7 Tit. X Nr. 21 Bd. 7: Acta der Universitäts-Irrenklinik zu Greifswald vom August 1927 bis Februar

GStA PK, HA I Rep. 76 VA Sekt. 7 Tit. IV Nr. 21 Adh. II Acta betreffend: das Disziplinarverfahren gegen den o. Prof. Edmund Forster in der Nervenklinik, August 1933–November 1933

GStA PK, HA I Rep. 76 VA Sekt. 7 Tit. IV Nr. 31 Bd. III: Acta betreffend die wissenschaftlichen Reisen der Dozenten von Januar 1929–November 1934

GStA PK, HA I Rep. 76 VA Sekt. 2 Tit. IV Nr. 50 Bd. X: Acta

betreffend die Privatdozenten in der Medizinischen Fakultät der
Universität zu Berlin vom Juli 1908–Juni 1910.

Universitätsarchiv Greifswald

UAG Kurator 449: Registratur des Universitätskuratoriums
   Greifswald Psychiatrische und Nervenklinik, 1928–1934
UAG Kurator 448: Registratur des Universitätskuratoriums
   Greifswald Psychiatrische und Nervenklinik, 1921–1927
UAG MF 77: Medizinische Fakultät, Akte Zador
UAG MF 221: Medizinische Fakultät: Beurlaubung von Dozenten
UAG MF 571: Medizinische Fakultät, Akte Geheim 1932–1944
UAG BM 40: Bereich Medizin 40, Fakultätsratsitzungen
UAG PA 2393 Personalakte Vorkastner
UAG PA 486 Personalakte Forster
UAG Kurator 454: Die Assistenzärzte der Psychiatrischen und
   Nervenklinik 1926–1935

Imperial War Museum (IWM) and Public Record Office (PRO) London

Official Diary of the 148th Brigade Royal Artillery, PRO W095
HQ 30th Division Artillery. War Diary, PRO WO 95 2317
War Diary of 6th Brigade Royal Garrison Artillery, PRO WO 95
   297
Brief History of the 30th Division
30th Division in France and Flanders. Compiled for the Imperial
   War Museum (Typescript)

Unpublished Dissertations

Armbruster, J. (1999). *Edmund Robert Forster (1878–1933): Lebensweg
   und Werk eines deutschen Neuropsychiaters.* Inaugural-Dissertation

zur Erlangung des akademischen Grades Doktor der Medizin, Medical Faculty, Ernst-Moritz-Arndt-Universität, Greifswald.

Lerner, P.F. (1996). *Hysterical Men: War, Neurosis and German Mental Medicine 1914–1921.* Graduate School of Arts and Sciences, Columbia University.

BIBLIOGRAPHY

Achille-Delmas, F. (1946). *Adolf Hitler: Essai de Biographie Psycho-Pathologique.* Paris, Librairie Marcel Rivière et Cie.

Aird, R.B. (1933). *Foundations of Modern Neurology: A Century of Progress.* New York, Raven Press.

Alexander, F.G.S. (1966). *The History of Psychiatry: An Evaluation of Psychiatric Thought and Practice from Prehistoric Times to the Present.* New York, Harper & Row.

Anonymous (1919). *A Brief History of the 30th Division.* London, War Narratives Publishing Company.

Anonymous (1919). *Military Operations – France and Belgium 1918. Vol. V 26th September–11th November.* Nashville, Imperial War Museum and the Battle Press.

Anton, J. (1987). *Korrektur einer Biographie Adolf Hitler 1908–1920.* Frankfurt/Berlin, Verlag Ullstein.

Artwinski, E. v. (1919). 'Uber traumatische Neurosen nach Kriegsverletzungen.' *Zeitschrift für die Gesamte Neurologie und Psychiatrie* Vol. 45, pages 242–60.

Aschaffenburg, G. (1915). 'Winke zur Beurteilung von Nerven- und psychisch-nervösen Erkrankungen.' *Münchener Medizinische Wochenschrift, Feldärztliche Beilage* Vol. 62, pages 931–3.

Barbasetti, L. (1896). *Ehren-Codex.* Vienna.

Barnett, C. (2000). *The Great War.* London, Penguin Books.

Beard, G.M. (1880) *A Practical Treatise on Nervous Exhaustion (Neurasthenia).* New York, William Wood.

Beard, G.M. (1881). *American Nervousness*. New York, Putnam.

Beckett, I. and Simpson, K. (eds) (1985). *A Nation in Arms: A Social Study of the British Army in the First World War*. Manchester, Manchester University Press.

Bennis, W.G. and Thomas, R.J. (2002). *Geeks and Geezers: How Era, Values and Defining Moments Shape Leaders*. Boston, Harvard Business School Press.

Berrios, G.P. and Porter, R. (eds) (1995). *A History of Clinical Psychiatry: The Origin and History of Psychiatric Disorders*. London, Athlone Press.

Binion, R. (1973). 'Hitler's Concept of *Lebensraum*: The Psychological Basis.' *History of Childhood Quarterly* Vol. 1, No. 20.

Binion, R. (1991). *Hitler among the Germans*. DeKalb, Northern Illinois University Press.

Binswanger, O. (1914). *Die Seelischen Wirkungen des Krieges*. Berlin, Deutsche Verlagsanstalt.

Birnbaum, K. (1916); 'Ergebnisse der Neurologie und Psychiatrie. Kriegsneurosen und Psychosen auf Grund der gegenwärtigen Kriegsbeobachtungen. Sammelbericht. III.' *Zeitschrift für die Gesamte Neurologie und Psychiatrie: Referate und Ergebnisse* Vol. 12, pages 317–88.

Bleuel, H.P. (1996). *Sex and Society in Nazi Germany*. New York, Dorset Press.

Bloch, E. (1941). 'My Patient Hitler, as told to J.D. Ratcliff.' *Collier's* 15 March, Vol. 11, pages 35–7; 22 March, pages 69–73.

Bonhöffer, K. (1933). 'Edmund Forster.' *Deutsche Medizinische Wochenschrift* Vol. 59, page 1516.

Brady, J.P.L. (1961). 'Experimental Analysis of Hysterical Blindness.' *Archives of General Psychiatry* Vol. 4, pages 331–9.

Braun, O. (1940) *Von Weimar zu Hitler 1930–1933*. New York, Europa.

Brazier, M.A.B. (1988). *A History of Neurophysiology in the 19th Century*. New York, Raven Press.

Brendon, P. (2001). *The Dark Valley: A Panorama of the 1930s*. London, Pimlico.

Brunner, J. (1919). 'Psychiatry, Psychoanalysis and Politics during the First World War.' *Journal of the History of Behavioural Sciences* Vol. 27, pages 352–65.

Bullock, A. (1961). *Hitler: A Study in Tyranny*. London, Bantam.

Bumke, O. (ed.) (1907). 'Über Melancholie, von Dr Edm. Forster in Berlin.' In Schmidt's *Jahrbücher der in-und ausländischen gesamten Medizin*. Leipzig.

Butler, A.G. (1943). *Moral and Mental Disorders in the War of 1914–1918*. Canberra.

Calic, E. (1968). *Ohne Maske. Hitler – Breiting. Geheimgespräche 1931*. Frankfurt, Societät Verlag.

Caplan, E.M. (1995). 'Trains, Brains and Sprains: Railway Spine and the Origins of Psychoneuroses.' *Bulletin of the History of Medicine* Vol. 69, pages 387–419.

Caplan, J. (1977). 'The Politics of Administration: The Reich Interior Ministry and the German Civil Service 1933–1943.' *The Historical Journal* Vol. 20, pages 707–36.

Chamberlain, H.S. (1913). *Foundations of the Nineteenth Century*. New York, John Lane Co.

Chertok, L. (1975). 'Hysteria, Hypnosis, and Psychopathy: History and Perspectives.' *Journal of Nervous and Mental Disorders* Vol.. 161, pages 367–78.

Cocks, G. (1985). *Psychotherapy in the Third Reich*. Oxford, Oxford University Press.

Collie, J. (1913). 'Malingering.' *British Medical Journal* Vol. 2, page 647.

Constantinesco, J. (1937). *Hitler Secret*. Paris, La Société Française de Librairie et d'Editions.

Crankshaw, E. (1956). *Gestapo: Instrument of Tyranny*. London, Putnam.

Cross, C. (1973). *Adolf Hitler*. London, Hodder & Stoughton.

Cruttwell, C.R. (1936). *A History of the Great War*. Oxford, Oxford University Press.

Cushing, H. (1936). *From a Surgeon's Journal*. Boston, Little, Brown and Co.

Davidson, E. (1966). *The Trial of the Germans: Nuremberg 1945–1946*. New York, Macmillan.

De Sales, R. de R. (1941). *Adolf Hitler – My New Order; Collected Speeches*. New York.

Drexler, A. (1923). *Mein Politisches Erwachen*. Munich, Deutscher Volksverlag.

Dunn, S. (1918). 'Report on the Nature of Lesions Produced in Experiments on Animals by Inhalation of Diphenyl-chlorarsine and Allied Compounds.' *MRC Chemical Warfare Medical Committee* Report No. 9, page 35.

Eksteins, M. (1989). *Rites of Spring: The Great War and the Birth of the Modern Age*. Boston, Houghton Mifflin.

Feder, G. (1932). *Das Programm der NSDAP und seine weltanschaulichen Grundgedanken*. Munich, Verlag Frz. Eher.

Feldman, G. (1993). *The Great Disorder: Politics, Economics, and Society in the German Inflation*. New York, Oxford University Press.

Fest, J.C. (1974). *Hitler*. (Translated by Richard and Clara Winston.) London, Weidenfeld & Nicolson.

Fischer-Homberger, E. (1975). *Die traumatische Neurose: Vom somatischen zum sozialen Leiden*. Bern, Hans Huber Verlag.

Flood, C.B. (1989). *Hitler – The Path to Power*. Boston, Houghton Mifflin.

Flower, N. (ed.) (1919). *The History of the Great War*. London, Waverley.

Flury, M. and Wieland, K. (1921). 'Ueber Kampfgasvergiftungen: Lokal reizende Arsenverbindungen.' *Zeitschrift für die gesamte experimentelle Medizin* Vol. 13, page 523.

Forster, E. (1917). 'Hysterische Reaktion und Simulation.' *Monatsschrift für Psychiatrie und Neurologie* Vol. 42, pages 298–324, 370–81.

Forster, E. (1918). 'Hysterische Reaktion und Simulation.' *Neurologisches Centralblatt* Vol. 37, pages 468–9.

Forster, E. (1930). 'Selbstversuch mit Meskalin.' In *Zeitschrift für die gesamte Neurologie und Psychiatrie.* (Edited by A.L.M. Alzheimer.) Berlin, Verlag von Julius Springer.

Forster, E. (1933). 'Für die Praxis.' *Münchener Medizinische Wochenschrift* Vol. 20, pages 766–9.

Foulkes, C.H. (1934). *Gas! The Story of the Special Brigade.* Edinburgh, William Blackwood.

Frank, H. (1953). *Im Angesicht des Galgens.* München, Gräfelfing.

Freimark, H. (1920). *Die Revolution als Massenerscheinung.* Wiesbaden.

Friedrich, O. (1972). *Before the Deluge.* New York, Harper and Row.

Fussell, P. (1975). *The Great War and Modern Memory.* New York, Oxford University Press.

Gardner, B. (ed.) (1965). *Up the Line to Death: The War Poets of 1914–18.* London, Methuen.

Gaupp, R. (1952). 'Some Reflections on the Development of Psychiatry in Germany.' *American Journal of Psychiatry* Vol. 108, pages 721–3.

Goebbels, J. (1948). *The Goebbels Diaries.* (Translated and edited by Louis P. Lochner.) London, Hamish Hamilton.

Goldschieder, A. (1915). 'Über die Ursachen des günstigen Gesundheitszustandes unserer Truppen im Winterfeldzuge.' *Zeitschrift für Physikalische und Diätetische Therapie* Vol. 19, page 170.

Goldstein, K. (1917). 'Über die Behandlung der Hysterie.' *Medizinische Klinik* Vol. 13, pages 757–8.

Goldstein, K. (ed.) (1953). *Carl Wernicke (1848–1905).* Springfield, Thomas.

Graf, O.M. (1928). *Prisoners All.* (Translated by Margaret Green.) New York, Knopf.

Greiner, J. (1947). *Das Ende des Hitler-Mythos.* Zurich/Leipzig/Vienna, Amalthea.

Grosz, H.J. and Zimmerman, J. (1965). 'Experimental Analysis of Hysterical Blindness: A Follow-up Report and New Experimental

Data.' *Archives of General Psychiatry* Vol. 13, pages 256–60.

Guillain, G. (1955). *J.M. Charcot 1825–1893: Sa Vie – Son Oeuvre*. Paris, France Masson et Cie.

Gun, N.E. (1969). *Eva Braun – Hitler's Mistress*. London, Bantam.

Haber, L.F. (1986). *The Poisonous Cloud: Chemical Warfare in the First World War*. Oxford, Clarendon Press.

Hanfstaengl, E. (1957). *Hitler: The Missing Years*. London, Eyre & Spottiswoode.

Hanser, R. (1971). *Prelude to Terror: The Rise of Hitler 1919–1923*. London, Hart-Davis.

Hanser, R. (1971). *Putsch*. New York, Pyramid Books.

Healy, David (2000). *The Creation of Psychopharmacology*. Cambridge, Massachusetts, Harvard University Press.

Hedin, S. (1915). *With the German Armies in the West*. London, John Lane, Bodley Head.

Heiber, H. (1972). *Goebbels*. New York, De Capo.

Heiden, K. (1935). *History of National Socialism*. New York, Knopf.

Heiden, K. (1939). *One Man against Europe*. Harmondsworth, Penguin.

Heiden, K. (1944). *Der Führer: Hitler's Rise to Power*. London, Victor Gollancz.

Heinz, H.A. (1938). *Germany's Hitler*. London, Hurst & Blackett.

Hellpach, W. (1915). 'Lazarettdisziplin als Heilfaktor.' *Medizinische Klinik* Vol. 11, pages 1207–11.

Heston, L.L.H.R.N. (2000). *The Medical Casebook of Adolf Hitler: His Illnesses, Doctors and Drugs*. New York, Cooper Square Press.

Hinton, D.B. (2000). *The Films of Leni Riefenstahl*. Lanham, Md., Scarecrow Press.

Hitler, A. (1933). *My Battle (Mein Kampf)*. (Translated by E.T.S. Dugdale.) Boston, Houghton Mifflin.

Hitler, A. (1933). *My Struggle*. London, Paternoster Library.

Hitler, A. (1936). *Mein Kampf*. München, Centralverlag der NSDAP.

Hitler, A. (1939). *Mein Kampf.* (Translated by James Murphy.) London, Hurst and Blackett.

Hitler, A. (1969). *Hitler's Mein Kampf.* (Translated by Ralph Manheim.) London, Hutchinson.

HMSO (1946). 'The Trial of German Major War Criminals: Part 1.' *Proceedings of the International Military Tribunal Sitting at Nuremberg Germany.* London.

Höhne, H. (1969). *The Order of the Death's Head: The Story of Hitler's SS.* London, Secker & Warburg.

Holden, W. (1998). *Shell Shock: The Psychological Impact of War.* London, Channel 4 Books.

Hull, I.V. (1982). *The Entourage of Kaiser Wilhelm II 1888–1918.* Cambridge, Cambridge University Press.

Infield, G. (1978). *Eva and Adolf.* New York, Grosset & Dunlap.

Jenks, W.A. (1960). *Vienna and the Young Hitler.* New York, Columbia.

Jetzinger, F. (1958). *Hitler's Youth.* Westport, Conn., Greenwood.

Joachimsthaler, A. (1992). *Hitler in München: 1908–1920.* Berlin, Ullstein.

Jones, N. (1999). *Rupert Brooke: Life, Death and Myth.* London, Richard Cohen.

Kater, M. (1985). 'Professionalization and Socialization of Physicians in Wilhelmine and Weimar Germany.' *Journal of Contemporary History* Vol. 20, pages 677–701.

Kaufmann, F. (1917). 'Zur Behandlung der motorischen Kriegsneurosen.' *Münchener Medizinische Wochenschrift* Vol. 64, pages 1520–3.

Kehrer, F. (1917). 'Behandlung und ärztliche Fürsorge bei Kriegsneurosen.' *Die Kriegsbeschädigtenfürsorge* Vol. 2, pages 158–64.

Kehrer, F. (1917). 'Zur Frage der Behandlung der Kriegsneurosen.' *Zeitschrift für die Gesamte Neurologie und Psychiatrie* Vol. 36, pages 1–22.

Kempner, R.M.W. (1969). *Das Dritte Reich im Kreuzverhör, Aus den unveröffentlichten Vernehmungsprotokollen des Anklägers.* München/Esslingen, Bechtle Verlag.

Kendell, R.E. (1983). 'Hysteria.' In *Handbook of Psychiatry: The Neuroses and Personality Disorders*. Cambridge, Cambridge University Press.

Kennedy, F. (1981). *The Making of a Neurologist* London.

Kershaw, I. (1987). *The 'Hitler Myth': Image and Reality in the Third Reich*. Oxford, Oxford University Press.

Kershaw, I. (1998). *Hitler: 1889–1936 Hubris*. London, Penguin Press.

Kipling, Rudyard (1940). *Rudyard Kipling's Verse*. London, Hodder & Stoughton

Kläger, E. (1910): *Durch die Wiener Quartiere*. Vienna.

Klein, A (1983), *Köln im Dritten Reich: Stadtgeschichte der Jahre 1933–1945*. Köln, Gauverlag Westdeutscher Beobachter.

Klein, A. (2000). 'Zum Tod von Herr Prof. Dr E. Forster.' *Rechtsmedizin: Organ der Deutschen Gesellschaft für Rechtsmedizin* Vol. 10 (3), page 14.

Kocka, J. (1984). *Facing Total War. German Society, 1914–1918*. Leamington Spa, Berg.

Kraepelin, E. (1904). *Psychiatrie: Ein Lehrbuch für Studierende und Ärzte*. Leipzig, Barth.

Kretschmer, E. (1917). 'Hysterische Erkrankung und hysterische Gewöhnung.' *Zeitschrift für die Gesamte Neurologie und Psychiatrie* Vol. 37, pages 69–91.

Kubizek, A. (1954). *Young Hitler*. London, Allan Wingate.

Lerner, P. (1996). 'Hystrerical Men: War, Neurosis and German Mental Medicine, 1914–1921.' Unpublished PhD thesis. Columbia University, Graduate School of Arts and Sciences.

Lorant, S. (1939). 'Is He Hitler's Successor?' *Picture Post* Vol. 5, pages 19–33.

Ludecke, K.G.W. (1938). *I Knew Hitler*. London, Jarrolds.

Lüdke, H. and Schlayer, C.R. (eds). (1922). *Lehrbuch der Pathologischen Physiologie. Für Studenten und Ärzte*. Leipzig, Engelmann.

Lutz, T. (1995). 'Neurasthenia and Fatigue Syndromes.' In *A History of Clinical Psychiatry: The Origin and History of Psychiatric*

Disorders. (Edited by G. Berrios and R. Porter.) New York, New York University Press.

McAleer, K. (1994). *Duelling: The Cult of Honour in Fin-de-Siècle Germany.* Princeton, Princeton University Press.

Mackintosh, W. (1919). 'Mustard Gas Poisoning.' *Quarterly Journal of Medicine* Vol. 13, page 201.

Macpherson, W.G., Herrington, W.P., Elliott, T.R. and Balfour, A. (eds) (1923). *Official History of the Great War*, Vol. II. London, HMSO.

Manvell, R and Fraenkel, H. (1960). *Doctor Goebbels: His Life and Death.* London, Heinemann.

Martin, J.P. (1981). 'Reminiscences of Queen Square.' *British Medical Journal* Vol. 2, pages 1640–2.

Maser, W. (1965). *Der Sturm auf die Republik: Frühgeschichte der NSDAP.* Frankfurt, DVA, Rev. und erg. Neuausg.

Maser, W. (1971). *Adolf Hitler: Legende, Mythos, Wirklichkeit.* München und Esslingen, Bechtle Verlag.

Maser, W. (1973). *Hitler.* London, Allen Lane.

Mehring, W. (1952). *Die verlorene Bibliothek: Autobiographie einer Kultur.* Hamburg, Ronholt.

Mendel, K. (1917). 'Die Kaufmannsche Methode.' *Neurologisches Zentralblatt.* Vol. 36, pages 181–93.

Mendelssohn-Bartholdy, A. (1937). *The War and German Society: The Testament of a Liberal.* New Haven, Yale University Press.

Merkl, P.H. (1992). *Political Violence under the Swastika.* Princeton, Princeton University Press.

Meyer, A. (1934). *Mit Adolf Hitler im Bayerischen Reserve-Infanterie-Regiment 16 List.* Neustadt, Aisch.

Micale, M.S. (1989). 'Hysteria and its Historiography: A Review of Past and Present Writings.' *History of Science* Vol. 27, pages 223–61, 319–51.

Micale, M.S. (1990). 'Charcot and the Idea of Hysteria in the Male: Gender, Mental Science, and Mental Diagnosis in Late

Nineteenth-Century France.' *Medical History* Vol. 34, pages 363–411.

Micale, M.S. (1995). *Approaching Hysteria, Disease and its Interpretations*. Princeton, Princeton University Press.

Middlebrook, M. (1983). *The Kaiser's Battle*. London, Penguin Press.

Middlemarch, M. (1980). *The Nuremberg Raid*. London, Allen Lane.

Mommsen, W. (1981). 'The Topos of Inevitable War in Germany in the Decade before 1914.' In *Germany in the Age of Total War*. (Edited by Volker Berghahn and Martin Kitchen.) London, Croom Helm.

Mosse, G.L. (1998). *The Crisis of German Ideology: Intellectual Origins of the Third Reich*. New York, Howard Fertig.

Muck, O. (1917). 'Über Schnellheilungen von funktioneller Stummheit und Taubstummheit nebst einem Beitrag zur Kenntnis des Wesens des Mutismus.' *Münchener Medizinische Wochenschrift Feldärztliche Beilage* Vol. 64, pages 165–6.

Myers, C.S. (1940). *Shell Shock in France 1914–1918*. Cambridge, Cambridge University Press.

Nonne, M. (1915). 'Soll man wieder traumatische Neurosen diagnostizieren?' *Archiv für Psychiatrie* Vol. 56, pages 337–9.

Nonne, M. (1922). 'Therapeutische Erfahrungen an den Kriegsneurosen in den Jahren 1914–1918.' In *Geistes-und Nervenkrankheiten*. (Edited by Karl Bonhoeffer.) Vol. 4. Leipzig, Barth.

Nonne, M. (1971). *Anfang und Ziel Meines Lebens*. Hamburg, Hans Christians Verlag.

Olden, R. (1936). *Hitler*. New York, Covici, Friede Inc.

Oppenheim, H. (1915). 'Der Krieg und die traumatischen Neurosen.' *Berliner Klinische Wochenschrift* Vol. 52, pages 257–61.

Oppenheim, H. (1916). *Die Neurosen infolge von Kriegsverletzungen*. Berlin, Karger.

Overy, R. (1984). *Goering*. London, Routledge & Kegan Paul.

Owen, H. and Bell, J. (eds) (1967). *Wilfred Owen: The Collected Letters*. Oxford, Oxford University Press.

Owen, W. (1963). *The Collected Poems of Wilfred Owen*. (Edited by C. Day Lewis.) New York, New Directions.

Payne, R. (1973). *The Life and Death of Adolf Hitler*. London, Jonathan Cape.

Pick, D. (1993). *War Machine: The Rationalization of Slaughter in the Modern Age*. New Haven, Yale University Press.

Post, D.E (1998). 'The Hypnosis of Adolf Hitler.' *Journal of Forensic Science* Vol. 43, pages 1127–32.

Pridham, G. (1973). *Hitler's Rise to Power: The Nazi Movement in Bavaria, 1923–1933*. London, Hart-Davis, McGibbon.

Priestley, M. (1918). *Report on the Length of Stay in Hospital in the United Kingdom and the Disposal of Gas Casualties*. Chemical Warfare Medical Committee Report No. 16, London.

Proctor, R. (1988). *Racial Hygiene: Medicine under the Nazis*. Cambridge, Mass., Harvard University Press.

Raether, M. (1917). 'Neurosen-Heilungen der "Kaufmann-Methode".' *Archiv für Psychiatrie* Vol. 57, pages 489–502.

Rather, L.J. (1965). *Mind and Body in Eighteenth Century Medicine*. London, Wellcome Historical Medical Library.

Rauschning, H. (1939). *Hitler Speaks*. London, Thornton Butterworth.

Read, C.S. (1918). 'A Survey of War Neuropsychiatry.' *Mental Hygiene* Vol. 2, page 60.

Redlich, F. (1998). *Hitler: Diagnosis of a Destructive Patient*. Oxford, Oxford University Press.

Repfennig, E. (1933). *Zehn Jahre Kampf um Pasewalk, die Lazarettstadt Adolf Hitlers*, Pasewalk. (*Ten years' struggle at Pasewalk, the hospital town of Adolf Hitler. An account of the local branch of the NSDAP, published to celebrate the tenth anniversary of the Pasewalk branch.*)

Ribbentrop, J. von. (1954). *The Ribbentrop Memoirs*. (Translated by Oliver Watson.) London, Weidenfeld & Nicolson.

Rice, F.A. (1939). 'We Hadn't Heard of Hitler.' *Picture Post* Vol. 2, pages 75–6.

Richter, D. (1992). *Chemical Soldiers: British Gas Warfare in World War I.* Kansas, University Press of Kansas.

Ritter, G. (1958). *The Schlieffen Plan: Critique of a Myth.* London, Wolf.

Rose, F.C. and Bynum, W.F. (1982). *Historical Aspects of the Neurosciences: A Festschrift for Macdonald.* Critchley, NY, Raven Press.

Rosenbaum, R. (1998). *Explaining Hitler: The Search for the Origins of his Evil.* New York, Random House.

Roth, E. (1915). 'Kriegsgefahr und Psyche.' *Ärztliche Sachverständigenzeitung* Vol. 21, pages 1–3.

Rothmann, M. (1916). 'Zur Beseitigung psychogener Bewegungsstörungen bei Soldaten in einer Sitzung.' *Münchener Medizinische Wochenschrift Feldärztliche Beilage* Vol. 63, pages 1277–8.

Rürup, R. (1984) 'Der Geist von 1914 in Deutschland. Kriegsbegeisterung und Ideologisierung des Kriegs in Ersten Weltkrieg.' In *Ansichten vom Krieg. Verleichende Studien zum Ersten Weltkrieg in Literatur und Gesellschaft.* Hain, Ferum Academicum.

Rushdie, Salman (2002). *Step Across this Line.* London, Jonathan Cape'.

Sänger, A. (1915). 'Über die durch den Krieg bedingten Folgezustände am Nervensystem. Vortrag im ärztlichen Verein in Hamburg am 26.1. und 9.11.15.' *Münchener Medizinische Wochenscrift.* Feldärztliche Beilage 62: 522–3; 564–7

Schacht, H. (1949). *Abrechnung mit Hitler.* Berlin, Michaelis-Verlag.

Schjerning, O. v. (1920). *Die Tätigkeit und die Erfolge der deutschen Ärzte im Weltkriege.* Leipzig, Barth.

Schmidt, W. (1915). 'Die psychischen und nervösen Folgezustände nach Granatexplosionen und Minenverschüttungen.' *Zeitschrift für die Gesamte Neurologie und Psychiatrie* Vol. 29, pages 514–42.

Schneck, P. (1993). 'Die Berufungs- und Personalpolitik an der Greifswalder Medizinischen Fakultät zwischen 1933 und 1945.' In *Akademische Karrieren im 'Dritten Reich'. Beiträge zur Personal- und*

Berufungspolitik an Medizinischen Fakultäten. (Edited by G. Gau and P. Schneck.) Institut für Geschichte der Medizin Universitätsklinikum Charité, Medizinische Fakultät, Humboldt-Universität, Berlin.

Schüller, L. (1917). 'Heilung der Erscheinungen der Kriegshysterie in Wachsuggestion.' *Deutsche Medizinische Wochenschrift* Vol. 43, pages 652–4.

Schwalbe, K. (1969). *Wissenschaft und Kriegsmoral: Die Deutschen Hochschullehrer und die Politischen Grundfragen des Ersten Weltkrieges.* Göttingen, Musterschmidt Verlag.

Schwarzschild, L. (1933). 'Die Woche.' *Das neue Tage-Buch*, Issue 1, pages 271–5.

Shakespear, L.C.J. (1921). *The 30th Division 1915–1918.* London, Imperial War Museum.

Shephard, B. (2000). *A War of Nerves: Soldiers and Psychiatrists 1914–1994.* London, Jonathan Cape.

Shirer, W. (1941) *Berlin Diary.* London, Hamish Hamilton.

Shirer, W. (1962). *The Rise and Fall of the Third Reich.* London, Secker & Warburg.

Shorter, E. (1992). *From Paralysis to Fatigue: A History of Psychosomatic Illness in the Modern Era.* New York, Free Press.

Singer, A. (1915). 'Über die durch den Krieg Bedingten Folgezustände am Nervensystem. Vortrag im ärztlichen Verein in Hamburg am 21.1 und 9.11.1915.' *Münchener Feldärztliche Beilage* Vol. 62, page 567.

Singer, K. (1915). 'Wesen und Bedeutung der Kriegspsychosen.' *Berliner Klinische Wochenschrift* Vol. 52, pages 177–80.

Singer, K. (1919). 'Die zukünftige Begutachtung traumatischer Nervenkrankheiten.' *Ärztliche Sachverständigen-Zeitung* Vol. 25, pages 330–49.

Smith, B.F. (1967). *Adolf Hitler: His Family, Childhood and Youth.* Stanford, Stanford University Press.

Smith, D.C. (1990). *Triumph of the Will: The Reich Party Rally of 1934.* Richardson, Tex. Celluloid Press.

Sombart, N. (ed) (1982). *The Kaiser in his Epoch: Some Reflections on Wilhelmine Society, Sexuality and Culture.* Cambridge, Cambridge University Press.

Sommer, R. (1916). *Krieg und Seelenleben.* Leipzig, Nemnich Verlag.

Sommer, R. (1917). 'Beseitigung funktioneller Taubheit, besonders bei Soldaten, durch eine experimentalpsychologische Methode.' *Schmidts Jahrbücher der in- und ausländischen Gesamten Medizin* Vol. 84, page 68.

Speer, A. (1969) *Erinnerungen.* Berlin, Propylaeen Verlag.

Sprecht, H. (1900). *Ein Geschichts – Stadt und Landschaftsbild.* Braunau-am-Inn, Austria.

Stone, M. (ed.) (1985). *Shell Shock and the Psychologists: The Anatomy of Madness.* London, Tavistock.

Störring, E. (1938). *Die Psychiatrie in Greifswald.* In H.Loeschke and A. Terbrüggen (eds.) 100 Jahre medizinische Forschung in Greifswald. Festschrift zur Feier des 75jährigen Bestehens des Medizischen Vereins. Greiswald 1938, pages 181–200.

Stromberg. R.N. (1982) *Redemption by War: The Intellectuals and 1914.* University Press of Kansas.

Temple-Bell, E. (1937). *Men of Mathematics.* New York, Simon & Schuster.

Terraine, J. (1965). *The Great War 1914–1918.* London, Hutchinson.

Toland, J. (1976). *Adolf Hitler.* New York, Doubleday.

Trevor-Roper, H.R. (1976). *Hitler's Secret Conversations.* London, Octagon Press.

Trillat, E. (1986). *Histoire de l'hysterie.* Paris, Seghers.

Trimble, M. (1981). *Post-traumatic Neuroses: From Railway Spine to the Whiplash.* Chichester, Wiley.

Tuchman, B.W. (1962). *August 1914.* London, Constable.

Ulrich, B. and Ziemann, B. (eds) (1992). *Frontalltag im Ersten Weltkrieg: Wahn und Wirklichkeit.* Frankfurt, Fischer.

Ulrich, B. and Ziemann, B. (eds) (1992). 'Nerven und Krieg. Skizzierung einer Beziehung'. In *Geschichte und Psychologie. Annäherungsversuche.* (Edited by B. Loewenstein) Pfaffenweiler, Centaurus.

Van den Bussche, H. (1999). 'Rudolf Degkwitz: Die politische Kontroverse um einen außergewöhnlichen Kinderarzt.' *Kinder- und Jugendarzt* Vol. 30, pages 425–31, 549–56.

Veith, I. (1965). *Hysteria: The History of a Disease*. Chicago, University of Chicago Press.

Wegener, Otto von (1985). *Hitler – Memoirs of a Confidant*. (Edited by H.A. Turner, Translated by Ruth Hein.) New Haven, Yale University Press.

Weichbrodt, R. (1917). 'Zur Behandlung Hysterischer Störungen.' *Archiv für Psychiatrie* Vol. 57, pages 519–25.

Weichbrodt, R. (1918). 'Einige Bemerkungen zur Behandlung von Kriegsneurotikern.' *Monatsschrift für Psychiatrie und Neurologie* Vol. 43, page 266.

Weiss, E. (1986; written 1938; first published 1963). *Der Augenzeuge*. Berlin, Aufbau-Verlag.

Weiss, E. (1977). *The Eyewitness*. (Translated by Ella R.W. McKee.) Boston, Houghton Mifflin.

Weller, W. (1920). *The Medical Aspects of Mustard Gas Poisoning*. London, Henry Kimpton.

Wessely, S. and Lutz, T. (1995). 'Neurasthenia and Fatigue Syndromes.' In *A History of Clinical Psychiatry: The Origin and History of Psychiatric Disorders*. (Edited by G. Berrios and R. Porter.) New York, New York University Press.

West, F. (1921). *Chemical Warfare*. New York, McGraw-Hill.

Wexberg, E. (1916). 'Neurologische Erfahrungen im Felde.' *Wiener Medizinische Wochenschrift* Vol. 66, pages 1410–11.

Whalen, R.W. (1984). *Bitter Wounds: German Victims of the First World War*. Ithaca, Cornell University Press.

Whitlock, F.A. (1967). 'The eetiology of Hysteria.' *Acta Psychiatrica Scandinavica* Vol. 43, pages 144–62.

Wiedemann, F. (1964). *Der Mann der Feldherr Werden Wollte*. Berlin, Blick und Bild Verlag.

Wilson, R. (1918). *Robert Wilson Diary, January–March 1918*. London, Imperial War Museum.

Wiltshire, H. (1916). 'A Contribution to the Etiology of Shell Shock.' *Lancet* Vol. 1, pages 1208–9.

Winter, D. (1988). *Death's Men: Soldiers of the Great War*. London, Penguin.

Winter, J.M. (1988). *The Experience of World War 1*. Oxford, Macmillan.

Winternitz, M.C. (1920). *Collected Studies on the Pathology of War Gas Poisoning*. New Haven, Yale University Press.

Wittkower, E. and Spillane, J.P. (eds) (1940). *The Neuroses in War*. New York, Macmillan.

Wollenberg, R. (1926). 'Hysterie oder Simulation.' *Psychiatrisch Neurologische Wochenschrift* Vol. 28, pages 211–12.

Wood, G. (1983). *The Myth of Neurosis*. London, Macmillan.

Wykes, A. (1970). *The Nuremberg Rallies*. London, Ballantine.

Zádor, J. (1933). 'Gleichgewichtsreaktionen bei Erkrankungen des Zentralnervensystems.' *Deutsche Medizinische Zeitschrift* Vol. 130, pages 25–43.

Zilboorg, K. (1941). *A History of Medical Psychology*. New York, W.W. Norton.

Zitelmann, R. (1998). *Hitler: The Politics of Seduction*. London, London House.

Zucker, K. (1928). 'Experimentelles über Sinnestäuschungen.' *Archiv für Psychiatrie* Vol. 33, pages 706–54.

INDEX

'active therapy' 132–40
Albert, King of Belgium 92–3
Amsterdam 46, 49
Antwerp 101
Ascherson, Neal 9
Austria 20, 169, 177–8
'awake or alert suggestion' 141

Babinski, Felix 126, 132–3
balance mechanisms of the human
  body 209
Basle 221–2
Baumann, Professor 169
Bayreuth 184
Beard, Charles 82
Beard, George M. 122–5
Bechstein, Carl 182–3
Bechstein, Helene 182, 190
Beckett, Ian F.W. 113
Bender, Arnold Siegfried 228
Benedikt, Moriz 81
Bennis, Warren 230
Berchtesgaden 161
Berlin 88, 178, 200–1
Berlin Neurological Society 198
Berliner Tageblatt 189
Beseler, Maximilian 86

Bickel, Heinrich 137
Binion, Rudolph ix–xi, 5, 55, 59,
  61–3, 218, 264–6
Binswanger, Otto 117, 126, 140
Bloch, Eduard 57–62
Blondi 24
Bomber Command 8
Bonhöffer, Karl 88, 122, 198,
  204, 273–5
Borchert, Ernst 87
Bormann, Martin 72
Brahms, Johannes 202
Braun, Edith 245–50, 254
Braunau-am-Inn 23–4
Brecht, Bertolt 131
Bredow, Lilly see Forster, Lilly
Brendon, Piers 9–10
Bretschneider, Mila see Forster,
  Mila
British Medical Association
  124
Brooke, Rupert 91–2
Brownshirts 173
Bruges 117
Brüske, Hermann 239, 256–7,
  268
Buck, Matthew 159

Chamberlain, Houston Stewart
184–5
Chamberlain, Neville 110–11
Charcot, Jean-Martin 127
Charité Nerve Clinic, Berlin 88,
113, 197–8, 201, 207–8
chlorine gas 152–3, 155, 160
Cochrane, Thomas 153
Constantinesco, Jean 72
Corinth, Lovis 202
Cruttwell, C.R.M. 154
Cushing, Harvey 147, 207

Daily Telegraph 180
Darling, Christian 16–17
Degkwitz, Rudolf 210
Deibner, K. 271
Dejerine, Jules-Joseph 133
Democritus 125
Dessauer, Heinrich 54
Diels, Rudolf 242–3
Dingfelder, Johannes 175
Döblin, Alfred 219–22
Drexler, Anton 168–70,
174, 178–9
duelling 85–8

Ebers papyrus 125
Eckart, Dietrich 170–1,
174, 190–2
Edinburgh University 47
educational system, German 33,
48–9, 75–6, 241
Ehrenburg, Ilya 200
Ehrensperger, Ernst 27
Einstein, Albert 48, 241
Eisner, Kurt 166
electrotherapy 82–3, 136–40
Elisabeth, Queen of Belgium 92
Engelhardt, Lieutenant-Colonel
106
Erb, Wilhelm 136

Erzberger, Matthias 199
Evening Standard 183
Ewald, Richard 76–7

Faist, Johann 44–5
Feder, Gottfried 169, 174
First World War
outbreak of 91–4, 98–9, 113
progress of 117–18
public and professional opinion
on 114–17
Foch, Ferdinand 109
Foerster, Otfried 207
Forster, Arne xi, 50, 203
Forster, Balduin 200, 258,
261–6, 270–3
Forster, Conrad 40–3
Forster, Dirk 47–50, 84, 202–3,
210–11, 222–5, 237, 254–5,
265, 270, 273
Forster, Edmund ix–x, 11
birth 39, 46
schooling 47–51
medical education 51, 75–7
early medical appointments
78–88
involvement in a duel 85–8
at the Charité Hospital, Berlin
88, 113, 144, 197–8, 201, 208
military service 77–8, 116–20,
145
views on First World War 116
views on treatment of hysterical
disabilities 88–9, 122, 126–7,
130, 143–4, 204, 213–14,
218, 230
views on Hitler and Nazism
211, 219–20, 235, 237–8,
245, 249, 251, 254
treatment administered to Hitler
18–22, 137, 212–19, 229–30
marriage 198–9

as Director of the Greifswald
Neurological Clinic 203–11
handing over of Hitler's hospital
file 220–3
Oklitz's denunciation of
235–6, 258
links with prominent Nazis
240–6, 254
plans for disgracing of
244–5, 252–3
'voluntary' resignation of
255–8, 268
death of 259, 261–4
reactions to death of 273–4
decorations awarded to 145
grave of 275
personality 87–8, 129, 198, 204,
206, 253–4, 264–5
Forster, Elise 40
Forster, Franz Joseph 39, 43–51,
75, 118
Forster, Johann Georg 40
Forster, Lilly 202, 221–2, 225,
248, 255, 270, 273–4
Forster, Mila 198–9, 210–11, 222,
252, 256–7, 261–3, 266–9
possible involvement in
Edmund's death 269–73
Forster, Pam 50, 273
Forster, Ruprecht 200, 261,
263, 270–3
Forster, Wilhelmina 39,
45–7, 221–2
Foulkes, C.H. 155–6, 159
Franck, James 241
Franco-Prussian War 44, 118
Frank, Bruno 226
Frank, Hans 27–8
Frank, Lorenz 168
Franz Ferdinand, Archduke 98
Freikorps 167, 200
Freud, Sigmund 82–3, 126, 222

Friedländer, A.A. 115
Friedrich Wilhelm IV of
Prussia 41
Friedrich, Otto 3, 48–9, 267
Fuchs, Walter 114
Führer, title of 190
Fürstner, Karl 76
Furtwängler, Wilhelm 202

Galvani, Luigi 77
gas warfare 147–8, 151–64
Gaupp, Robert 89, 117–18, 124
Geneva University Pathological
Institute 78–9
German National Socialist
Workers' Party (NSDAP)
178–80, 183, 192–6
German Psychiatric Association
127
German Workers Party (Deutsche
Arbeiterpartei) 168–71
Gestapo, the 242–3, 251–2, 261,
266, 272
Gildisch, Kurt 272–3
Glassl-Hörer, Anna 29
Godin, Lieutenant-Colonel 109
Godl, John 110–11
Goebbels, Joseph 9–10, 165, 194
Gohrbandt, Erwin 198
Goldschieder, Alfred 126
Goldstein, Kurt 141
Gordon, Paul 231–2
Göring, Hermann 1–2, 9, 187–8,
191, 221, 240–3, 262
Graf Zeppelin 203
Graf, Alfred 95, 187–8
Graff, Oskar Maria 139
Great Depression 195–6
Great Macdermott, the 39
Greifswald 203–6, 266
Greiner, Josef 70
Grosz, George 131

Grosz, Hanus J. 13, 127
Gürnter, Franz 188

Haber, Fritz 153, 241
Hague Convention (1907) 153
Haig, Sir Douglas 158
Halle University 83–5, 88
Hammond, William Alexander 81
Hanfstaengl, Ernst 'Putzi' 181–2,
    188, 191
Hanisch, Reinhold 69, 71–2
Harrer, Karl 168–9, 172
Hedin, Sven 148
Heer, Hermann 14
Heidelberg University 79–80
Heiden, Konrad 34, 53, 172, 177
Heinz, Heinz A. 152
Heisig, Helmut 165, 196
Held, Heinrich 192–3
Hellpach, Willy 126, 128
Henneberg, Richard 294–5
Hepp, Ernst 101
Hess, Rudolf 173, 187, 190
Heydrich, Reinhard 273–4
Hiedler, Johann Georg 25–30
Himmler, Heinrich 27, 242
Hindenburg, Paul von 116, 165
Hinze, Klaus-Peter 226
Hitler, Adolf
    birth 23
    father of see Schicklgruber, Alois
    mother of see Pölzi, Klara
    early life 31, 36
    intense relationships as an
        adolescent 53–7
    applications to enter
        Viennese Academy
        of Fine Arts 57–9,
        66–7, 73
    living in Vienna 63–73
    living in Munich in 1913–14
        95–7

in First World War 2, 4–5,
    13–14, 95–102
award of Iron Cross 109
temporary blinding of 147–8,
    151–3, 159, 163, 231
at Pasewalk Lazarett 11, 14–17,
    20–2, 152, 163, 230–1
living in Munich in 1918–19
    166–7
early political career 168
as propagandist 180
trial and imprisonment for
    attempted putsch (1923–24)
    188–90
banned from speaking in public
    (1924–27) 193–5
appointment as Chancellor
    165, 196
leadership qualities 4–5, 104,
    108, 230–1
supposedly divine inspiration
    and mission 7–11, 177,
    185, 231
charismatic presence 10,
    182, 194
oratory 168, 172, 176–7,
    180–1, 191
appeal for women 181–2
anti-Semitism 20, 72, 175, 183,
    192, 214
Mein Kampf 69, 73, 95, 147–8,
    152, 160–1, 163, 190, 193
Hitler, Alois Jr 30–3
Hitler, Alois Sr see Schicklgruber,
    Alois
Hitler, William Patrick 27, 32–3
Hoffmann, Heinrich 28, 99, 190
Höhne, Heinz 272–3
Holmes, Gordon 128–9
Holocaust, the 5
Home for Men, Vienna
    69–73

Hösslin, Wilhelmina (Mina) von
    see Forster, Wilhelmina
Hötzendorf, General 96
Hull, Isabel 87
Hütler, Johann Nepomuk 25–30
hypnosis 133–5
hysteria 82, 125–30, 132–44 passim
    Forster's views on treatment
        of 88–9, 122, 126–7, 130,
        143–4, 204, 213–14, 218, 230
    Nazi view of 219–20
hysterical blindness x, 13–15,
    18, 163

inflation 201
iodoform, use of 59–61

Jackson, Robert H. 2
Janet, Pierre 125–6
Jaurès, Jean 93
Jetzinger, Franz 55
Jolly, Frederick 83
Jones, Ernest 82
Jones, Nigel 91

Kafka, Franz 225–6
Kähler, Wilhelm 240
Kahr, Gustav von 185–7, 272
Kaiser, Gottfried von (pseud.) 227
Kantzow, Karin von 241–2
Kanya, Johann 70–1
Karajan, Herbert von 202
Kaufmann, Fritz 136–8
Kempner, Robert 1–4, 242
Kiel-Wik Naval Hospital 116–17
Kitchener, Lord 47, 92
Kläger, E. 68
Klausener, Erich 272–3
Klintzsch, Johann Ulrich 173
Kocher, Emil Theodore 222–3
Korth, Klar 239

Kraepelin, Emil 79, 83
Kreisselmeier, Hermann 232
Krisch, Professor 249–50
Kroll, Friedrich Wilhelm 207–8
Kroner, Karl x, 17–18, 229
Kubizek, Gustl 53–67 passim

L'Allemand, Sigmund 58
Landsberg-am-Lech prison
    189–90
Laplace, Pierre Simon de 80
Lattner, Konrad 206, 253
Lechfeld 100
Leonding 33, 36
Lerner, Paul 114, 119, 137, 140
Leybold, Oberregierungsrat 190
Lidz, Ruth 262
Liebknecht, Karl 114
Lindau 221
Linz 36–7, 53, 56–7, 59, 97–8
Little, Brown and Co. 226
Livens, William Howard 159–60
Lloyd George, David 5
Ludecke, Kurt 176–7
Ludendorff, Erich 185–9
Ludwig III of Bavaria 100
Lutz, Tom 123
Lutze, Viktor 261

McAleer, Kevin 87
Mahler, Gustav 65
malingering 127, 130, 143
manic depression 264
Mann, Thomas 225–6, 228, 232
March Revolution (1848) 40–1
Marne, the, Battle of 94, 101
Martin, Jean 81
Marx, Karl 41
Matzelsberger, Fanny 29–30
Maurice, Emil 182
Max II of Bavaria 41
May, Hugo and Agatha Amalie 43

May, Karl 35
Mayr, Karl 167–8, 173, 176
Medical Record 81
Mehring, Walter 222–3
Meinecke, Friedrich 93
Meisner, Wilhelm 256–7, 273
Meissner, Otto 3
Mendel, Kurt 116
Mendelssohn-Bartholdy, A. 132
mental illness 82–3, 115–21, 125;
  see also hysteria
mescaline 209
methylene blue 82
Meyer, Victor 156
Meyers, Charles 121–2
Mitchell, Silas Weir 125
Muck, Otto 135–6
Müller, Adolf 190
Munich 45–6, 73–6, 95–7, 100,
  108, 122, 167, 242
Munich *putsch* (1923) 186–91, 203
Munich Tourist Association 193
Munich University 168
Mussolini, Benito 185
mustard gas 152–3, 156–64,
  215–16; see also Yellow-Cross
  gas

National Socialism 7–8, 179–80,
  183–6, 192–3, 196
Neumann, Hermann 272
neurasthenia 122–6
neurology 80–3
New York Neurological Society 81
New York Times 274
'Night of the Long Knives' 272
Nightingale, Florence 206
Niklashausen 215
Nissen, Professor 265
Nissl, Franz 83
Nonne, Max 133–5
Nonnenhorn 40–5

Nürnberg 5–9

Oklitz, Eugen 235–40, 256–7,
  266–7
Oklitz, Louise 239–40, 244, 248
Olden, Rudolf 226
Oppenheim, Hermann 119–22

Paris 132–3, 232
Pariser Tageszeitung 226
Pasewalk *Lazarett* ix–x, 11, 14–17,
  20–2, 145, 152, 163, 223,
  229–31
Passau 25
Péguy, Charles 93
Pels-Leusden, Friedrich 204–8
Petz, Friedrich 106
Philippi, Mark (*pseud.*) 228
La Pitié Hospital, Paris 132
Pitt, Barrie 7
placebo effect 141
Pointecker, Franziska 23
Pölzi, Klara 23–5, 29–32, 35–6
  illness and death 57–63, 66
Pönitz, Karl 128
Popp, Josef (and Frau Popp)
  95–6, 102
Porton Down 155
Pridham, Geoffrey 193
Probst, Ignaz 23–4
psychiatry 81, 83, 115, 118, 127

Raether, Max 138
'railway brain' 119, 122
Rätz, Johanna 239
Raub, Hans 106–7
Rawlinson, Sir Henry 109
Redl, Alfred 95–6
Reichardt, Martin 205
Reichstag fire 165, 196, 243, 254
Ribbentrop, Joachim von 10–11

Riefenstahl, Leni: *Triumph of the Will* 7–9
Rietzkow, Fräulein 210, 247–51, 258
Roger, Sidney 3
Röhm, Ernst 9, 173, 187
Romberg, Wilhelm 81
Roosevelt, Eleanor 232
Rothmann, Max 141
Russo-Japanese War 118
Rust, Bernhard x, 221, 235, 239–41, 254, 261, 271

Sacks, Oliver 80
Sackur, Otto 153
Saltpêtrière hospital, Paris 133
Salzburg 98
Sänger, Alfred 115–16
Schacht, Hjalmar 172
Scheubner-Richter, Max von 187–8
Schicklgruber, Alois 23–6, 28–35
Schjerning, Otto von 127
Schlieffen Plan 94
Schmidt, Ernst 108, 166–7
Schmidt, Willy 272
Schnabel, Artur 201
Schnoering, G.M.R. 244
Schröder, Paul 203–4
Schroeder, Wilhelm 17–18
Schurz, Carl 42–3
Schützenhaus, Pasewalk 16–17
Schutzstaffel (SS) 173
Schwarz, Hanns 198
Schwarzchild, Leopold 222–5, 266
Schwedendick, Pastor 274
Schweyer, Magdalena 174
shell-shock 119–22
Shirer, William 6–7, 240
Simpson, Keith R. 113
Singer, Kurt 115
Smith, B.F. 31

Sommer, Dr (Curator, Greifswald University) 244–5, 249–58 *passim*, 263–9 *passim*
Sommer, Robert 92, 142–3
Spatny, Colonel 106–7
Stefanie 56–7
Steyr 35–6
Stier, Ewald 140
Stokes, Wilfred 159
Strasbourg 47
Strasser, Gregor 194
Streicher, Julius 5, 188
swastika symbol 178, 181, 194, 232
syphilis, study of 208

Tandey, Henry 110–11
Le Temps 274
Thom, Johannes 17
Thomas, Robert 230
Thürk, Max 249
Tieck, Ludwig 6
'tilting-table' experiments 209–10, 244, 250, 252
The Times of London 180, 189, 274
Trommler, the 214–16
Tuchman, Barbara 93–4

Urban, Karl 57

van der Lubbe, Marinus 165
vesicants 156
Victor Emmanuel III of Italy 185
Vienna 65–9
Voit, Anna Juliana 45
Voits, Karl von 44, 76
Völkischer Beobachter 177, 194–5
Vorkastner, Willi 204–5

Wagner, Richard 65, 214
Die Meistersinger 6–7

Wagner family 184, 190
Wahnfried 184
Wall Street Crash 195
Warburg, Otto 241
Weichbrodt, Rafael 139
Weiss, Ernst x, 222–5
    death 232–3
    The Eyewitness (*Der Augenzeuge*)
        217–18, 226–31
Weizsäcker, Ernst von 8
Wernicke, Carl 83–5, 88
Wervicq 148–51, 158
Westdeutscher Beobachter 259
Westenkirchner, Ignaz 105, 108–9,
    151–2, 160–1, 229
Whateley, William 110
White Star gas 155, 161, 164, 229
Wiedemann, Fritz 2–5, 108
Wiegand, Karl II von 11
Wieland the Smith 66
Wilhelm II, Kaiser 93, 113–15,
    184, 186
Wilhelmstrasse Trial 3
will-power 89, 115, 126–8, 137,
    144, 214, 217, 219
    Hitler's 9
Willstätter, Richard 241
Wilmanns, Karl 262

Wilson, Robert 91
Wiltshire, Harold 120–1
Wolf, Johanna 24
Wolfschanze and Wolfsschluchut
    24
Wollheim, Fred 225, 288
Wollheim, Mona 225–8, 230
Wood, Garth 75, 77
Wundt, Max Wilhelm 79
Wykes, Alan 6

Yellow-Cross gas 147–8, 151–2,
    156; *see also* mustard gas
Ypres, First Battle of 101

Zádor, Julius 209–10, 218, 221,
    236–8, 246–50
Zahn, Frederick 78
Zahnschirm, Josef 26
Zakreys, Maria 63–8
Zech, Count 102
Ziehen, Professor 85
Zimmerman, J. 13, 127
Zucker, Konrad 209–10, 247–50
Zürn, Ludwig 275
Zutt, Jürg 230
Zweig, Stefan 225–8